# Financial Laws & Regulations

# Financial Education Is Your Best Investment

Published March 08, 2019
Revision 2.1
Â© 2014-2019 Financial Terms Dictionary - Thomas Herold - All rights reserved
Financial Terms Dictionary

I0491553

## Copyright And Trademark Notices

Unless otherwise expressly noted, none of the individuals or business entities mentioned herein have endorsed the contents of this book.

## Limits of Liability and Disclaimer of Warranties

The materials in this book are provided "as is" and without warranties of any kind either express or implied. The Author disclaims all warranties, express or implied, including, but not limited to, implied warranties of merchant-ability and fitness for a particular purpose.

The Author does not warrant that defects will be corrected, or that that the site or the server that makes this eBook available are free of viruses or other harmful components. The Author does not warrant or make any representations regarding the use or the results of the use of the materials in this book in terms of their correctness, accuracy, reliability, or otherwise. Applicable law may not allow the exclusion of implied warranties, so the above exclusion may not apply to you.

Under no circumstances, including, but not limited to, negligence, shall the Author be liable for any special or consequential damages that result from the use of, or the inability to use this eBook, even if the Author or his authorized representative has been advised of the possibility of such damages.

Applicable law may not allow the limitation or exclusion of liability or incidental or consequential damages, so the above limitation or exclusion may not apply to you. In no event shall the Author's total liability to you for all damages, losses, and causes of action (whether in contract, tort, including but not limited to, negligence or otherwise) exceed the amount paid by you, if any, for this eBook.

Facts and information are believed to be accurate at the time they were placed in this book. All data provided in this book is to be used for information purposes only. The information contained within is not intended to provide specific legal, financial or tax advice, or any other advice whatsoever, for any individual or company and should not be relied upon in that regard. The services described are only offered in jurisdictions where they may be legally offered. Information provided is not all-inclusive and is limited to information that is made available and such information should not be relied upon as all-inclusive or accurate.

You are advised to do your own due diligence when it comes to making business decisions and should use caution and seek the advice of qualified professionals. You should check with your accountant, lawyer, or professional advisor, before acting on this or any information. You may not consider any examples, documents, or other content in this eBook or otherwise provided by the Author to be the equivalent of professional advice.

The Author assumes no responsibility for any losses or damages resulting from your use of any link, information, or opportunity contained in this book or within any other information disclosed by the author in any form whatsoever.

## About the Author

Thomas Herold is a successful entrepreneur, mediator, author, and personal development coach. He published over 20 books with over 200,000 copies distributed worldwide and the founder of seven online businesses.

For over ten years Thomas Herold has studied the monetary system and has experienced some profound insights on how money and wealth are related. After three years of successful investing in silver, he released 'Building Wealth with Silver - How to Profit From The Biggest Wealth Transfer in History' in 2012. One of the first books that illustrate in a remarkable, simple way the monetary system and its consequences.

He is the founder and CEO of the 'Financial Terms Dictionary' book series and website, which explains in detail and comprehensive form over 1000 financial terms. In his financial book series, he informs in detail and with practical examples all aspects of the financial sector. His educational materials are designed to help people get started with financial education.

In his 2018 released book 'The Money Deception', Mr. Herold provides the most sophisticated insight and shocking details about the current monetary system. Never before has the massive manipulation of money caused so much economic inequality in the world. In spite of these frightening facts, 'The Money Deception' also provides remarkable and simple solutions to create abundance for all people, and it's a must read if you want to survive the global monetary transformation thatâ€™s underway right now.

## For more information please visit:

Financial Terms Dictionary

## Financial Dictionary Series

There are 12 books in this financial terms series available. Click the link below to see an overview and available formats on Amazon.

Thomas Herold Author page on Amazon

## Please leave your review on Amazon:

This book is self-published and the author does not have a contract with one of the five largest publishers, which are able to support the author's work with advertising. If you like this book, please consider leaving a solid 5-star review on Amazon.

# 1035 Exchange

A 1035 Exchange is an exchange process that permits individuals to replace their existing life insurance policy or annuity contract with a similar new contract or policy. Thanks to a provision in the tax code, this can be affected without suffering any negative tax repercussions as part of the trade off exchange. The Internal Revenue Service permits those who hold these kinds of contracts to update their old policies and annuities with those more modern ones that include better benefits, superior investment choices, and lower fees.

The 1035 Exchange is also called a Section 1035 Exchange after the tax code section for which it is named. It literally permits policyholders to transfer their funds out of an endowment, life insurance policy, or annuity into a newer similar vehicle. The way it works is to allow holders to defer their gains. When all of the received proceeds of the original contract become transferred to the newer contract (as there are simultaneously not any loans outstanding on the prior policy), no tax becomes due at point of exchange. Should these proceeds be received and not exchanged according to the 1035 Exchange rules, then all gains obtained out of the first contract become taxable like ordinary income, and not as capital gains.

Gains do not refer to all money received. Instead they are the result of subtracting the gross cash value from the premium tax basis. This basis refers to the original dollar amount put into the contract itself minus the premiums paid for extra benefits or any distributions which qualify as tax free.

In order for this 1035 Exchange to make sense, it has to benefit the policy holder either economically or personally. It is also important for holders to never terminate their in place insurance policies until the newer policy has been fully issued and becomes effective. The holders need to contemplate any health changes since the original policy started. It might cost extra premiums in order for the newer policy to cover them. They might even receive a denial of coverage if the changes in health are too drastic. Similarly, if the holder is well advanced in age, the premium rate may increase.

Some policies also have surrender charges that must be considered. There may be different guarantees, provisions, and interest crediting in the newer policy as well. Most importantly, benefits of the newer policy have to be carefully reviewed. These may change negatively in some cases.

There are rare cases where simply surrendering an existing insurance policy or annuity is more advantageous than engaging in a 1035 Exchange. These primarily occur when the existing contract offers no gain. Sometimes outstanding loans on the initial policy also decrease the benefits of an exchange. In other cases, the original policy may have a "market rate adjustment" type of provision. This would cause the exchange proceeds to be less than those offered in a surrender.

It is usually the case that such a 1035 Exchange will be slower and more involved than simply surrendering the holder's original policy. It can even require a few months much of the time. This is why the conditions that affect the practicality of the exchange include financial conditions of the initial policy carrier, the country's economic climate at the time, and the intentions of the policy holder.

The IRS only deems certain exchanges to be considered "like kind" and allowable. These include life insurance for life insurance, life insurance for non-qualified annuity, life insurance for endowment, endowment for non-qualified annuity, endowment for endowment, and non-qualified annuity for non-qualified annuity. They also will allow multiple numbers of existing contracts to be changed into a single newer contract. It does not work in reverse. A single existing contract can not be exchanged in for multiple newer contracts, per the IRS rules and regulations.

# 403(b) Plan

403(b) plans were created for employees of schools, churches, and tax exempt organizations. Individuals who are eligible may establish and maintain their own 403(b) accounts.Â  Their employers can and often do make contributions to the employeesâ€™ accounts. Individuals are able to open one of three different types of 403(b)s.

The first is an annuity plan that an insurance company establishes. These types of plans are sometimes called TDAs tax deferred annuities or TSAs tax sheltered annuities. A second plan type is an account which a retirement custodian offers and manages. With these 403(b)s, the account holders may only choose from mutual funds and regulated investment companies that the custodian allows. The final type is a retirement income account. These accounts accept a combination of mutual funds or annuities for the investment choices.

Employers have some control over these accounts. They are able to decide which financial institution will hold the employeesâ€™ 403(b) accounts. This determines the kind of plan that the employees are able to set up and fund. Employers receive several advantages from choosing to offer a 403(b).

The benefits which they get to offer their employees are worthwhile. This helps to ensure valuable employees stay with the organization. They also enjoy sharing the funding costs between themselves and their employees. Employers may also choose for the 403(b) to only accept employee contributions if they do not wish to participate financially in the account.

Employees also experience several benefits from these types of retirement vehicles. They may contribute tax deferred dollars from their income. They may also contribute taxed dollars to the accounts. In these Roth 403(b)s, all of their earnings accrue tax free for the entire life of the account. Deferred tax payments until retirement typically allow for the employees to pay fewer taxes as they are often in a more advantageous tax bracket at retirement point.

Employees may also obtain loans from their 403(b) accounts as they need them.

A variety of non profit organizations may choose to establish such a 403(b) plan for their employees. This includes any 501(c)(3) tax exempt organization, co-op hospital service organizations, public school systems, ministers at churches, Native American public school systems, and (USUHS) Uniformed Services for the University of the Health Sciences.

Such 403(b) plans can obtain a variety of contribution types. Employees may have elective deferral contributions taken out of each paycheck. These are taken out in a pretax dollars arrangement. Employees also have the ability to contribute taxed dollars to the accounts. They have these deducted from their payrolls as well.

Employers may also choose to make contributions which are either discretionary or fixed amounts as they desire. Employees and employers may make contributions to Roth 403(b) accounts. These 403(b) accounts may also receive any combination of the previously mentioned contribution types, which demonstrates their flexibility.

Employees have generous annual contribution limits with these plans. In 2016, they may contribute up to $18,000 (or $24,000 if they are over 50 years old and catching up on contributions for retirement). For 2016, employers may also deposit as much as $53,000 (up to 100% of the employee compensation) as an annual contribution.

Regarding distributions, the rules are comparable to the other types of retirement savings vehicles. Distributions of deferred taxed dollars become taxable like regular income when the employee receives them. If these are taken before the employee turns 59 Â½, then the withdrawn dollars are assessed the standard 10% penalty for early withdrawals. There are some exceptions to this penalty for which an employee may qualify. One of these exceptions is if the employee terminates the job even before reaching the age of retirement.

# 457(b) Plan

A 457(b) plan is a retirement savings vehicle. It derives its name from the Internal Revenue Service code that regulates the plans in its section 457(b). Many times this retirement account name is simply shortened to 457 Plan.

There are many similarities between these 457 Plans and tax deferred, employer provided retirement vehicles including 403(b) and 401(k) plans. All of these retirement vehicles are defined contribution plans. People who participate in these 457 Plans set up payroll deductions so that a portion of their income is put into this investment account that is tax free.

The government established these 457 Plans in 1978. They were set up to be another defined contribution account that would help two particular kinds of employers. They are intended for both government employers and non government employers which are tax exempt as with hospitals and charities.

Despite this fact, a few different rules apply for the government plans as opposed to the non government plans. The principle difference revolves around funding. Government 457 Plans have to be funded by the employer in question. The non government 457 Plans are practically all funded by employees. The vast majority of 457(b) plans that private not for profit companies use they only offer to well paid employees usually in upper level management.

With 457 Plans, there must be both a plan administrator and a plan provider. Each plan provides its own limited choices for investment options which are particular to the plan.

Rollover rules are different for these 457 Plans as well. The non government versions can not be transferred over to qualified retirement plans which include IRA and 401(k)s. Instead they can only be rolled over to other tax exempt 457 Plans. The rules are different with government sponsored employer plans. These may be transferred into another employer's 401(k), 403(b), or 457(b) plan as well as to an IRA account. The new plan must permit account holders to make such transfers.

Withdrawals are easier for government sponsored plans as well. Individuals may do early withdrawals before they reach the 59 ½ year old age of retirement and not have to suffer the 10% early withdrawal penalty. The full withdrawn amount would be taxed as regular income. Employees who are switching jobs may also keep the money where it is assuming the plan permits this.

Rollover rules on 457(b) plans are pretty standard. If funds are dispersed to the account owner, he or she has a maximum of 60 days to finish the rollover process. Beyond this time, the IRS considers this money to have been distributed and to be taxable. Owners are also restricted to doing a single rollover in a calendar year with these retirement vehicles.

The date on which the owners receive their 457 Plan distribution is when the one year rule commences. While the money is in the 60 day process of being rolled over, it may not be invested. Direct rollovers avoid the dangers of the 60 day rule. An account holder never obtains a distribution check (as with indirect rollovers) in this type of transfer. Instead, the plan provider will directly transfer all money to the new IRA or retirement plan.

Investment choices in 457 Plans are more limited than with Self Directed IRAs or Solo 401(k) plans. The plan provider will restrict choices to ones that fit their plan. If they permit them, owners may invest their funds in individual bonds and stocks, fixed or indexed annuities, exchange traded funds, and mutual funds.

Gold bullion can not be purchased by these plans. Paper gold investments such as stocks of gold mining firms, mutual funds containing gold mining companies, or gold ETFs like GLD and mining ETFs may be purchased instead.

# 501(c)

501(c) designations refer to incorporations of entities which are established as charitable not for profit corporations. These charitable operations are companies which are founded in order to offer the benefits of a community service instead of attempting to make profits for their founders or managers.

When such an outfit is incorporated it becomes legal. This gives it responsibility for the actions it carries out within its community. This legal status is critical for the founder. It takes away much of the legal responsibility of the individual who starts up the company. Any people who set up these 501(c) companies do so with the goal of having all legal liability for any damages removed from them. Instead, the responsibilities transfer over to the 501(c) itself so that the founder's own personal assets are protected from any lawsuits or creditors.

Every state has its own particular set of rules for creating a 501(c) company. This is why participants are encouraged to seek out qualified financial and legal advice before they incorporate under this status. The expenses involved in establishing such a corporation are different depending on how large the corporation proves to be. The larger the outfit, the more expensive it is to establish.

The 501(c) status refers to the Internal Revenue Service code section that pertains to the charitable company rules. The document itself is a very dense and difficult read. This helps to explain how the not for profits earned such a non creative and cumbersome name associated with this type of company.

These 501(c)s do not have to pay any income tax to the federal, state, or local governments. The trade off for such a benefit is that they are not allowed to participate in election campaigns with a goal of helping a single candidate to be chosen versus another one. The companies are also forbidden to provide any material or financial benefits to the owners or officers of the organization itself. Such rules apply to the not for profit for its entire life span. This means that companies can not switch their status back to and from 501(c).

11

Any not for profit organization that is no longer such an outfit must be disbanded.

This type of corporate designation proves to be a critical method for individuals who wish to establish organizations to help their overall community. It protects them from personal risks to their assets in the process. It also permits charity outfits to expand to a big enough company that they can affect major changes. These operations can grow far larger than the person who started them and can also outlive him or her.

The Internal Revenue Service has a variety of rules that individuals must observe in order to properly organize and operate under the 501(c) designation. Not a penny of the earnings may go into the hands of an individual or shareholder. The outfit must also not endeavor to sway any federal, state, or local legislation as a mainstay of its daily activities. They similarly may not be involved in political campaigns either for or against any candidates in the election. These organizations must be entirely charitable organizations in order to qualify for this tax exempt status.

Such operations also may not be created or run to benefit any personsâ€™ private interests. For any not for profit that participates in excess benefit transactions with groups or people who have significant influence in the operation, they may suffer from the government levying an excise tax against the manager or individual who agreed to such a transaction in the first place.

# Bretton Woods Agreement

The Bretton Woods agreement represents the outcomes of a three week conference that the United Nations held to set up a new monetary system at the end of World War II. The U.N. organized this meeting called the United Nations Monetary and Financial Conference for July 1 to July 22 of 1944. They held it at Bretton Woods in New Jersey, which gave its name to the deal that ultimately resulted from the conference. The agreement itself proved to be a famed framework that set up a new exchange rate system.

Three significant outcomes resulted from this conference. Two of them are still a major part of the world financial system today. First the group agreed on the Bretton Woods Agreement which set up a new foreign exchange system. Besides this, the United Nations authorized forming the International Monetary Fund and also the International Bank for Reconstruction and Development.

A new foreign exchange system had been called for in the wake of World War II. The international economic system had been destroyed by the already more than five years of fierce global fighting. Allied nations decided even before they successfully concluded the war they needed to come up with a new currency and a plan to rebuild the devastated nations and world economy.

The conference saw 730 delegates attend from all of the 44 Allied countries. They met at the Mount Washington Hotel and spent three weeks coming up with the new currency system and financial institutions. On the last day of the conference on July 22, they signed the Bretton Woods agreement.

The new system rested on several key proposals. One of these involved currency convertibility. All currencies had to be converted for trade purposes and to settle current account transactions. The U.S. sat in a position of commanding strength as it controlled fully two thirds of all the gold in the world.

This gave it the basis to call for a new system of pegging foreign exchange to both gold and the U.S. Dollar. The final agreement had the currencies pegged to gold, but more countries added the U.S. dollar as it became clearer over the subsequent years that it was the world's new reserve currency.

Naturally not everyone felt satisfied with these outcomes to the agreement. Soviet Union (Russia and surrounding republics) representatives came to the conference and participated. They accused the institutions that the conference had created of being mere branches of Wall Street.

As a result, they refused to ratify the final important agreements. Many nations including those of Western Europe, South America, Canada, Australia, the U.S., and eventually Japan after the war did sign on to the agreements and these new institutions began operating in 1945 after enough nations ratified them.

Meanwhile, countries began to exchange their currencies at rates based on the set quantity of gold they held. Whenever an imbalance of payments would occur as a result of the artificial currency pegging system, the International Monetary Fund had the powers to intervene and adjust as necessary. This encouraged foreign trade and global economic growth. It caused expansion in the majority of the developed world following the war.

Besides the International Monetary Fund, the conference also created the International Bank for Reconstruction and Development that eventually evolved into the World Bank. These two organizations still thrive today and promote financial stability and international trade. They encourage worldwide monetary cooperation and economic growth that is sustainable. They also help to reduce poverty and push for higher employment.

Europe and other damaged parts of the world engaged in a long era of rebuilding and development after the war ended with the aid of these institutions. The Bretton Woods system itself became abandoned in 1971 when the U.S. unilaterally left the gold standard. It was replaced by today's free floating currency exchange system.

# British Bankers Association (BBA)

The British Bankers Association turns out to be the members' representative for the biggest international banking cluster in the world. This main trade association for the British banking sector boasts over 200 member banks headquartered in both the U.K. and more than 50 other countries that run operations in over 180 jurisdictions around the globe. As such fully 80% of all the systemically critical banks on earth carry membership with the BBA. This is the voice of UK banking.

The BBA claims the greatest and most comprehensive policy resources for those banks operating in the UK. They represent membership not only to the government of the U.K., but also throughout Europe and globally. Besides this impressive membership roster, their network also is comprised of more than 80 of the foremost professional and financial services organizations in the world.

The BBAâ€™s members collectively manage over Â£7 trillion (British pounds) of British bank assets. The members employ almost half a million people throughout the country. Their contributions to the British economy every year are more than Â£60 billion. Members loan in excess of Â£150 billion out to business based in the U.K.

The British Bankers Association works to encourage both initiatives and policies that promote the interests of not only banks but also the overall public. They have three principal priorities in their work. The first is to help out customers. This includes both businesses and consumers. The second is to encourage growth. By this they intend to support Britain as the worldâ€™s global financial center. Finally they are interested in improving standards in the industry on both an ethical and professional level.

The BBA works with two strategic aims in mind. The first is to encourage a superior and improving banking sector for the overall U.K. They do this by working alongside banks and other beneficiaries to increase trust in the banking industry, by raising standards, by encouraging growth, and by assisting customers. They promise to facilitate public approval and overall awareness of the important position banks play in the economy. They are also aspiring to build appreciation for the advantages of hosting an internationally critical banking sector.

Chief among their public relations tasks are to encourage acknowledgement of the substantial improvements the sector has gone through since the global financial crisis. The BBA’s goal is to be understood as an agent of positive change that makes a better banking industry by its non members and members alike. They strive to be a trusted partner of both banking regulators and the government. They also take the initiative to impact international and national debates on banking issues.

Their second strategic aim is to be the banking industry’s trade association that is world class. They are the principal trade association for the foremost sector of the British economy as well as the main trade group for the foremost banking cluster in the world. This is why they aim to be best in class in their operations.

Before September in 2012, the BBA both compiled and published the LIBOR London Interbank Offered Rate, the most important interest rate in the world. They lost their role in managing the rate after the Barclays scandal erupted that showed the bank had been consistently manipulating the rate for a number of years. As lobby organization for the rate submitting banks, the Bank of England decided the BBA’s conflict of interest was too great.

Nowadays the BBA puts on training and events throughout Britain. These include training classes, briefings, and forums besides their annual industry dinners and conferences. They also publish a monthly report that covers figures on high street banking. This is used in their Annual Abstract of Banking Statistics that they produce every August. BBA furthermore runs the GOLD Global Operational Loss Database for members. This serves as a helpful tool in helping to manage risk from operations.

# Bureau of Engraving and Printing (BEP)

The Bureau of Engraving and Printing is the Treasury Department entity that actually makes the United States’ currency. Their mission centers on creating and producing American currency notes which are trusted around the world. They have a vision to be considered the world standard for securities printing. This is so that they can deliver the public and their customers with the best products that are exceptionally well designed and manufactured.

The main activities of the BEP are to print up billions of Federal Reserve notes (or dollars) every single year. They then deliver these to the Federal Reserve System for distribution into the economy. It is the Federal Reserve that exists to be the American central bank. They bear the responsibility to be certain that sufficient coins and bills currency are in active circulation. The BEP handles all of the U.S. printed bills but does not make any coins. United States coins are always minted at the U.S. Mint.

When various federal agencies have concerns or questions about document security, they turn to the BEP for help and advice. The BEP also engages in research and development for improving their utilization of automation processes in production. They are always seeking out technologies to deter counterfeiters of U.S. currency and security documents as well.

It is no understatement to say that currency creation at the BEP offices has changed drastically from its origins in 1862. In those early years, they used the basement in the Treasury building. Here a handful of individuals worked with hand cranked machines to print and separate notes. Today's BEP does not engage in an easy process or job.

Nowadays making the currency bills takes greatly skilled and expertly trained craftspeople who work with specially designed equipment. They utilize both sophisticated and world leading technology alongside the time tested old world printing methods. Producing the currency takes numerous specific steps. This starts with designing, engraving, and making the plates. The specially sourced paper is then plate printed and inspected. Bills are numbered and re-inspected again before being packaged and shipped to their customer the Federal Reserve Bank.

The Bureau of Engraving and Printing also offers redemption of mutilated currency services and the sale of shredded currency. BEP will redeem such mutilated currency for free for the public. If the bills are so damaged that the value can not be conclusively determined, they can be sent on to the BEP so that their trained experts can examine them. After their determination is made, they will redeem the currency for full face value.

They accept currency that has been mutilated by water, fire, chemicals, or explosives; deterioration or petrification from burying; or insect, animal, or rodent damage. Bills missing security features are also treated as mutilated. For them to consider these bills without supporting documentation and explanations for what happened, at least half of the note has to be identifiable as American currency and remain.

If less than 50% is present, Treasury will require proof that the rest of the currency has been destroyed. Each year the department examines 30,000 mutilated currency claims and redeems them for more than $30 million.

The BEP also sells bags of shredded currency as novelty souvenir items. The Fort Worth and Washington, D.C. BEP visitor centers offer them in pre-packed small amounts for those who just want to have some. The D.C. visitor center and online store of the BEP also sell larger five pound bags of such shredded currency. In order to obtain larger quantities, individuals must get permission from the Treasury department and obtain them from one of the Federal Reserve Banks.

# C Corporation

C Corporations refers to the primary subchapter under which American businesses decide to incorporate themselves in order to restrict the total financial and legal liabilities of the owners. Such C Corporations prove to be the principle alternatives to S Corporations, whose profits are able to pass directly through to the owners and so only become taxable on the individual level. Limited liability companies are the other main choice to the C corporations. They deliver all of the legal safeties of corporations yet become tax treated as if they were sole proprietorships.

Unfortunately for C Corporations, they do suffer the effects of double taxation. Yet they do also permit the businesses to reinvest their profits back into the firm with a lower corporate tax rate penalty. The majority of incorporated companies within the United States turn out to be C Corporations.

Organizing a corporation starts with the new owners selecting the new entity's name (and in many states registering or reserving it with the secretary of state) of the new business enterprise. The owners must draft up the articles of incorporation and file them with the appropriate state business department. The first shareholders will then be issued their stock certificates once the business is established. Every C Corporation has to first file the Form SS-4 in order to get their EIN employer identification number. Every jurisdiction has its own varying requirements for these obligations, yet the corporations generally must file income, state, payroll, disability, and unemployment taxes for their employees.

Such C Corporations must hold minimally one meeting per year for the benefit of both the directors and the shareholders. These must have meeting minutes kept in order to transparently display the ways and means in which the business functions. There will have to be voting records maintained of the company directors as well as a full list of all owners' names and their ownership percentages in the firm. The company bylaws are required to be kept on the business headquarter premises at all times. Such enterprises also have to file all necessary financial disclosure reports, annual reports, and relevant financial statements with the SEC.

There are many benefits to such C Corporations. Most importantly for owners, they first limit the liability of all shareholders, directors, officers, and employees. It is not possible for the legal and debt obligations from the company to transfer over to one or more individuals under this type of corporate structuring. Even if each of the company owners become changed out, the corporation continues its existence. There is no limit to the numbers of shareholders and owners with this kind of corporation either as there would be with an S Corporation. Yet these must be registered properly with the SEC

Securities and Exchange Commission once they reach a certain number of shareholders.

The primary downside to the C corporations centers on the idea of double taxation. As the firm generates its income, it will have to file a corporate tax return with the IRS Internal Revenue Service. Once the appropriate business expenses (including salaries) have been deducted from the gross income, the rest becomes subjected to corporate income taxes. Much of the remaining net income will then be distributed out to shareholders in what is called dividends. The income to the shareholders must be reported on the recipients' tax returns. This means that the C Corporation profits are being twice taxed, once at the corporate tax rate level and a second on the individuals' tax rate level. That income which is retained earnings will avoid double taxation only. It helps to explain why mega corporations like Apple hold on to billions of dollars in retained earnings routinely.

# Certificate of Occupancy

A certificate of occupancy is a local government issued document. These papers give permission for tenants or residents to occupy a new building or even a residence. The reason that local governments mandate such certificates is because of building codes. The certificate proves that a building inspector has certified the building to be safe so that it can be occupied. It means that the structure complies with all present building codes.

Local governments will inspect and then issue such a certificate of occupancy any time that a construction company puts up a new building in the local government's jurisdiction as defined by the city limits. Even buildings that are opened outside of city limits can requires these before people can use them. In these cases, it might be the parish or county government that would issue the certificate. Local government will give these after they are satisfied with the results of the inspection. Inspectors look at all of the basic elements in the building including wiring, construction basics, plumbing, and other features to ensure they meet up to date code standards. Then they can sign off on a building being safe to inhabit.

Upgrades and additions to building that already exist can also require a new certificate of occupancy. In these cases, the owner of the building will have to apply to the local government for a new certificate after he has finished the changes and improvements. Inspectors will also check over all features of the structure to make sure that both existing and new parts meet the codes, as they would with a new building. After they finish such an inspection, the building department will have to sign off before the government agency can issue the certificate.

The owners of the building are not generally the parties responsible for requesting an inspection. Professional contractors and renovators will contact the responsible government entity so that the department can schedule the inspection. They also go through any necessary arrangements to make sure the certificate of occupancy becomes issued. The builder or contractor will receive the certificate first. They will provide copies of the document to the building owner. They keep copies in the construction company files too.

Other copies will be delivered to appropriate parties as well. One of these would be a lender. Should the building owner wish to use the property as collateral for an application on a loan, he will likely have to furnish a certificate of occupancy copy to the lender along with the application. A great number of lenders will refuse to make the loan until they have a proper copy of the certificate of occupancy on file.

In the event that a building fails an inspection, a certificate of occupancy will not be issued at first. Whatever modifications the inspector insisted on will have to be made. The building has to be brought up to current code before they can request another inspection. After successfully passing a second or later inspection, the certificate will then be issued by the appropriate department.

# Certificate of Title

A certificate of title represents a document which states who the owners or owner of real estate or personal property actually are. It is issued by a municipal or state government. This certificate gives evidence of any ownership rights.

In general a title insurance company will issue a certificate of title opinion on a house or piece of property. This is their statement of opinion regarding the status of a title. They draft this opinion after carefully looking through public records pertaining to the property.

Such a certificate of title opinion will not necessarily assure the buyer of a clean title. It will list out any encumbrance on the property. Encumbrances are often items that keep the property from being freely sold. These could include easements or liens. The title companies will issue such certificates to financial institutions which are making the loan. Many of these lenders must have such documents in hand before they will approve a mortgage loan for a house or piece of property.

Certificates of title are extremely important with real estate. This is why a title company will issue their opinion that the person selling the property actually owns it. Personal property is easier to give to another person than is land. Where land is concerned, a person might be living on a given property and yet not own it. This makes the certificate opinion from the title company critical. It promises that the company has performed the complete background check regarding who owns the land and so has the right to sell it.

This certificate of title is a statement of fact when a state or municipal government actually issues it. These documents contain a good deal of useful information on them. All of them will have the name and address of the owner of the property. They also have information that identifies the property itself in some specific way.

If the certificate pertains to a real estate property, then it will have the location of or address for the land in question. If it is instead for a car or other vehicle, it will have the license plate number and possibly the vehicle identification number. These certificates will also state what the encumbrance is on the property if there is any. If there is a lien on a vehicle or mortgage on the house or land, this will be noted.

State agencies will also issue certificates of title on a variety of vehicles. This covers such things as buses, trucks, motorcycles, trailers, motor homes, boats and watercraft, and airplanes. When a lender makes a loan on such a vehicle, it is able to keep the title in its possession until the debt has been paid in full. They then release the lien at this point and send back the title certificate to the actual owner.

Certificates of title should not be confused with deeds though they share certain common characteristics. Each of these two documents offers a proof of ownership for the property in question. The certificate of title has sufficient information to specifically identify the property itself and any relevant encumbrances. Deeds have additional information on the real property. This includes any conditions for the ownership as well as more detailed information on and about the property. Deeds are critical elements in any transfer of real estate.

# CFA Institute

The CFA Institute stands for the Chartered Financial Analyst institute. This global organization was formerly called the AIMR Association for Investment Management and Research. This institute is made up of over 70,000 individual members (from 137 different member societies located in 60 countries) who have the CFA Chartered Financial Analyst designation or who instead agree to be bound up by the organizationâ€™s rules. The principal mandate of the group lies in setting forth and ensuring that there is a lofty standard for the members of the investment and financial advisory universe.

The CFA Institute boasts an active membership in nearly all nations of the world, 150 countries and territories specifically. Their board of governors is steered by 20 individual board members. The majority of these become elected by the votes of the members of the institute for three-year long terms. The institute counts important offices in the United States, the United Kingdom, and Hong Kong. It also staffs satellite offices in Mumbai, India, and Charlottesville, Virginia in the United States. It crafts and releases such important industry guidelines as the financial industry's GIPS Global Investment Performance Standards.

Ultimately, the aims of the CFA Institute are to encourage and foster the greatest possible standards in education, ethics, and excellence in the profession for the worldwide investment industry. As such, the Institute itself works to help out financial professionals via offering professional development, education, and also networking possibilities and opportunities. It also concentrates on becoming the world leader in best practices for the industry, highest investment ethics, and integrity for the capital markets of the globe.

The CFA Institute developed its famed Code of Ethics and Standards of Professional Conduct. This is the worldwide benchmark for investment professionals throughout the globe, whatever their particular roles in the industry may prove to be. The members of the Institute as well as the CFA charter holders and candidates for this designation must abide by the gold standard document so long as they are practicing. The Institute similarly strives to influence and direct the public policy and practices of the industry in such a way as to make sure the interests of the investors come first.

The CFA Institute does a lot of great work in the industry, but the educational programs are among the most important. These programs lead to designations of various kinds. The most important, widely recognized, and popular of these accreditations is the CFA Chartered Financial Analyst. The program itself offers an important foundation in investment analysis and portfolio management skills.

In fact, this CFA designation proves to be the preferred professional accreditation for more than 31,000 different investment companies around the world. Attaining this designation mandates that the prospective candidates successfully complete three consecutive exams which deal with professional and ethical standards, economics, quantitative methods, corporate finance, financial reporting, equity, derivatives, fixed income, portfolio management, and alternative investments.

The CFA Institute also purveys its CIPM, the impressive Certificate in Investment Performance Measurement. This designation provides candidates with risk evaluation and investment performance credentials that are based on actual practice. These various skill sets are considered to be useful and relevant on a global scale. In this program, the participants learn useful subjects such as measurement, attribution, appraisals, selection of managers, reporting standards, and ethics.

Another program of the CFA Institute is called the Claritas Program. This course addresses the important elements of ethics, finance, and investment roles. It is also interesting for being a self study program which was specifically designed to help those individuals who already work for financial services and investment firms. This includes professionals in marketing and sales, information technology, and/or human resources.

# Chapter 11 Bankruptcy

Chapter 11 Bankruptcy proves to be a specific type of bankruptcy. This kind has to do with the business assets, debts, and affairs being reorganized. The business reorganization filing was named for the Section 11 of the United Statesâ€™ Bankruptcy Code. Corporations commonly file it that need some time to rearrange the terms of their debts and their business operations. It gives them a fresh start on repaying their debt obligations. Naturally the indebted company will have to stick to the terms of the reorganization plan. This proves to be the most highly complex type of bankruptcy filing possible. Companies have been advised to only entertain it once they have contemplated their other options and analyzed the repercussions of such a filing.

This Chapter 11 bankruptcy rarely makes the news unless it is a nationally known or famous corporation which is filing. Among the major corporations that have filed such a Chapter 11 bankruptcy are United Airlines, General Motors, K-Mart, and Lehman Brothers. The first three successfully emerged from it and became as great or stronger than they were before falling into hard times financially. In reality, the vast majority of these cases are unknown to the general public. As an example, in the year 2010, nearly 14,000 separate corporations filed for Chapter 11.

The point of this Chapter 11 Bankruptcy is to assist a corporation in restructuring both obligations and debts. The goal is not to close down the business. In fact it rarely leads to the corporation closing. Instead, corporations like K-mart, General Motors, and tens of thousands of others were able to survive and once again thrive thanks to the useful process of protection from creditors and reorganization of business debts.

It is typically LLCs Limited Liability Companies, partnerships, and corporations that make application for Chapter 11 Bankruptcy. There are cases where individuals who are positively saddled with debt and who are not able to be approved for a Chapter 13 or Chapter 7 filing can be qualified for Chapter 11 instead. The time table for successfully completing Chapter 11 bankruptcy ranges from several months to as long as two years.

Businesses that are in the middle of their Chapter 11 cases are encouraged to keep operating. The debtor in possession will typically run the business normally. Where there are cases that have gross incompetence, dishonest dealings, or even fraud involved, typically trustees come in to take over the business and its daily operations while the bankruptcy proceedings are ongoing.

Corporations in the midst of these filings will not be permitted to engage in specific decisions without first having to consult with the courts to proceed. They may not terminate or sign rental agreements, sell any assets beyond regular inventory, or expand existing business operations or alternatively cease them. The bankruptcy court retains full control regarding any hiring and paying of lawyers as well as signing contracts with either unions or vendors. Lastly, such indebted organizations and entities may not sign for a loan that will pay once the bankruptcy process finishes.

After the business or person files their chapter 11 bankruptcy, it gains the right to offer a first reorganization plan. Such plans often include renegotiating owed debts and reducing the company size in order to slash expenses. There are some scenarios where the plan will require every asset to be liquidated in order to pay off the creditors, as with Lehman Brothers.

When plans are fair and workable, courts will approve them. This moves the reorganization process ahead. For plans to be accepted, they also have to maintain the creditorsâ€™ best interests for the future repayment of debts owed to them. When the debtor can not or will not put forward a plan of their own for reorganization, then the creditors are invited to offer one in the indebted company or personâ€™s place.

# Chapter 7 Bankruptcy

Chapter 7 bankruptcy is a form of protection from creditors. Unlike Chapter 13 bankruptcy, it does not have any repayment plan. In the Chapter 7 a bankruptcy trustee determines what eligible assets the debtor individual or company has. The trustee then collects these available assets, sells them, and distributes proceeds to the creditors against their debts. This is all done under the rules of the Bankruptcy Code.

Debtors are permitted to keep specific property that is exempt, such as their house. Other property that the debtor holds will be mortgaged or have liens put against it to pledge it to the various creditors until it is liquidated. Debtors who file chapter 7 will likely forfeit property in partial payment of debts.

Chapter 7 bankruptcy is available to corporations, partnerships, and individuals who pass a means test. The relief can be granted whether or not the debtor is ruled to be insolvent.

Chapter 7 bankruptcy cases start when debtors file their petitions with their particular area's bankruptcy court. For businesses, they use the address where the main office is located. Debtors are required to give the court information that includes schedules of current expenditures and income and liabilities and assets.

They are also required to furnish a financial affairs statement and a schedule of contracts and leases which are not expired. The debtors will also have to deliver the trustee tax return copies from the most current tax year along with any tax returns which they file while the case is ongoing.

Debtors who are individuals also have to furnish their court with other documents. They are required to file a credit counseling certificate and any repayment plan created there. They must also file proof of income from employers 60 days before their original filing, a monthly income statement along with expected increases in either, and notice of interest they have in tuition or state education accounts. Husbands and wives are allowed to file individually or jointly. They must abide by the requirements for individual debtors either way.

The courts are required to charge debtors who file $335 in filing, administrative, and trustee fees. Debtors typically pay these when they file to the clerk of court. The court can give permission for individuals to pay by installments instead. When the income of debtor's proves to be less than 150% of the amount of the poverty level, the court can choose to drop the fee requirements.

Debtors will have to provide a great amount of information in order to complete their Chapter 7 filing and receive a discharge of debts. They have to list out each of their creditors along with the amounts they owe then and the type of claim. Debtors have to furnish a list of all property the own. They must also give the information on the amount, source, and frequency of income they have to the court.

Finally, they will be required to provide an in depth list of all monthly living expenses that includes housing, utilities, food, transportation, clothing, medicine, and taxes. This helps the court to determine if the debtor is able to set up a repayment plan instead of discharging the debts.

From 21 to 40 days after the debtor files the petition with the courts, the trustee hosts a creditorsâ€™ meeting. The debtor will have to cooperate with the trustee on any requests for additional financial documents or records. At this meeting, the trustee will ask questions to make sure the debtor is fully aware of the consequences of debt discharge by the bankruptcy court. Sometimes trustees will deliver this in written form to the debtor before or at the meeting. Assuming the trustee makes the recommendation for discharge, the Federal bankruptcy court judge will discharge the debts when the process is completed.

# Commodities Futures Trading Commission (CFTC)

The CFTC is the regulatory agency whose acronym stands for the Commodities Futures Trading Commission. This group arose as a direct result of the Congressionally enacted Commodity Futures Trading Commission Act of 1974. Since that time, the group has carried the responsibility of regulating both the commodity options and futures markets. Their goals range from protecting investors from manipulative endeavors of firms to promoting fair, efficient, and competitive futures markets to stopping fraud and other abusive trading practices.

This regulatory group with vast powers is a fully independent agency under the umbrella of the United Statesâ€™ government. Besides their core objectives listed above, they seek to use their considerable powers to safeguard against systemic risk and to encourage transparent and financially viable markets. Following the Global Financial Crisis of 2007-2009 they have been working towards greater transparency and more stringent regulation of the swaps market, a multiple trillion dollar enterprise. The Dodd Frank Wall Street Reform and Consumer Protection Act of 2010 gives them this authority and ability to transition into this additional role as safe guardian of the swaps markets.

Five different committees comprise the CFTC. Each of these governing groups reports to a commissioner. The President of the United States appoints these commissioners directly which the Senate must then approve. The areas of concentration for the five committees include global markets, technology, agriculture, energy and environmental markets, and cooperation with the SEC Securities Exchange Commission. Each committee is made up of people with backgrounds in and connections to various industries and their interests. This includes the commodities exchanges, the futures exchanges, traders, the environment, and consumers.

The history of regulation of these futures and commodities markets stretches back nearly a century. While these contracts have been trading in the United States for longer than 150 years, they have only been Federally regulated from the 1920s. The original Congressional act that gave the government the authority to regulate and monitor these high stakes and leveraged markets was the Grain Futures Act of 1922. This authority was expanded by the Commodity Exchange Act of 1936.

With the advent of technological advances in the 1970s, the futures and commodity contracts trading has rapidly grown well beyond the original agricultural and other physical types of commodities. It now spans a dizzying range of financial instruments. Among these are the securities of foreign (and American) governments, foreign currencies, and foreign and American stock indices, and even individual company shares. Because of this rapid and spiraling expansion into countless other arenas, Congress decided to act to ensure that the oversight functions of these markets were adequate to handle the vast array of new activity.

They passed the Commodity Futures Trading Commission Act of 1974 in order to establish the CFTC. This new agency took the place of the U.S. Department of Agriculture and its Commodity Exchange Authority with regards to regulating both commodity futures and options exchanges and markets throughout the U.S. This new Act enabled vast changes to the old simple powers which the Commodity Exchange Act of 1936 had granted.

When their original mandate expired around the year 2000, Congress updated it with the Commodity Futures Modernization Act of 2000. This act mandated that the CFTC and the SEC begin to establish a combined regulatory authority for the relatively new single stock futures. These financial instruments had started trading in November of 2002. By 2003, such swaps had massively and exponentially expanded from the time when they had been originally introduced in the latter years of the 1970s.

As with the SEC, the CFTC does not exercise direct regulatory control for individual companies in the commodity and futures markets and their corporate financial soundness. The exception to this general rule pertains to huge swap participants and the now-regulated swap dealers. For these organizations, the CFTC actually sets the minimum capital standards as mandated by the Dodd-Frank Act.

Since 2014, the Commodities Futures Trading Commission has also gained oversight over the DCM designated contract markets. This includes the derivatives clearing organizations, swap execution facilities, swap dealers, swap data repository, commodity pool operators, and futures commission merchants, as well as other intermediary groups. This regulatory body also coordinates its efforts with major international counterparts, such as the British regulatory group the Financial Conduct Authority that oversees the London Metal Exchange.

# Commodity Futures Modernization Act (CFMA)

In the year 2000, the U.S. Government passed the Commodity Futures Modernization Act. The act did several things. First it reaffirmed the regulatory authority of the Commodity Futures Trading Commission over all American futures markets. This authority became extended for a period of five years with this act.

A second and more significant result of the act came about as the government allowed Single Stock Futures to be traded for the first time in the United States. Other countries already allowed their investors to trade these particular types of futures when Congress passed this act. In America up to this point where the CFMA passed, it was illegal for investors to participate. Yet investors were eager to gain the leverage that these futures delivered.

Single Stock Futures are popular precisely because they do allow significant exposure to equity markets. A single stock future is a special kind of futures contract. The instrument allows a buyer to trade a certain number of shares in a single company at a price that they agree on now for a particular date in the future. The price is known as the strike price or futures price. The future date that the two parties set is the delivery date.

Buyers of these contracts are long the future in the stock. Sellers of the contract are short the stock in question. The buyer makes money if the price of the underlying stock increases, while the seller makes money if the value of the underlying stock declines. There is no cost to open the contract besides commissions and fees.

Single Stock Futures trade typically in contracts of 100 shares. Buying the contract does not cause any dividend or voting rights to transfer from the seller to the buyer. Futures trade using margin and provide tremendous leverage. There are no short selling rules applied to them as there are to stocks themselves.

Other countries adopted the Single Stock Futures trading ahead of the United States. The American market was not allowed to trade them before the passage of the Commodity Futures Modernization Act of 2000. This was because there was conflict between the two regulatory agencies the U.S. Securities and Exchange Commission and the Commodity Futures Trading Commission. The two could not work out which agency would regulate these new Single Stock Futures products and trading.

When the government passed the CFMA of 2000 into law, they agreed to a compromise. Both of these agencies decided to share the jurisdiction under a plan that allowed the Single Stock Futures to finally start trading on November 8 of 2002. This allowed the United

States based traders to catch up with other countries who were already trading these instruments.

The Commodity Futures Modernization Act brought the United States into a global market of the Single Stock Futures that included Great Britain, Spain, South Africa, India, and other countries. The South African market has traditionally been the largest of the single stock futures marketplaces. Their average numbers of contracts amount to 700,000 each day.

Though the CFMA allowed single stock futures to be traded, this did not establish a marketplace for them on which they could be traded in the U.S. Two different companies began trading them initially. One of these closed. The remaining company trading these types of futures in the U.S. is now known as the One Chicago. This is a joint venture of the main Chicago commodities and futures exchanges the Chicago Mercantile Exchange, the Chicago Board Options Exchange, and the Chicago Board of Trade.

# Congressional Budget Office (CBO)

The Congressional Budget Office was created by Congress in 1975. Since that time, it has continuously developed and published its own independent analyses for economic and budget related issues. Its goal is to support the process of making Congressional budgets. Ever year the agency puts together literally hundreds of estimates for costs of proposed legislation as well as dozens of routine reports.

The CBO is religiously non partisan so that it can engage in unbiased and objective analysis. It only hires staff based on their professional abilities and does not consider their political affiliations. CBO never engages in recommending policies. It is concerned with all of its reports and price estimates explaining its analytical methodology.

The CBO produces Baseline Budget and Economic Projections. It does this regularly to come up with predictions for economic and budget outcomes. These estimates assume that the present conditions for revenues and spending will continue. Such baseline projections extend for 10 year time frames as utilized in the process of Congressional budget making.

Long Term Budget Projections are another item that the Congressional Budget Office offers Congress. These extend well beyond the usual 10 year budget forecasts to cover the next 30 years. They reveal the impacts of economic developments, demographic trends, and increasing health care expenses for federal deficits, spending, and revenues.

With the Cost Estimate analyses, the Congressional Budget Office delivers estimates in writing for the expenses created by every bill which the committees in Congress approve. They reveal the ways the bill will impact revenues or spending for the coming five to 10 years.

The CBO also develops Analytic Reports which consider specific elements of the tax code, programs of federal spending, and economic and budget constraints. Such reports pertain to a number of elements of federal policy. This includes economic growth, health care, social insurance, taxes, income security, the environment, energy, national security, education, financial issues, infrastructure, and other areas.

Once the President submits his Presidential Budget, CBO get involved. It re-estimates the impacts of it. The office does this by using its particular methods for economic estimating and forecasting.

From time to time, the CBO comes up with a volume on Budget Options. This reference work provides a number of ways that the government could reduce its budget deficits. The options are varied and come from a number of sources. They include raising additional revenues and lowering spending.

The Congressional Budget Office also produces Sequestration Reports. They must put out estimates of funding caps on discretionary programs in every fiscal year that goes through 2021. They consider these numbers to determine if cancelling the pre-allocation of budgeted resources is necessary.

The CBO knows what it should study because of its mandates. It's responsibilities are to assist the Senate and House Budget Committees in their jurisdictional affairs. They also are directed to support various other committees of the Congress. This includes especially the Finance, Ways and Means, and Appropriations Committees as well as the leadership of Congress. They are required by law to produce many of the annual reports which they create. The best known of these remains the Budget and Economic Outlook.

# Consumer Data Industry Association

Consumer reporting has become a huge business in the United States. It makes sense that they would have a large and important trade association. The Consumer Data Industry Association is this organization that functions as the industry trade association for credit reporting companies in the United States.

While they have over 140 different corporate members, they represent approximately 200 companies in the consumer data business. These companies provide a wide range of services. Among these are risk management, fraud prevention, and mortgage and credit reports in the data reporting business.

Other companies offer additional services that are newer in nature. These cover employment and residential screening services, collection services for companies and individuals, and even check verification and check fraud services. Naturally the major consumer reporting agencies are important pillar members of the CDIA. These include Experian, Equifax, TransUnion, and Innovis.

This Consumer Data Industry Association works to provide education to all parties involved in the learning process of consumer data and information. This includes regulators, legislators, the media, and consumers. Their goal is to teach about the proper utilization of such information.

The members of this association also deliver analytical tools and data to help companies provide safe, fair transactions for their customers. Their products and services encourage competition and make better opportunities for the economy as a whole and their customers.

The products and services produced by the members of the Consumer Data Industry Association are enormously utilized. They are a part of over nine billion transactions that are processed every year. The goal of these companies is to offer better access to consumers. They also strive to create products and services which are centered on the needs of the consumers. Finally, they try to offer innovation in an industry that is constantly changing to keep up with rapidly expanding technology and the times.

The history of the Consumer Data Industry Association goes back to 1906. Its founders established it in Rochester, New York as the National Association of Retail Credit Agencies. The organization arose because American consumers were requiring more credit. At the same time, Americans were moving around like never before. Creditors needed a standardized and consistent form of credit information on these consumers. This way they would be able to assess their history of credit payment.

The CDIA underwent numerous name changes over the decades before settling on their present one as the services provided by their membership gradually evolved. In 1907 they became the National Association of Mercantile Agencies. After World War I this organization changed to the Associated Credit Bureaus of America. Under this identity they created the very first standardized system for credit data reporting following World War II.

In the 1960s they began computerizing the industry to keep better track of credit records. Nearly all credit became accessed through such automation by the end of the 1960s. The agency again changed its name at this time to Associated Credit Bureaus as it had expanded to become international. The government took notice of all this activity and passed the first of the consumer reporting industry regulatory laws the Fair Credit Reporting Act in 1971.

In 1991 they moved the office to Washington, D.C. to be near the regulatory and legislative bodies of the U.S. A final name change came about in 2001 as the group evolved to its present Consumer Data Industry Association. Today the organization is the representative body for all companies that deal with analyzing and managing credit data for consumers. Since the 1990s this has grown beyond credit reports to include background screening and employment reporting.

# Consumer Financial Protection Bureau (CFPB)

The CFPB is the Consumer Financial Protection Bureau. Congress created this government agency in 2008 as one of the reactions it took to the devastating financial crisis and Great Recession, the worst financial shocks to the system since the end of the 1930s era Great Depression.

The idea was to erect an organization that would protect consumers from risks and predatory practices of Wall Street and the mega banks which already had been determined as â€œtoo big to fail.â€ The Dodd-Frank Wall Street Reform and Consumer Protection Act actually set up this new entity the CFPB.

The role of this new twenty-first century organization is to assist consumers in the financial markets through creating rules that are more efficient and fair, by continuously and equitably enforcing the rules, and by helping consumers to be able to gain additional command over their own economic futures and affairs.

The Consumer Financial Protection Bureauâ€™s goal is to ensure that the various financial markets function fairly and appropriately for providers, consumers, and the all around national economy. To this effect they strive to safeguard consumers from deceptive, predatory, abusive, and unfair activities in the marketplaces. They enforce action on any companies which break the laws. The CFPB provides people with the tools and information they require to make decisions that are smart for their own situations.

The Consumer Financial Protection Bureau believes in and labors towards a financial market that works fairly. This means that the terms, risks, and prices of any deals must be transparent and obvious in advance so that all consumers are able to know their choices and fairly and effectively comparison shop. They work to see that all corporations abide by the identical consumer protection rules. Each company must fairly compete to provide high quality goods and services.

To see this vision become reality, the Consumer Financial Protection Bureau strives to empower, enforce, and educate. Empowering means that they develop tools, answer commonly posed queries, and offer helpful tips for consumers who are interested in making their way through the various financial options to shop around for the deal that best meets their needs. They pride themselves on their effective enforcement of the rules against predatory operations and actions that break the law.

The CFPB has obtained and returned literally billions of dollars in damages to customers who were wronged. Education means that the CFPB fosters consumer abilities and educational opportunities from a young age extending on to retirement. They inform financial companies of their legal and ethical responsibilities and publish research to help out consumers.

The Consumer Financial Protection Bureau operates in several core functions. They acknowledge that the government created them to offer one accountability agency to enforce the laws for federal consumer finance and to safeguard consumers in the financial arena. This used to be the purview of a number of different agencies. Among the CFPB's core functions are receiving complaints from consumers, enforcing the discrimination laws in consumer finance, and creating and enforcing rules to rid the market of abusive, deceptive, and predatory actions by companies.

They also foster financial education among consumers, regulate and oversee the financial markets for upcoming risks for consumers, and do research on consumer's experiences in utilizing financial services and products. They do this to try to locate problems lurking in the financial marketplace so that more fair ultimate outcomes can be achieved for American consumers everywhere.

As of 2016, Richard Cordray is the Consumer Financial Protection Bureau's first director. Before he assumed this important responsibility, he served in the role as head of the Bureau's Office of Enforcement.

# Corporation

A corporation refers to a business entity where it is distinctive and separated from the owners. Such corporations may take on many responsibilities similar to individuals. They can borrow and loan out money, make and execute contracts, hire and terminate employees, sue or become sued, pay taxes, and own cash and assets. This is why corporations are many times referred to by the phrase of legal person.

A corporation is a legal construct that controls and runs businesses of all types all over the globe. There may be differing legal arrangements from one government jurisdiction to the next, but they all have the attribute of a limited liability. With this protection, shareholders enjoy important rights like benefitting from dividends as a result of profits and price appreciation from successful business endeavors. While enjoying these advantages, limited liability means that they do not carry any of the personal responsibility for payment of the company's debts.

Practically every famous business and brand in the world is a part of a corporation. This includes such internationally recognized entities as Coca-Cola, McDonalds, Microsoft, and Toyota Motors. Corporations can also do business under a different name. A classic example of this is Alphabet Inc. that runs Google.

Corporations are established as a group of stock holders choose to incorporate. They pursue this follow up after a common goal in their ownership of the business. Such corporations may be charitable as well as for profit. The overwhelming majority of such companies are founded with the ambition of earning positive returns for the stock holders. These shareholders own some percentage of the corporation in exchange for paying for their shares. If they obtain them directly from the company, then their payments remit to the treasury of the company itself.

Corporations sometimes possess thousands of shareholders, especially when they are publicly traded companies. These entities could also have only a few or even one shareholder. The most common corporations within the United States are called "C Corporations."

Shareholders use their one vote per share to vote for the company board of directors every year. This group is responsible for naming the management which they oversee. The managers run the daily activities of the company. It is the corporation's board of directors which must carry out the business plan of the entity. They also do not bear responsibility for the company's debts, but have a fiduciary responsibility to care for the corporation. If they do not fulfill the duty faithfully, they may become personally liable for mistakes. There are tax statutes that allow for board of directors members to be personally liable.

As these corporations fulfill their goals, they can be wound down through a process also known as liquidation. In this process, they appoint a liquidator to sell off the company assets, pay the creditors, and share out all cash assets which remain among the stockholders. This can be done as a result of an involuntary or a voluntary procedure. Creditors can force liquidation when a company can no longer pay its debts. This often leads to corporate bankruptcy.

# Debt Forgiveness

Debt Forgiveness refers to the action of writing off all or some of a debt which a debtor has outstanding and usually simply cannot hope to repay. This act of forgiving debt can occur for the purpose of reducing the total sum of loss which the lender will otherwise incur because of defaults. From time to time, this idea has been pursued to strengthen the national economy in countries that would rather write down their debt against resources they borrowed on in prior years.

There are definite advantages for a lender or creditor in choosing to pursue debt forgiveness with their borrowers. When they grant this forgiveness of debt, they can save huge amounts of resources and wasted time trying to collect on a bad debt. This means that such resources are then freed up for more productive activities going forward. In a number of countries, the regulations and laws concerning credit and debt permit the creditor to claim an associated tax deduction for at least some if not all of the debt which they forgive. This enables them to additionally reduce the revenue loss from the anticipated income stream of the borrower's payments.

In these scenarios, debtors receive the opportunity to escape from part of even all of the debt in question. This can significantly help them to ease their financial case especially after they have suffered from various dramatic financial setbacks and can no longer honor the previously negotiated debts. One downside is that many sovereign governments choose to tax any and all debt forgiveness as real income. This means that while the debtor may enjoy a temporary form of relief from the burdensome debts, they may become categorized according to a higher tax bracket at least for that particular year. This could lead to a hefty tax bill which they cannot settle with the taxing authorities. It can create a whole host of new problems in place of the older and now forgiven ones.

The process of debt forgiveness even happens between one nation and another creditor country. It always helps to consider concrete examples of these concepts to better understand them. Nations which are recovering form devastating natural disasters could not be able to pay debts or even interest owed on them for a few years after such a disaster occurs. Instead of destroy the nation's fragile economy at that point and time, creditor nations will often decide instead to simply write off the loan. This is not an atypical event when it is clear that the economy of the nation will collapse otherwise, especially as this often impacts the entire global economy should it occur.

It is not important as to whether such debt forgiveness is actually applied to individuals, companies, or nations. The process is generally the same. It is also rarely pursued before all other potential avenues are fully explored. Usually what will happen is that debt will not be written down or off if there is any practical possibility that the financial condition for the debtor in question will improve in an acceptable to the creditor time frame. Yet in the end, this debt forgiveness will typically prove to be the most intelligent and ultimately practical form of action if the debtor's financial condition does not look like it will improve any time soon so that the debtor can actually resume their debt and interest payments in an reasonable time frame going forward.

# Debt Relief

Debt relief refers to the effective reorganizing of any form of debt so that the indebted party experiences at least some debt forgiveness. This could be complete or partial relief of debt from a large or even overwhelming burden. It is possible for it to take a wide range of scenarios. Relief might be offered in the form of lowering the aggregate principal in whole or in part. It might also be accomplished through lengthening the loan term or reducing the total interest rate and payments of loans which are due.

Debt relief also relates to debt forgiveness in order to stop the growth of the principal or at least to slow it down. This can be done for groups ranging from individual people to companies or multinational corporations to entire nations. From the days of the ancient world up to the 1800s, it primarily pertained to individual and household debt. This especially meant freeing of slaves from indebtedness or forgiving agriculture debts.

In the last years of the 1900s, the use of the phrase changed to cover mostly debt of the Third World. This began with the skyrocketing debt from the Latin American Debt Crisis that included such countries as Mexico and Argentina. By the early years of the 2000s, the phrase had greater application to individuals in wealthy countries that had been ravaged by housing and credit bubbles.

Debt relief in the 20th century came to apply to nations after the devastating effects of the First World War. Those debt payments from the allies of the United states were suspended in the dark depths of the Great Depression from 1931. Finland was the only country to repay these debts in full. Germany also received debt relief of its war reparation burdens from the United States, Britain, and France with the Agreement on German External Debts in 1953. This represented one of the first large scale applications of debt relief on an international scale.

By the 1990s, debt relief had become an urgent need for those under-developed nations which were heavily in debt. This became a mission in the 1990s for a number of Christian organizations, Non Governmental Organizations focused on development, and others partners who worked in an enormous coalition which called itself Jubilee 2000. As part of the campaign to push for debt forgiveness and relief, there were demonstrations at meetings like the G8 Summit in Birmingham, England in 1998. This helped the agenda for debt relief to reach the radar of international organizations like the World Bank and IMF International Monetary Fund as well as Western developed nationsâ€™ governments.

It actually became public policy through an initiative called the HIPC Heavily Indebted Poor Countries program. This initiative started out in order to offer consistent help in the form of debt relief to those most impoverished nations of the world. It worked strenuously to make certain that the money donated went for reduction of poverty and did not get siphoned off to infrastructure or military buildup programs.

This World Bank-supervised project involved conditions which were much like those accompanying loans from the World Bank and IMF International Monetary Fund. They mandated strict structural reforms that often involved privatizing public utilities including electricity and water. The prospective nations had to institute Poverty Reduction Strategies and demonstrate substantial macroeconomic stability for minimally a year.

In order to cut inflation, there were nations goaded into reducing their expenditures on important sectors such as education and health. The World Bank may have deemed the HIPC protocols a triumph for the twin goals of poverty and debt reduction, but many scholars and analysts offered significant criticisms of the program.

Despite critiques though, the HIPC became extended through the MDRI Multilateral Debt Relief Initiative. After the Gleneagles G8 meeting of 2005 in July, the wealthy creditor nations signed on to the MDRI. This provided full, complete elimination of all HIPC countriesâ€™ multilateral debts which they owed to the IMF, World Bank, and African Development Bank.

# Debt Relief Order

A Debt Relief Order (also known by their acronym DRO) refers to a British legal system type of insolvency method which is relatively new. It was Chapter 4 from the Tribunals, Courts, and Enforcement Act 2007 that actually created these new orders. The advantage that such DROs offer is a less expensive, faster, and simpler means of receiving bankruptcy styled relief in Great Britain.

The DRO works well for those indebted individuals who possess no or very few assets (under 1,000 British pounds without owning a home), and who count tiny disposable income levels (which have to be under 50 pounds sterling each month). Individuals who meet these criteria and several others may pay only a 90 pounds one time fee and then make application for the Debt Relief Order without a court appearance. Participants can even pay this fairly reasonable fee in a period of installments before they file the application for the order. Such DROs took the full force of law for both England and Wales on April 6th of 2009.

There are a range of specific requirements that individuals must meet in order to qualify for such a Debt Relief Order. It must be clear the persons can not pay their debts. They must not owe more than 20,000 pounds in total unsecured bills. Homeowners do not qualify, nor do those who have over 1,000 pounds in total gross assets. They can only keep their car if its value is under 1,000 pounds. The debt holder has to live in Wales or England or at least have been resident or engaged in business in either place within the past three years. They also may not have been issued a DRO in the prior six years.

Besides this the indebted individuals may not be part of any other kind of insolvency proceedings. These include bankruptcies which are not yet discharged, voluntary individual arrangements, present debt relief restrictions, present bankruptcy restrictions, a bankruptcy petition, or an interim order. It is true that these Debt Relief Orders are still insolvency forms that will be publicly listed in the insolvency services website.

In order for Debt Relief Orders to be successfully implemented, there must be a government approved intermediary who handles the event with the relevant authorities. For intermediaries to be approved, they generally have to be debt advice organization personnel which have experience as debt advisors. Some of these approved organizations include the Consumer Credit Counseling Service, one of the Citizens Advice Bureaus, Baines and Ernst National Debtline, Think Money, Payplan, the Institute of Money Advisers, and members of the entity Advice UK. Any of these approved intermediaries are able to consider the information of the persons applying, discern if they are DRO eligible, and finally make an online application on their behalf. These intermediaries who are approved do not charge fees to submit such applications.

The Official Receivers are able to issue the Debt Relief Orders after they obtain both the fee and the application. No court involvement is necessary if the applicant is eligible. Otherwise they will reject the application out of hand. These Official Receivers also have the authority to rescind these DROs if more relevant information on the debtors' financial conditions appears after the order has been granted. There are also criminal charges and penalties allowed by the British law if the applicants knowingly perjure themselves or provide deliberately misleading information on their financial conditions, assets, debts, and other personal financial costs.

Back in November of 2014, the New Policy Institute released data (research funded by the Trust for London) on the quantities of debt relief orders throughout different parts of the United Kingdom. Unsurprisingly, the total numbers of these DROs for London in the years of 2009 to 2013 proved to be vastly less than the rest of Englandâ€™s average.

# Deed in Lieu of Foreclosure

A deed in lieu of foreclosure represents an alternative option to a standard foreclosure on a house. In this deed in lieu arrangement, the owner of the property decides to hand over the property in question to the lender on a completely voluntary basis. In exchange for agreeing to this, the lender cancels out the mortgage loan. The deed to the house becomes transferred from the owner to the lender. As part of this conciliatory arrangement, the mortgage lender guarantees that it will not start the foreclosure process on the owner. If there are any foreclosure actions that have already begun, the lender will also terminate these. It is up to the lender to decide if they will forgive any extra balance that the sale of the home does not cover.

There are some tax issues that can arise with a deed in lieu of foreclosure deal. One potential downside to this type of debt forgiveness involves the consequences of it with the IRS. Federal law in the United States requires creditors to file 1099C forms for tax purposes when they choose to forgive any loan balance that amounts to more than $600. This debt forgiveness is then considered to be income and it becomes a tax liability for the home owner.

Fortunately for many home owners during the financial crisis, Congress passed the Mortgage Forgiveness Debt Relief Act of 2007. This delivered tax relief on a number of loans that banks forgave in the years starting from 2007 till the end of 2013.

The main issue and advantage that a deed in lieu of foreclosure offers centers around this excess balance debt forgiveness. Anyone who enters into such a voluntary agreement should carefully review the contract to learn how the deficiency balance topic will be addressed. Sometimes the documents are not clear on this point.

In this case, the homeowner should take the deed in lieu document to a lawyer who specializes in property law. It is not inexpensive to have a lawyer review such a contract document. The money it can save the home owner in the future for signing a contract he or she does not understand and may suffer significantly from will make the fees seem reasonable by comparison.

There are a number of requirements in order for a deed in lieu of foreclosure to be accepted. First the house would have to be on the seller market for a minimum number of days. Ninety days is usual. There also may not be any liens on the house. The property typically could not be in the process of foreclosure already. Finally, the deed in lieu offer has to be voluntary on the part of the home owner.

Another option that can be pursued in place of this deed in lieu of foreclosure is a short sale. Short sales have the same requirements as do the deed in lieu arrangements with several additional stipulations. The home seller must be suffering from financial hardship. The home itself has to be offered at a reasonable price.

In an alternative short sale, the mortgage lender will consent to receiving a lesser amount from the sale than the remaining mortgage balance that the owner still owes. It is up to the bank and the contract if any additional balance which exists will be forgiven or not. The same tax issues apply if the lender agrees to forgive more than $600.

# Deed of Priority

Deed of Priority refers to a deed or other form of contract where two or more creditors concur between themselves on the order that their security for a debtor in common will rank. In other words, they set out the rights which each of them will have pertaining to recovering the debts which the specific debtor in question owes them all should said debtor choose to default.

Many times in practice this phrase is interchanged with the similar term inter-creditor agreement. It is true that both kinds of documents look to arrange the order of precedence rank between a group of creditors. There are important differences between these two types of documents though. For one, the inter-creditor agreement is usually a more complicated document. It tends to detail equity and debt provider rights as well as the rights to obtain payments in advance of a debtor going insolvent and the rights to seize security.

Deeds of Priority are also referred to as Waiver Arrangements in Britain, and as Ranking Arrangements in Scotland. Both businesses and consumers have opportunities to source finance from multiple sources. Each lender will want some form of security with which to back the loan naturally. This might amount to any business assets or only specific ones. The second lender will also wish to obtain security in the form of some of the business assets regarding the loan they are issuing.

It is critical for every lender involved in the project, both original ones and new ones, to be aware of the different security arrangements which have already been made between the customer and earlier lenders. In other words, the various lenders will need someone to act as liaison between them so that each lender is able to ascertain and confirm its part of the secured assets, as well as its ranking for them. They will require such assurances before they actually issue the funds in the agreed upon loan.

There are a means by which they could attempt to effectively do this. One of them is the waiver arrangement. Another is using the deed of priority discussed in this article. The deed of priority is usually preferable since it spells out clearly and concisely the terms which pertain between each and every lender in the case of this specific borrower. It helps them all to understand how the various company or personal assets will be fairly and equitably distributed and shared out in the case of a default on one or more of their repayment agreements with the borrowing customer.

These scenarios will most commonly arise when a business already had a financing arrangement in place with a traditional bank. The business may then open negotiations with what is known as an alternative lender to borrow additional capital. Naturally this alternative lender will then want an arrangement hammered out with the other lender so that it can be sure of obtaining some level of collateral security over assets which are already pledged in part or whole to the original lender.

They will then sit down to fine tune the priority ranking of the various securities of the business, or to establish a release of assets from the existing security in play with the original lender. Paperwork must be drawn up, legalized, and signed off on by all lenders involved typically as swiftly as possible.

Fortunately for British- based businesses, there is a protocol in place to handle these matters. The British Bankers Association (or BBA) has compiled a PDF document called the â€œDeeds of Priority and Waivers: What You Need to Know as a Small or Medium Sized Business and What the Major Banks Are Committed to.â€

All of the major British banks have signed on to the terms of this protocol, making it far easier for British businesses to work out the deeds of priority arrangements so that they can obtain their supplementary financing from the second institutions.

# Deed of Trust

A Deed of Trust refers to a critically important document which is associated with purchasing a house. Coupled with the promissory note, these are arguably the two most important documents which get signed in a closing on a home. The deed of trust proves to be the loan security. It is similarly the one which becomes recorded with public records in the local area governing jurisdiction. This deed can be numerous pages long.

There are three component parties to the deed of trust. The trustor is ultimately the borrower. The beneficiary proves to be the lender on the deal. The trustee is that third party entity that maintains the ownership of the title throughout the terms of the loan. These instruments will identify many important terms to the mortgage and the loan arrangements. Among these is the principal amount of the loan, the names of the various parties, and the property's legal description which ultimately secures the mortgage. It also details the mortgage requirements and provisions, the loan's maturity date and inception date, the legal proceedings, and the late fees associated with the account. Finally, the deed will cover alienation and acceleration clauses along with riders that pertain to clauses such as adjustable rate mortgages and prepayment penalties that may apply.

It is critically important to understand who or what the trustee is on a given mortgage. Mortgages themselves do not come with a trustee. Yet the deeds of trust do. This must always be a neutral third party which neither represents the interests of neither the lender nor the borrower. It would often be an entity or organization like the title company. Such a group will maintain the rights known as the "Power of Sale" should the borrower default. Once the deed has been paid off fully, the trustee will reconvey the property. The trustee has the duty to file the Notice of Default should the borrower default. Generally though, such a trustee will bring in another trustee to arrange the foreclosure terms in what is called a Substitution of Trustee.

In either case, following 90 day periods while the public records are updated and the subsequent 21 day publication in the major area circulating newspaper, the trustee has the rights to sell the property directly from the steps of the courthouse without undergoing standard court proceedings. Up to this point, the borrower could reclaim the property by catching up on all missed back payments and covering the fees the trustee has assumed to that point. After a trustee sells the property in the Trustee Sale, this is considered to be binding and final.

The promissory note should never be confused with the Deed of Trust. The deed secures both the debt and the property. The promissory note is further secured by the deed itself. This comprises the debt's evidence of existence. Besides this, the promissory note represents the borrower's promise to repay the mortgage debt. It will contain all applicable terms like payment obligations and interest rates. Though it is not usually recorded, this note will be stamped â€œpaid in fullâ€ and given back to the appropriate borrower with the recorded Reconveyance Deed. It is the lender who holds the promissory note up to the point when the borrower fully repays the loan. Borrowers do receive copies of these important documents.

With Deeds of Trust and Promissory Notes, borrowers should thoroughly read both documents before signing them. It is critically essential to review a number of items covered by both documents. These include the all-important loan balance principal, the trustorsâ€™ names spelling, the interest rate, the amount of monthly payments, address of the property in question, and any prepayment penalties associate with the mortgage itself.

# Defeasance Clause

A defeasance clause refers to a mortgage contract. It is the statement in a mortgage loan that explains what will happen once a borrower has repaid all of the outstanding loan amounts. At that point, the lender usually will be required by law to hand over the title of the property to the owner. These defeasance clauses are not utilized in every part of the country. Instead they are a part of mortgages where they are not issued on a lien basis. When such liens are used instead, lenders keep their interest in the house. This gives them the right and ability to foreclose on the property in case the borrower does not make the payments according to the loan terms and agreement.

When a loan contains a defeasance clause, borrowers should carefully read through it. They must be certain that the lender interest in the house will come to an end after the loan is fully paid off including principle, interest, and other costs. This is the standard and accepted practice in the industry.

As mortgages are set up using a defeasance clause, lenders keep a special form of title called a defeasible title. These conditional titles may be revoked in specific scenarios. It is the defeasance clause itself found in the mortgage contract that determines when the lender will give up the title to the property after the borrower has fulfilled all of the loan obligations. The clause may also detail additional information. This can include penalties for prepayment should the loan come with them.

After the home buyers have completely repaid their loan, they can redeem their property's title. The one time borrower then becomes the home owner with title. Having the title is important for many reasons. It allows owners to refinance the home, sell it, rent it out, pledge it for a line of credit, or keep and live in it indefinitely. These titles are supposed to be free and clear after the interest of the lender terminates. An exception to this might be if the title had other issues hanging over it that had nothing to do with the mortgage loan with which the buyer purchased it. This might be from a tax lien or other problem.

It is the paperwork associated with the mortgage which usually spells out such things as defeasance clauses. Such paperwork should come with terms and conditions that are spelled out in great detail. For example, this contract contains all of the relevant information that pertains to the forecast repayment date, total amount to be paid back throughout the loan, and other issues. Buyers should carefully review all of this for accuracy. If any of it does not appear to be as expected by the borrowers, then they need to talk with the lender before signing any contracts.

There are several different ways that titles can be released by the lender. A defeasance clause may stipulate that the lender needs to release the title at once to the borrower after the loan has been completely paid. In other cases, the borrower might need to file paperwork for the release before the title comes back. The title should be cleared when the loan is paid off in full. Should any problems with this title arise, it can be a serious issue in the future when the owner wants to sell or refinance the house. Clearing up issues and mistakes on a title can take time, so these should be addressed as soon as possible.

# Deferred Annuity

A Deferred Annuity refers to a specific kind of annuity contract. These types of annuities delay income payments (in the form of either a lump sum or installments) to the point where the investor chooses to obtain them. There are two principal stages in these kinds of annuities. These are the savings phase and the income phase. In the savings phase, individuals put money into the contract. The income phase is the one after the annuity becomes converted so that the payments are distributed as arranged. With deferred annuities there are several sub-types. These include fixed, variable, equity-indexed, and longevity.

A Fixed Deferred Annuity operates similarly to a CD Certificate of Deposit. The main difference lies in how the interest income must be claimed. With these annuities, it becomes long-term deferred until the owners take disbursements from the contract. These fixed contracts come with a guaranteed rate of interest that all funds earn. The insurance company stands behind the guarantee. These are attractive choices for those investors who are averse to risk and who do not require any interest income until after they turn 59 and Â½ or older.

A variable Deferred Annuity is something like an assortment of mutual funds. With annuities, they refer to these as sub-accounts. Each owner has personal control over the investment risk he or she engages in through selecting particular sub-accounts which may cover both stocks and bonds. The returns on these investments will influence how well the annuity performs. For most investors, it benefits them more to purchase shares in several index mutual funds. This is because deferring taxes to retirement could mean that the owners will possibly pay higher taxes when they are retired than when they are working. The fees can also be as high as greater than three percent each year with many variable annuities.

Equity indexed annuities work much like the fixed annuities but also have variable annuity-like features. They possess two features. The first proves to be a guaranteed minimum return. The second is the ability to obtain a higher return than this by gaining from a formula which is based on one of the popular indices of the stock market like the S&P 500 or the Dow Jones Industrial Average. The downside to this type is that it typically comes with expensive surrender charges that can last over a ten to fifteen consecutive year long period.

Buying one of these last categories, the longevity annuity, is akin to obtaining insurance for a long life expectancy. It is helpful to consider a real life example to better understand how this works out in practice. An investor who is 60 might decide to pay in $150,000 to one of these longevity annuities. In exchange for this consideration, the insurance company which backs it will promise to pay out a set dollar amount of income for the rest of the holderâ€™s life beginning 25 years later at age 85. The advantage to this type of arrangement is that the retirees can then spend their other retirement assets because they feel comfortable that there will be a steady income stream that will support them guaranteed the rest of their lives. All income and taxes would be deferred to the distribution age when the money begins being disbursed.

It is important to realize with these annuities that any early withdrawals realized before the owners reach their legal retirement age will come with a full 10 percent penalty tax on top of the regular income taxes which the IRS will assess. The income tax rate would be based on the tax bracket of the individual when they receive the distribution.
These deferred annuities have many interesting (but often expensive) options and features which the buyers can obtain. Some of these include future income guarantees and death benefits.

# Defined Benefit Plan

A defined benefit plan is a pension plan that serves as a vehicle for retirement. These plans give owners who are retiring benefits that are already pre-determined when they are established. These plans turn out to be a win-win situation for all parties.

Employees like the set benefit towards retirement that this provides. Employers also appreciate particular features of the plan. An employer is able to make larger contributions with this type of plan than with a defined contribution plan. Businesses can deduct the amounts they contribute from their tax liabilities. These types of plans are more complicated than the defined contribution plans. This is what sets the two types of plans apart. Defined benefit plans are more expensive to set up and to maintain than are alternative employee benefit plans.

What makes these plans more helpful to employees is the contributor. Employers usually contribute the most to them. Cases exist where employees can make voluntary contributions of their own. Occasionally the plan requires employees to make contributions. Whoever contributes, the benefits delivered by the plan are limited. The IRS sets and changes these limits every few years.

There are numerous distinctive features to these types of plans. An advantage to defined benefit plans is that plan participants can be allowed to take a loan against the value of the plan. Distributions before the participant reaches 62 are usually not allowed while the employee is still working for the company. The employees with the defined benefit plans are allowed to participate in other retirement plans.

Businesses have certain requirements with these plans as well. Companies of all sizes can participate in one. They are able to offer other types of retirement plans as well. Participating companies need to have an actuary who is enrolled in the plan decide how much the funding levels should be. Businesses also may not decrease the plan benefits after they have set them.

There are many advantages to defined benefit plans. Companies can confer significant retirement benefits on employees in a small amount of time. Employees can earn these benefits in a similarly short time frame. Even early retirement does not eliminate the ability to access these benefits. Employers appreciate that they can put more into these plans than with alternatives plans Employees love the predictable dollar benefits that the plans deliver. They also are happy to have a retirement account whose benefits do not depend on investment returns.

The schedule for becoming vested in the money of this benefit account varies. It can be set up for immediate full vesting. Schedules for vesting can stretch to as long as seven years with defined benefit plans as well. Some employers use the flexibility with these accounts to provide an early retirement package. Offering special benefit packages for early retirement is achievable with defined benefit plans.

There are also several downsides to these types of plans. They are the most complicated plan to administer and run. Defined benefit plans are also the most expensive kind of retirement benefit plan that a company can offer.

The IRS penalizes companies that do not make their minimum contribution requirement for a year. They do this using an excise tax when the minimums are not met. Some companies may wish to make larger contributions to the plan than they need to do. They might be motivated by the larger tax breaks. If a company over contributes, than an excise tax also applies.

# Department of the Treasury

The Department of the Treasury is an American Federal government department which is tasked with financing the spending of the United States. It bears the responsibility for raising funds by issuing and selling treasury bills, notes, and bonds to banks and investors.

The treasury department has oversight for a number of other important government agencies. Beneath its umbrella and authority are the U.S. Mint, the Internal Revenue Service, the Secret Service, and the Bureau of Alcohol and Tobacco Tax. As such Treasury and its subsidiary government agencies wear many hats which include protecting both the President and Vice President of the U.S.

The Treasury itself has a variety of functions which both it and the bureaus under it perform. Among these are printing postage, bills, and Federal Reserve notes. It also enforces the government tax laws, collects taxes (via the IRS), and manages the Federal government spending accounts and debts. Treasury also must oversee the various U.S. banks alongside the Federal Reserve. Besides this the U.S. Secretary of the Treasury carries the responsibilities for financial policy, international monetary policy, and intervention in the foreign exchange rate of the U.S. dollar.

This cabinet level department in the United States was originally intended to encourage and facilitate economic security and growth in the country. The origins of the department itself go back to the United States First Congress that sat on March 4 of 1789 after the states ratified the Constitution. This makes it among the oldest and most important departments in the country. As a cabinet level post, the American President nominates the U.S. Secretary of the Treasury. It is the responsibility of the U.S. Senate to vet and confirm this nominee.

Once the U.S. Constitution received ratification in 1789, a much stronger centralized Federal government arose. It became necessary for the new government to have a centralized Treasury Department to manage its expenses and income.

The first Treasury Secretary proved to be Alexander Hamilton. He served the country well in this capacity until 1795. Hamilton accomplished numerous important achievements as secretary. He assumed American Revolution debts from the states to the Federal government. Hamilton made provision to pay off the war bonds the new country had issued during the war for independence. His greatest achievement probably lay in the new system he set up to collect Federal government taxes.

The Treasury Department today finances an enormous and increasing portion of the United Statesâ€™ spending by borrowing money. It does this constantly by issuing longer term Treasury Bonds and shorter time frame Treasury Bills. The bonds can take as many as 30 years to reach maturity.

Treasury Bonds and Bills are guaranteed by the full faith and credit of the federal United States government. This makes them extremely popular around the globe. Other government central banks, individuals, corporations, commercial banks, and institutions alike all invest in these interest paying debt instruments.

Government Treasury Bonds and Bills pay extremely low interest rates because they are considered by the major ratings agencies Moody's, Standard & Poor's, and Fitch to be guaranteed safe investments. These U.S. Federal debt issues traded in a world wide market estimated at $12.9 billion at the end of the year 2015.

Once the Department of the Treasury issues these bonds and bills, it is up to the Federal Reserve Bank to work alongside them to manage them. The Federal Reserve Bank utilizes these government debt instruments by buying and selling them from banks. This way they are able to manage the money supply for the United States as they determine the interest rates for the country.

# Dodd-Frank Act

The Dodd-Frank Act is fully entitled the Dodd-Frank Wall Street Reform and Consumer Protection Act. This enormous law served to reform the financial world following the financial crisis and Great Recession that began in 2008. President Obama's administration passed it through congress in 2010.

This Dodd-Frank Act legislation is literally thousands of pages long and contains numerous provisions. The regulations of this Dodd-Frank Act law are set for implementation over the course of a number of years. They were meant to reduce the obvious risks for failure in the American financial system. In order to oversee and carry out the numerous parts of the act it addresses, the controversial legislation created a range of new government agencies.

The first of these new agencies is the Financial Stability Oversight Council and Orderly Liquidation Authority. This group is tasked with overseeing major financial firms whose continued financial stability is necessary for the proper and continuous functioning of the U.S. economy.

These companies were negatively referred to as "too big to fail." The agency also handles necessary restructurings or liquidations of such firms in an orderly fashion should they become too unstable. They are charged with preventing these firms from being propped up with tax dollars. This council has great authority. They can even break apart banks which they deem in their judgment to be so big that they pose a risk to the banking system. It may also order higher reserve requirements for such banks. Another new group the Federal Insurance Office is similarly tasked with identifying and overseeing insurance companies which are too important to fail.

The CFPB Consumer Financial Protection Bureau was created to stop predatory forms of mortgage lending by the lenders. They are also responsible for increasing the simplicity of mortgage terms so that consumers can understand what they are signing before they complete the contracts. The group stops mortgage brokers from obtaining larger commissions when they close loans that have higher interest rates and fees.

It states that originators of mortgages may not direct possible borrowers to loans which provide the largest payouts to the loan originators. This group also governs various other kinds of lending to consumers. Their domain includes debt and credit cards and consumer complaints. They insist that lenders provide information in a manner that is simplest for consumers to comprehend. Credit card application simplified terms are an example of their work.

One potent rule that emerged from this Dodd-Frank Act legislation proved to be the so-called Volcker Rule. Named for the former Federal Reserve Chairman Paul Volcker, the rule was intended to reduce the amount of speculative trading, while simultaneously banning proprietary trading, by banking institutions. Banks have complained that these changes in the business model will make it more difficult to stay profitable.

The rule addresses regulating the derivatives like the infamous credit default swaps that majorly contributed to the financial meltdown in 2008. This rule also limits the ability of financial companies to utilize derivatives. The goal is to stop the systemically critical institutions from building up enormous risks that could ruin the banking system and overall economy.

The Dodd-Frank Act further created the new SEC Office of Credit Ratings. This group received the job of watching the credit agencies to ensure that the credit ratings they provide for various entities prove to be both dependable and reliable. Credit rating companies received a lot of blame for the financial crisis for falsely dispensing investment ratings that were misleading and overly positive.

Critics of the Dodd-Frank Act legislation claim the law will hamper economic growth and lead to higher unemployment in the future. Fans of the act insist that over time it will reduce the chances of the economy suffering from another 2008 styled crisis all the while safeguarding consumers from the abuses that eventually led to the crisis.

# Due Process Oversight Committee (DPOC)

Within the structure and organization of the IFRS International Financial Reporting Standards, the trustees have various bodies that help them to perform their duties. The Due Process Oversight Committee is the one that carries the responsibility to monitor the procedures for effective due process. They also do this for the IASB International Accounting Standards Board and its Interpretations Committee.

This Due Process Oversight Committee generally holds meetings four times per year on the sidelines of the usually quarterly IFRS Foundation trustees meeting. When they require additional meetings, the DPOC usually handles them via conference call. Each year, they select different international locations for their meeting places. One of their quarterly meetings is usually held in London. In May and June of 2016, the IFRC Trustees and DPOC met in Jakarta and

London, respectively. The Trustees and committee met in Beijing in October of 2015, London in June of 2015, Toronto in of April 2015, and Zurich in February of 2015.

There are a number of different responsibilities that the Due Process Oversight Committee carries out for the IFRS and the IASB. These are all spelled out within the Interpretations Committee Due Process Handbook of both the IFRS and the IASB. The first of these is to review the standard setting activities in which the IASB and staff of the IFRS Foundation engage. They do this review of due process activities routinely and with expediency as their mandate requires.

The Due Process Oversight Committee is also responsible for reviewing the Due Process Handbook that governs the committee among other things. They are to suggest updates to it that are in order. These updates would pertain to developing new and reviewing old standards, their various interpretations, and the Taxonomy of the IFRS itself. They do this to make sure that the procedures of the IASB are the best practice possible.

Besides this the Due Process Committee is tasked with reviewing the consultative groups of the IASB. They check who makes up the groups to ensure that the perspectives included are well balanced. They wish to have representation from the various relevant sub-disciplines. It is the committee's aim to ensure that these consultative groups are effective in their duties.

When outside parties request information on any due process issues, this Due Process Committee is the one that has to respond to them. They work with the technical staff of the Director for Trustee Activities to cohesively do so.

The IFRS Foundation bodies are also monitored for effectiveness by the Due Process Oversight Committee. They check up on the activities that involve standard setting at both the Interpretations Committee and the IFRS Advisory Council. Other groups within the IFRS Foundation which address the setting of standards are also followed up on by this Due Process Committee.

Finally, this important oversight committee is responsible for coming up with and issuing its recommendations to the IFRS Trustees about changing the committees. When the Due Process Oversight Committee determines that the makeup of these various committees that deal with due process needs to be changed, they let the Trustees know so that the committees can be appropriately re-balanced.

The Due Process Oversight Committee issues summaries of all of its meetings. These and any other papers and reports which they author are all found on their websites which are sub-pages of the International Financial Reporting Standards and the International Accounting Standards Board.

# Environmental Protection Agency (EPA)

The Environmental Protection Agency is the United Statesâ€™ environmental enforcement group. It is not a cabinet level department, though its Administrator typically receives cabinet status and rank. The president appoints the administrator after the individual is approved by the Congress. The EPA is headquartered in Washington, D.C. It also operates ten regional offices and 27 laboratories throughout the U.S.

President Richard Nixon originally proposed the EPA and created it by signing an executive order. It started operating December 2nd of 1970. President Nixonâ€™s order received ratification from Congress via committee hearings in the Senate and the House of Representatives.

The mission of the Environmental Protection Agency lies in protecting human health and the environment. To do this, it engages in research and environmental assessments. The group also promotes education. It carries the responsibility for enforcing environmental standards as provided in the national laws. The EPA does this by consulting with the federal, state, local, and tribal governments. Some of this enforcement, monitoring, and permitting it delegates out to the fifty states and the recognized Indian tribes.

The powers of the EPA allow it to issue sanctions and levy fines. Whenever possible it works with the government and industries to prevent pollution voluntarily. It also promotes efforts to conserve energy throughout the country.

The Environmental Protection Agency has a number of priorities in its mission. First and foremost it is interested in protecting Americans from substantial risks to their health as well as the environment in which they work, live, and learn. To do this, they carry out the best scientific research so that environmental risk can be effectively reduced on a national level. They also work to enforce the federal laws which safeguard the environment and health fairly and efficiently.

The EPA feels that every individual and group in society should be able to access correct information for taking care of environmental risks and health. This includes businesses, people, communities, and local, state, and tribal governments. They want to see environmental protection treated as a critical priority in all American policies. Energy, economic growth, natural resources, transportation, health, industry, agriculture, and foreign trade should all be taken into consideration when making environmental policy.

Making the protection of the environment help with sustainable and economically productive development is another concern of the Environmental Protection Agency. They make it their business to ensure that the U.S. is leading other nations in protecting the world's environment as well.

The EPA carries out a number of activities in order to see through their mission and goals. The primary one is to develop and enforce the environmental regulations. Congress passes laws that the EPA puts into effect by writing regulations. They set national standards for state and tribal governments to enforce on their own. They also help these groups if they can not achieve the national standards. Enforcing such regulations becomes necessary if they are not able to convince offenders voluntarily.

The EPA gives many grants out to educational groups, state programs, not for profits, and others. Almost half of their budget is devoted to this. These finance everything from cleaning up communities to paying for scientific studies. They also sponsor dozens of partnerships as part of this. Some of these help to recycle solid waste, lower greenhouse emissions, and conserve energy and water.

The group spends a lot of time and effort studying environmental issues. In their over two dozen labs around the country, they find and attempt to solve these problems. They also share the findings with academic circles, the private sector, other government agencies, and foreign countries. The Environmental Protection Agency publishes online and written materials regarding what they learn and their various activities.

# Equal Credit Opportunity Act (ECOA)

The Equal Credit Opportunity Act is also known as the ECOA. Congress created this regulation in order to provide all legal American residents with a fair and reasonable opportunity to obtain loans from banks or other financial institutions that make loans.

The act clearly states that such organizations may not discriminate against individual people for any reason that does not directly pertain to their credit history and file. It makes it illegal for lenders and creditors alike to take into consideration such factors as the consumerâ€™s color, race, ethnicity, nation of origin, religion, sex, or marital status when they are determining whether or not they will accept the credit or loan application.

Besides this, the law prohibits denying any credit application because of the age of the applicant. This assumes that the person applying has attained the legal minimum age and demonstrates the mental abilities necessary to execute such a contract. Finally, companies making loans may not reject an applicant because he or she receives public assistance funds from the government.

The governmental agency responsible for enforcing this Equal Credit Opportunity Act turns out to be the FTC Federal Trade Commission. As the consumer protection agency for the country, the FTC monitors lending organizations to make sure that they are not in violation of any of these discriminatory rules. Creditors are allowed to ask applicants for such information as their color, race, religion, sex, ethnicity, nation of origin, age, or marital status.

They are not allowed to consider any of these factors when determining whether or not to extend credit or even when deciding the terms of the credit which they are offering. The fact remains that not all people applying for credit will receive it or will obtain it on equal terms. Many factors are taken into consideration by lenders in ascertaining a person's creditworthiness, such as expenses, income, credit history, and levels of debts.

This Equal Credit Opportunity Act specifically protects consumers when they transact with investors or organizations that routinely offer credit. This includes loan and finance companies, banks, department or retail stores, credit unions, and credit card companies. Every party who is a part of the credit granting or terms setting decisions has to abide by the rules of the ECOA. This includes even the finance arrangers such as real estate brokers.

As a person applies for a mortgage, lenders will routinely inquire about some of the elements of information that are forbidden to be considered in the ultimate application decision. Because of this, applicants do not have to respond to these questions. The only considerations which they are allowed to employ in judging the merits of the individual must be information that is financially relevant, like the person's income, credit score, and present debt levels.

The Equal Credit Opportunity Act will not allow lenders to make approval decisions because of an individual's present or past marital status. They will require that applicants inform them of any child support or alimony payments which they are making. Persons receiving such substantial payments as part of their income should also disclose this so that they can obtain the loan. Companies may refuse to provide a loan because the individual's financial obligations along with child support payments are too high to pay back the loan under the required terms. This does not mean that a person can be turned down for a loan because he or she is or has been divorced.

The penalties for violating the Equal Credit Opportunity Act are severe. Class action lawsuits can be brought against them. Organizations found guilty of ignoring this act can be made to pay damages that amount to either $500,000 or a percent of the applicant's net worth, whichever is less.

# Equity of Redemption

Equity of redemption refers to a property owner's legal rights. This term represents the right of a home owner to reclaim his or her property which a mortgage loan secures. Such a right pertains to the period before the bank or lender has foreclosed on the home when the home owner is in default on the mortgage payments that include principle and interest.

As a home owner gets behind on his or her monthly mortgage payments, the lender has the right to accelerate the loan. They will generally not do this until they have attempted to work with the owner to help them get caught up on the mortgage. It is everyone's best interest for the home owner to remain in the home. Banks often lose money on houses which they sell through foreclosure.

Accelerating the loan means that the bank demands payment in full. It is still possible that the lender may be willing to let the behind home owner catch up on the mortgage payments which are in arrears at this point. Otherwise, if the owner does not meet this demand or make full payment, then foreclosure on the property begins in earnest.

In order to meet this order for full payment, home owners are permitted to find an alternative source of funds to pay off the original mortgage principle, interest, and late fees. If they are able to secure such a funding source, then the equity of redemption gives them the rights to keep the house. The problem for most home owners is that if they are in financial trouble and can not pay their mortgage, then they probably will be unable to secure another loan with which to pay off the first one.

This equity of redemption right only lasts until the home has been foreclosed upon and sold. The equity of redemption is also considered to be a valuable interest in the property and a legal estate in and of itself. This means that the home owner can sell or even transfer away this right to another individual or a company.

Equity of redemption should never be mixed up with the statutory right of redemption. The right of redemption is a separate legal right that is not universal throughout the United States. Some of the states allow for this separate right of redemption which gives home owners significantly greater maneuvering room and legal avenues.

In fact a right of redemption means that for an amount of time determined by state law, the owner is able to redeem his or her house and property simply by paying all principle, interest, costs, and fees. This right is for the period after foreclosure or seizure for unpaid taxes has already occurred. By paying the amounts demanded, the right of redemption means that the owner is able to reclaim his or her home, even if it has already been sold.

How long the statutory right of redemption period lasts depends on the state in question. This amount of time could be for several months. In other states and scenarios, it could stretch on for several years after the foreclosure has been completed. Investors who buy houses in states with this legal right must be aware of the repercussions.

Those who buy seized or foreclosed upon houses could run into a situation where the original owner comes up with the money to pay off the entire original obligation on the house. In this case, the original owner would receive back his or her home. The investor would be left to work out compensation for the lost property with the lender from whom they had purchased it.

# ESOP

An ESOP stands for the Employee Stock Ownership Plan. These are not exactly retirement savings accounts in the traditional sense. They are critical investment vehicles with tax advantages. With these types of accounts, employers establish a trust fund for the employee. The employer is then able to transfer shares of its own stock to this fund.

They might alternatively allocate cash with which the employees' account can purchase already existing shares of stock. These ESOPs prove to be the most typical means for employees gaining part ownership in their company within the United States.

Every company has its own unique formulas for allocating shares to its participating employees. The shares come out of the company trust account and transfer over to the appropriate individual employee accounts. As with other benefits for employees that are employer sponsored, vesting rules apply.

Gaining full vesting in stock option accounts requires the employee to reach a minimum number of years at the company. Once this seniority level and vesting is obtained, the employee fully owns the shares and may sell them at will. When employees part with the company, the vested shares of stock have to be purchased from them at the full market price.

There are also tax benefits to these stock option plans. Companies that issue them accrue the advantages of tax deductions for the stock value. Employees do not have to pay any taxes on employer offered contributions. They are also able to transfer the distributions to IRAs or other qualified retirement vehicles. This will help them to avoid realizing capital gains or income taxes.

These stock option plans do have limitations and rules pertaining to rollovers and withdrawals. Distribution rules can be different from one employer to the next. In general the distributions are allowed to be rolled over to other retirement plans which are qualified. Any person with an ESOP will find the distribution rules detailed in the Summary Plan Description section.

As with 401(k)s and other types of retirement vehicles, penalties for early withdrawals do apply. An employee must be 59 Â½ to begin receiving non penalized distributions. These distributions become mandatory on the April 1st that follows the year the employee reaches 70 Â½. Companies have the choices of making these account distributions with cash, stocks, or a combination of the two.

Regardless of the way they give them out, employees are always allowed to sell back vested stock shares. The proceeds from these sold shares can be transferred into self directed or traditional IRAs to defer taxes. They may also roll or transfer their distributions to a different companyâ€™s qualified retirement savings vehicle. The money will only become taxable at ordinary income tax rates once it is withdrawn later.

Participants in these stock option plans are not able to purchase any types of gold investments with the distributions. The only exceptions are when an employee has obtained diversification rights from his or her employer. Normally only employees of gold mining companies would be able to acquire either paper or physical gold in such a retirement savings account.

Because of these limitations, rolling over distributions from a stock option account to a self directed IRA makes sense. Once the funds are in a self directed account, the holders will be able to choose where they invest these funds. They will then have a variety of tax free alternative investments such as gold and other precious metals.

There are a few downsides to the employer established and funded profits sharing plans. Investment choices are as limited as can be imagined. The account owner also has to complete the companyâ€™s vesting schedule. This means that the employees can only access their funds once the vesting period of years has elapsed. ESOP’s also carry risks specific to the employee’s company. Should the employer go bankrupt, the plan may become closed. An employee might no longer be allowed to contribute to the plan or account at this point.

# European Central Bank (ECB)

The European Central Bank is responsible for the European Union’s monetary system and for maintaining the euro currency. The EU created this central bank of European central banks in June of 1998. It works alongside the various national banks of the EU member states to come up with unified monetary policy. This policy is intended to help achieve price stability throughout the countries in the EU.

The ECB became responsible for the EU’s monetary police on January 1 of 1999. This was the point in time when the euro currency became adopted by the various EU nations. This landmark event was the culmination of 20 years of steps towards a currency union.

In 1979, eight of the EU nations created the EMS European Monetary System. It effectively fixed the exchange rates between the eight participating nations. By 2002, the ECB had become more entrenched. Twelve EU nations signed on to a common monetary policy and formed the European Economic and Monetary Union that year.

The European Central Bank is independent of political groups in the various institutions of the EU such as the European Commission, European Parliament, and European Council. It handles all EU monetary issues and policies. Maintaining price stability is the first goal of the central bank. It also sets the important interest rates for the Eurozone and area.

Besides creating monetary policy for the Eurozone block, the ECB also engages in foreign exchange, holds reserve currencies, and authorizes euro bank note issues. Euro currency is actually created, printed, and maintained by the European System of Central Banks, also known as the ESCB.

The ECB has become involved in some controversial activities which were beyond the scope of its original role. It has further expanded its mandate in recent years by buying up bonds of financial companies like banks and also sovereign countries whose bonds are not finding enough interested subscribers at competitive low rates.

They have been practicing this quantitative easing and injecting money into euro area economies in an effort to encourage growth and to increase financial liquidity in the banking system. Keeping the interest rates down on sovereign national bonds also improves the budgets and balance sheets of the euro area countries which are struggling. The result of these activities has led to negative real interest rates in Europe.

Individual EU countries collect their own taxes. They also determine their own national budgets. The ECB has nothing to do with these activities. National governments work together at the EU level to come up with uniform rules on public finances. This helps them to cooperate better on policies for employment, growth, and financial stability.

The financial crisis that broke out around the globe in 2008 hit some European countries especially hard. It created a need for the ECB to work closely with the European Commission and the national governments of the EU and Eurozone members in a series of coordinated, sustained actions.

These groups are continuing to strive together to promote employment and growth, keep credit flowing to consumers and businesses at affordable prices, safeguard savings, and to guarantee inter-European financial stability. This has led to the accusation of critics of the European institutions that they only work effective when there are crises, as in a management by crisis style.

Despite these ongoing and best efforts of the ECB and other European institutions, severe imbalances and problems remain in several Eurozone countries. As of 2016, unemployment in Spain still sat at over 25% and Greece teetered on the brink of yet another recession and potential insolvency.

# European Monetary System (EMS)

In 1979 a few European nations linked their currencies together in an arrangement and system to stabilize exchange rates called the European Monetary System. This system endured until the EMU European Economic and Monetary Union succeeded it.

As an important institution within the European Union, the EMU established the euro. The origin of the EMS lay in an effort to reduce significant changes in exchange rates between the European nations and to reign in inflation. It led to the creation of the European Central Bank in June of 1998 and the euro in January of 1999.

After the failure of the defunct Bretton Woods Agreement in 1972, the Europeans wanted to create a new exchange rate system of their own to help encourage political and economic unity throughout the EU. They came up with the EMS in 1979 as a means of moving towards the common currency of the future.

The EMS eventually formed its successor the European Currency Unit. With the ECU, exchange rates could be formulated by methods that were official. In the first year of the EMS, currency values proved to be uneven. Adjustments had to be made to lower weaker currencies while increasing the stronger currency values. In 1986 they came up with a more stable system of altering national interest rates instead.

Crisis broke out in the EMS in the early years of the 1990s. Germanyâ€™s reunification created political and economic conditions that made the exchange rate bands less workable. Britain withdrew permanently from EMS in 1992. They became more independent from the central EU this way and banded together with

Denmark and Sweden in refusing to become members of the eurozone.

This did not stop other nations within the EU from continuing to push for closer economic integration and a common currency. They formed the European Monetary Institute in 1994 to set up an orderly transition to the ECB that arose in 1998. The main tasks of the new ECB were to come up with one interest rate and monetary policy by laboring alongside the national central banks.

The ECB was not given the role originally of lending money to governments in financial crises or increasing employment rates like the majority of central banks. This would later cause delays and problems in bailing out struggling countries in the financial crisis that began in earnest in 2008.

The end of 1998 saw the majority of nations in the EU cut their interest rates at the same time to encourage economic growth while preparing to implement the Euro currency. This is when they established the EMU to succeed the EMS as the primary economic policy mechanism in the European Union. The adoption and subsequent circulation of the euro by the eurozone countries proved to be a significant step towards the aimed for European political unity. The EMU has helped member nations attempt to work toward lower inflation, less public spending, and lesser government debts.

Hidden weaknesses in the European Monetary System became obvious during the global financial crisis of 2008 and the following years. Member nations like Greece, Portugal, Spain, Ireland, and Cyprus ran up high deficits that later erupted in the European sovereign debt crisis.

Because these countries did not have national currencies to devalue, they could not increase their exports. The EMU forbade them from spending additional money and running higher deficits to help increase employment. EMS policies had expressly forbidden eurozone bailouts to any countries whose economies were in trouble.

After months of arguments from the larger economy members such as Germany and France, the EMU at last came up with bailout policies that allowed aid to be dispensed to peripheral members who were struggling. They set up the European Stability Mechanism as a permanent pool of money to help out economies of struggling EU member states in 2012. This allowed a few of the countries in trouble like Spain, Portugal, and Ireland to make some progress on recoveries.

# European Monetary Union (EMU)

The European Monetary Union is also known by its long-time acronym of EMU. The full name of this is the European Economic and Monetary Union. This refers to the succeeding protocol to the original EMS European Monetary System. It means the combining of European Union member nations into a frame work for a centralized economic policy set and system. The most visible and greatest representation of this union is the euro currency, which has become the national currency for more than half the EU member states.

It was via a three-staged process that the EMU succeeded the EMS. The final third phase included the adopting of the euro currency which replaced the long-time national currencies such as the franc, peso, and mark. It was successfully concluded by all of the original EU members besides Denmark and the United Kingdom. Both of these countries received opts-outs from taking on the euro in place of their beloved sovereign national currencies.

The real history of such an economic and monetary union began with the French Foreign Minister Robert Schumanâ€™s speech, which became known as the Schuman Declaration on May 9th of 1950. He reasoned that the one sure way to ensure the peace lasted in Europe that had suffered from devastating world wars two times in only thirty years was to craft Europe into one single economic polity. It was his landmark speech that gave rise to the Treaty of Paris in 1951. This actually forged the ECSC European Coal and Steel

Community betwixt signatories Germany, Italy, France, Belgium. Luxembourg, and the Netherlands.

This original treaty strengthened through the subsequent Treaties of Rome that led to the creation of the EEC European Economic Community. Next came the Treaty of Paris that lasted through 2002. In the 1960s and 1970s, the politicians across Europe adopted the Werner Plan, yet later economic disruptions including the Saudi oil embargo and break down of the Bretton Woods agreement meant that they could not merge economically any further at this point.

The Maastrict Treaty of 1992 created a literal timeline to establish the European Monetary Union. By 1998, they had successfully formed the ECB European Central Bank which established conversion rates that were fixed between all of the member state currencies. This led to the rise of the euro single currency that started physically circulating in 2002.

Yet there were hidden flaw in the EMU design. Greece became the first severe example of these. It was revealed by 2009 that Greece had been intentionally under reporting the amount of its severe budget deficits it ran since they started using the Euro in 2001. As a result, the nation experienced what amounts to the most serious economic crisis in modern history. The proud country had no choice but to agree to two painful bailout and austerity packages from the EU and ECB in only five years. Continued bailouts remained essential to Greece being able to repay its massive debts to its many creditors.

The unemployment rate in Greece rose to as high as 25 percent (in general) and 50 percent (for people less than 25 years old). The countyâ€™s government was forced to instill capital controls to prevent monetary flight and also launch a bank holiday to limit the amounts of euros which depositors could withdraw from the banking system in any given day. The only way out of their still ongoing crisis would be to leave the EMU and return to their ancient currency the Drachma. This would allow them to severely devalue their currency and increase the competitiveness of their exports abroad.

# European Stability Mechanism (ESM)

The European Stability Mechanism is a significant part of the financial stability and safeguard mechanisms in the Euro Zone area. It replaced the EFSF European Financial Stability Facility in 2013. This original EFSF was never intended to be permanent. Instead it was designed as a temporary solution to financial problems within the EU.

The European Stability Mechanism that took over for it was better established to deliver financial help to those Eurozone member countries that found themselves either threatened by or actually experiencing financial difficulties.

These two financial facilities ran concurrently from October of 2012 through June of 2013. Beginning in July of 2013 the EFSF could no longer begin new programs for financial support or help. The program still exists to manage and collect repayments of debts that are outstanding.

Once all of the existing loans that the EFSF program made have been repaid and all funding instruments and guarantors have received full payment for their contributions, then the EFSF will cease to exist entirely. This makes the replacing ESM the only and ongoing internal means for delivering aid in response to new calls for financial assistance from Eurozone member nations.

The European Stability Mechanism proves to be the principal means of resolving crises for nations which participate in the Euro. It obtains its money by issuing debt obligations. This permits it to fund financial aid and loans to the member countries of the Euro area. The European Council actually created the ESM in December of 2010. Participating Euro member states came together and signed a treaty between the governments on February 2 of 2012. October 8 of 2012 was the day they inaugurated the new ESM.

This ESM has great flexibility in funding its distressed member states. As various conditions are met, it is able to deliver loans as part of a program for macroeconomic adjustment. The mechanism is also able to buy member countries’ debt in either the secondary or primary markets.

It can help to recapitalize banks of member states by loaning the governments money for this purpose. It can also deliver credit lines as a means of providing financial help as a precaution. In worst case and last resort conditions, the facility is allowed to recapitalize banks and other financial institutions directly. This is limited to times when resolution funds and bail ins are not enough to make the bank financially viable again.

The resources of the ESM are considerable. It has a capital base that has been subscribed in the amount of â,¬704.8 billion. Of this amount, â,¬80.5 billion has been paid in to the facility. The remaining â,¬624.3 billion is classified as callable capital when it is needed. The fund is able to loan out a maximum total of â,¬500 billion.

The ESM is based in Luxembourg. It is governed by public international law as an intergovernmental organization. It has only government shareholders making up its ownership. These are the 19 member countries that make up the Euro area. In 2016, 153 staff members worked under the direction of Klaus Regling the managing director.

European countries which are in trouble have other outside recourses for help besides the ESM. The principal other provider of assistance is the International Monetary Fund. The EU has supported having its own ESM, along with the predecessors the EFSF and the European Financial Stabilization Mechanism because it feared the consequences of some of its member states’ problems with debt. Not all of the EZ countries suffered from debt issues. One EZ country failing could have contagious effects and widespread repercussions on the other national economies’ health.

# Exchange Rate Mechanism (ERM)

Exchange Rate Mechanisms are systems that were established to maintain a certain range of exchange for currencies as measured against other currencies. These ERMs can be run in three different ways. On one extreme they can float freely. This permits the systems to trade without the central banks and governments intervening.

The fixed Exchange rate mechanisms will do whatever it takes to maintain rates pegged at a specific value. In between these two extremes are the managed ERMs. The best known example of one of these is the European Exchange Rate Mechanism known as ERM II. It is in use today for those countries who wish to become a part of the EU monetary union.

The European Economic Community formally introduced the European ERM system to the world on March 13, 1979. It was a part of the EMS European Monetary System. The goal of this new system centered on attaining monetary stability throughout Europe by reducing the variable exchange rates. This was set up to prepare the way for the Economic and Monetary Union. It also paved the way for the Euro single currency introduction that formally occurred on January 1, 1999.

The Europeans changed their system once the Euro became adopted. They introduced ERM II as a way to link together those EU countries who were not a part of the eurozone with the euro. They did this to boost extra eurozone currencies' stability. A second goal was to create a means of evaluating the countries who wished to join the eurozone. In 2016 only a single currency uses the ERM II. This is the Danish krone.

The European ERM ceased to exist in 1999. This was the point after the eurozone country European Currency Units exchange rates became frozen and the Euro began trading against them. ERM II then replaced the initial ERM. At first the Greek drachma remained in the ERM II alongside the Danish currency. This changed when Greece adopted the Euro in 2001. Currencies within the newer system may float in a fairly tight range of plus or minus 15% of their central exchange rate versus the euro. Denmark does better than this. Its Danmarks Nationalbank maintains a 2.25% range versus the central rate of DKK 7.46038.

In order for other countries that wish to join the Euro to participate, they are required to be a part of the ERM II system for minimally two years before they can become members of the eurozone. This means that at some point, a number of currencies for member states that joined the EU will have to be in the system. This includes the Swedish krona, Polish zloty, Hungarian forint, Czech Republic koruna, the Romanian leu, Bulgarian lev, and Croatian kuna. Each of these is supposed to join the system according to their individual treaties of accession.

In the case of Sweden, the situation is more complicated. The country held a referendum on becoming a part of the mechanism to which the citizens voted no. The European Central Bank still expects that Sweden will join the system and eventually adopt the euro. This is because they did not negotiate for an opt out of the currency as did the U.K. and Denmark. The Maastricht Treaty requires that EU member states all eventually join the exchange rate mechanism.

Britain participated in the mechanism from 1990 until September of 1992. On September 16, 1992 the British famously crashed out of the system on what became known as Black Wednesday because of manipulation of the pound by currency speculators led by Hedge Fund Billionaire George Soros.

# Fair Credit Billing Act

Congress passed the Fair Credit Billing act back in 1975. They enacted this national law in order to safeguard consumers from unfair or prejudiced billing actions. It created mechanisms for dealing with billing errors that affect credit accounts which are open ended. This includes credit cards and charge card accounts.

There are many different and all too common types of billing errors that the Fair Credit Billing Act specifies and protects against in its statute. Charges which are an incorrect amount are one. It also covers charges showing up on a bill that the consumer did not process. These are often known as unauthorized charges. Consumers can never be responsible for more than $50 of these. The act also covers the costs of any goods that did not come as they were supposed to when the consumer bought them, as well as for those goods that the consumer never received.

Consumers are similarly protected by the Fair Credit Billing Act from errors in calculation. They can not be held responsible for billing statements which the companies send out to the wrong address. Changes of address are required to be submitted by the account holder in writing and received by the creditor more than 19 days before the billing period ends. Consumers are similarly protected against any charges which they request proof of or clarification for on a statement. They may also not be held liable for a creditor improperly showing payments or charges to their credit accounts.

Customers are able to avail themselves of the protections spelled out in the Fair Credit Billing Act. To do so, they have to begin the process by writing the creditor at their business address specified for billing inquiries. They must include their name and address, account numbers, and any information on the billing dispute in question. The letter must be received by the creditor within 60 days or less of the original bill mailing date.

Such a letter should be dispatched by certified mail with return receipt so that the consumer has conclusive proof of when the creditor received it. All relevant copies of receipts and supporting documents need to be included with the letter. The creditor concerned is required by law to acknowledge that they have received the letter of complaint in 30 days or less after they receive it. The creditor then has up to 90 days (as in two billing cycles) to research and resolve the dispute per the terms of the Fair Credit Billing Act.

The Fair Credit Billing Act also governs what happens when a bill is placed in dispute by a consumer. The person is allowed to not make payments on any charges pertaining to the disputed amount in question. Such a period of withholding only applies throughout the time frame in which the investigation is ongoing. All remaining portions of the bill and relevant interest amounts have to be paid as per the governing credit agreement and terms. The creditor may not engage in any legal action or collection activity against the borrower so long as the investigation phase is ongoing. The account of the borrower is not permitted to be closed or restricted in this phase.

The creditor is also forbidden to make threats against the borrowersâ€™ credit ratings when charges are under investigation and in dispute. The dispute itself can be reported to the credit ratings agencies. Creditors are not allowed to discriminate by withholding credit approval from any consumer who uses his or her rights to dispute a credit charge. This means in practice that consumers may not be refused credit because they have filed disputes against charges on a bill.

# Fair Housing Act

The Fair Housing Act of 1968 is officially known as Title VIII from the Civil Rights Act of 1968. It makes it illegal to discriminate with regards to renting, selling, or financing homes or apartments. No one may consider color, race, sex, religion, or national origin in these activities.

Congress amended the Fair Housing Act of 1968 with the Fair Housing Amendments Act in 1988. These amendments expanded the rulings of the original act in a number of important ways. No one was permitted to discriminate with housing because of an individualâ€™s disability or based on their family status. This meant that home sellers or renters could not disallow families with pregnant women or who had children less than 18 years of age living with them.

To prevent disability discrimination, the act included construction and design accessibility rules for some multifamily homes. Those that were to be occupied initially after March 13, 1991 had to comply with the accessibility provisions for disabled people.

The amendments also created new means of enforcing and administering the rules. HUD Housing and Urban Development attorneys were now able to take cases to administrative law judges for victims of such housing discrimination. The jurisdiction of the Justice Department became expanded and revised in such a way that it could file suits in Federal district courts for discrimination victims.

HUD has been tasked with the principal responsible to administer the Fair Housing Act of 1968 since the government adopted it. Thanks to the amendments in 1988, the department has become substantially more involved in enforcing the provisions. This is because the newly protected families and disabled brought many new complaints. The department also had to move beyond investigating and conciliating. They were tasked with mandatory enforcing the rules.

Any complaint regarding the Fair Housing Act of 1968 that individuals file with HUD becomes investigated. The FHEO Fair Housing and Equal Opportunity office handles this responsibility. When complaints can not be resolved voluntarily, the FHEO decides if there is sufficient evidence for a reasonable case of discrimination in housing practices. If they find reasonable cause, then HUD issues a Determination and Charge of Discrimination to the complaint parties. Hearings are next scheduled in front of a law judge for the HUD administration. Either the complaining party or the accused can terminate this procedure to instead have the matter resolved in Federal courts.

At this point, the Department of Justice assumes HUD's responsibility for the aggrieved party's complaints. They act as counsel that seeks to resolve the charges. The matter then becomes a civil case. In either the case of the HUD law judge hearing or the civil action held in the courts, the U.S. Court of Appeals can review the outcome.

The Fair Housing Act of 1968 proved to be historic as the final major act in the civil rights movement legislation. Despite this, housing remained segregated throughout much of the United States for decades. During the thirty years from 1950 through 1980,

Americaâ€™s urban centersâ€™ black population grew from 6.1 million up to 15.3 million people.

At the same time, white Americans continuously abandoned the cities in favor of the suburbs. With them went a great number of the jobs that the black population needed to communities where they did not find welcome. The result of this ongoing trend caused urban America to be filled with ghettos. These are the communities inside the American inner cities where many minority populations live. They have been dogged by consistently high crime, unemployment, drug use, and other social problems.

# Federal Deposit Insurance Corporation (FDIC)

The U.S. government started The Federal Deposit Insurance Corporation back in 1933. They created it because of the literally thousands of failed banks that went down in the 1920s and 1930s. The FDIC began insuring bank accounts at the beginning of 1934. Since then, no depositors have lost any insured bank account money despite a consistent number of banks failing every year.

The first role of the FDIC is to insure and to increase the publicâ€™s confidence in the American banking system. They do this in several ways. The FDIC insures minimally $250,000 in bank and thrift accounts. They watch for and take action on any risks to the deposit insurance funds. They also stop the spread of any bank failures when one of the banks does fail.

The Federal Deposit Insurance Corporation only insures deposits. This means that it does not cover mutual funds, stocks, or any other investments that some banks offer to their customers. They offer a standard $250,000 amount for each depositorâ€™s account. This single limit amount does not apply to other types of account ownerships and accounts at other banks. To help individuals understand if the insurance provided is enough to cover their various kinds of account, the FDIC provides its Electronic Deposit Insurance Estimator.

Another important role of the FDIC lies in its supervisory position. The outfit oversees over 4,500 different savings and commercial banks to make sure that they are operationally safe and sound. This represents more than half of the banks. Those banks that are set up as state banks may choose to become a member of either the Federal Reserve System or the FDIC. Any banks that are not overseen by the Federal Reserve System are watched over by the FDIC.

Another job of the FDIC is to check on the various banks to make sure they abide by the government's consumer protection laws. These laws include The Fair Credit Reporting Act, the Fair Credit Billing Act, the Fair Debt Collection Practices Act, and the Truth in Lending Act.

Lastly, the FDIC checks banks to make sure the different institutions are abiding by their responsibilities under the Community Reinvestment Act. This law ensures that banks help the communities where they were started to achieve their needs for credit.

Despite all of these roles, the only one that members of the public really encounter on a personal basis is the FDIC protecting insured depositors. When a bank or thrift goes down, the FDIC immediately reacts to the situation. They come in fast with the group that chartered the bank to close it down. The charter group could be the Office of the Comptroller of the Currency or the state regulator.

The next step is for the FDIC to wind up the failed bank. In their preferred method, they sell both the loans and the deposits of the bank to another banking institution. Customers rarely feel the transition in the majority of the cases. This is the FDIC's goal, to make sure that people do not lose access to their accounts and money.

The FDIC carries out its several mandates through six regional branches. It has more than 7,000 staff members that help it to carry out these goals. The organization is based in its headquarters in the capital Washington, D.C. Besides these locations, they also have various field offices throughout the nation.

The leadership of the FDIC is supplied by the Federal Government. The President appoints the board which the Senate confirms. There are five members of their Board of Directors. No more than three of them may belong to one political party to ensure bipartisanship in the decisions.

# Federal Housing Finance Agency (FHFA)

The Federal Housing Finance Agency is a government regulating agency. They are independent and responsible for overseeing several agencies within the secondary mortgage market. These include Freddie Mac, Fannie Mae, and the Federal Home Loan Banks. They work to keep these critical government sponsored organizations, along with the entire American housing financial system, in good health.

As such, the FHFA labors constantly to build up and safeguard the secondary mortgage markets in the United States. They do this through their leadership in and delivering excellent research, dependable data, strong supervision, and pertinent policies. The three government sponsored entities of Freddie Mac, Fannie Mae, and the Federal Home Loan Bank system together deliver over $5.5 trillion in financial institutions and mortgage markets funding throughout the United States.

The FHFA helps to keep this all possible by providing their independent regulation and careful oversight of these vital mortgage markets. Besides this, they are also the conservator of both Freddie Mac and Fannie Mae since the financial crisis and Great Recession that began in 2007-2008 wreaked havoc on the two giant government sponsored agencies along with the housing market they guaranteed.

The Federal Housing Finance Agency is concerned with creating a better market of secondary mortgages for the countryâ€™s future. To this effect, they are working on a sequence of strategies and initiatives to boost the housing financial system in the future. Among these new ideas is the construction of a new and improved database called the Common Securitization Platform. This will have dual roles. It will take the presently outdated infrastructures and modernize them. It will also allow for the possibilities of other players in the market choosing to utilize this same infrastructure.

The FHFA considers itself to be in a partnership. They strive alongside the entities they regulate to keep home ownership alive and affordable through a variety of programs. These include the HARP Home Affordable Refinance Program and the HAMP Home Affordable Modification Program. The two programs deliver significant and tangible aid to both communities and their homeowners. So far such programs have assisted literally millions of home owning Americans to keep or stay in their houses.

The FHFA does not have a long history. It is a new organization that grew out of the housing market collapse and Great Recession. President Obama signed the Housing and Economic Recovery Act of 2008 to create the Federal Housing Finance Agency back on July 30, 2008.

The ongoing mission of the FHFA is to make certain that the government sponsored enterprises for housing function in a manner that is both economically viable and safe. This is so that they can continue to provide a dependable source of both funds and liquidity for investment in communities and the financing of home purchases. As part of this, they envision a housing financial system that is stable, dependable, and liquid for both the present and the future.

The FHFA values four virtues. They prize excellence in all areas of their work. The organization appreciates respect for their team members, resources, and the information they collect. They value integrity and commit themselves to the greatest possible professional and moral standards. The group also encourages diversity in all of their business dealings and employment arrangements, as well as in the entities which they regulate and for whom they are the conservator.

FHFA is also an important member group of the Financial Stability Oversight Council. Chief among their tasks is to identify financial stability risks in the U.S., to respond to rising threats to the American financial system, and to encourage discipline in the market. They serve on this council with fellow members that include The Federal Reserve governors, CFTC, FDIC, Comptroller of the Currency, SEC, and Treasury Department.

# Federal Open Market Committee

The Federal Open Market Committee is a group within the Federal Reserve, the central bank for the United States. This central bank is more commonly known as the Fed. They carry out actions of monetary policy. This impacts the cost and readily available quantity of money and credit. The Fed uses these tools to foster the countryâ€™s economic goals. Thanks to the Federal Reserve Act of 1913, the Fed gained the authority to set the national monetary policy.

Under the mantle of the Federal Reserve are three different monetary policy tools. These are reserve requirements, the discount rate, and open market operations. It is the Federal Reserve System Board of Governors that carries out the task of setting the reserve requirements and the discount rate. The Federal Open Market Committee handles the Fedâ€™s open market operations.

With these three different tools, the Fed is able to influence the supply of and demand for balances that the financial institutions keep inside the Federal Reserve Banks. This is how it affects the federal funds rate. This is the interest rate that banks and other financial institutions are willing to loan money from their Federal Reserve accounts to other such institutions on an overnight basis.

When the federal funds rate changes, this sets off events which impact foreign exchange rates, other types of shorter term interest rates, longer term interest rates, and the quantity of money and credit in the economy. Eventually this affects a number of important economic indicators like economic output, employment, and the costs for goods and services.

Open market operations are the main tool that the Federal Reserve uses to carry out American monetary policy. Specifically they buy and sell government securities like Treasuries and T-Bills. They do this in the open market so that they can contract or expand the quantity of money that exists in the banking system. When they buy securities, it puts money into the banking system. This boosts growth in the economy. When they sell their securities, they withdraw money from the system. This shrinks the economy. Ultimately it is the federal funds rate the Federal Open Market Committee is trying to adjust with these operations.

The Federal Open Market Committee is made up of twelve members in total. These are comprised of the Federal Reserve System Board of Governorsâ€™ seven members, the Federal Reserve Bank of New York President, and four of the other eleven Presidents of the Reserve Banks. These other Reserve Bank Presidents rotate in and out serving one year terms. Rotating seats have a special order in which they are filled. There are four groups of Banks which each contribute a Bank President to the voting Federal Open Market Committee. The groups are Richmond, Philadelphia, and Boston; Chicago and Cleveland; Dallas, Atlanta, and St. Louis; and San Francisco, Kansas City, and Minneapolis.

Those Reserve Bank Presidents who are not voting members of the committee in a given year still attend all of the committee meetings, make their contributions to the economy and policy choices assessments, and take part in all discussions.

Every year the Federal Open Market Committee engages in eight routinely scheduled meetings. In these meetings, the committee does a number of important activities. It reviews national financial and economic conditions, considers the risks to maintainable economic growth and long term price stability, and decides on its monetary policy appropriate stance.

The FOMC legally is authorized to set its own internal organization. They have a tradition of electing the Board of Governors Chair to be the Chair of the FOMC and selecting the New York Federal Reserve

Bank President to be the vice chair. The eight annual meetings occur in Washington D.C.

# Federal Reserve

The Federal Reserve, also known as the Fed, or the Federal Reserve Board, proves to be the United States' central banking system. This central bank came about in 1913 as a result of Congress passing the Federal Reserve Act. Congress created the organization because of a number of serious financial panics that culminated in the severe panic of 1907.

With time, the Federal Reserve's roles and areas of responsibility have grown as the organization has expanded. Economic events such as the Great Depression have only served to encourage this.

The Federal Reserve today counts among its duties many responsibilities. Among these are regulating and overseeing the country's banks, managing the country's monetary policy and supply, assuring the financial systems' continuance and stability, and offering a variety of financial services to depositing banks, foreign central banks, and the United States government.

The Federal Reserve's structure is made up of a number of different components. Among these are the Federal Reserve Board of Governors, all of whom are appointed by the President. The Federal Open Market Committee, also known by its acronym of FOMC, sets the monetary policy, like the interest rates, for the nation. There are also Federal Reserve Banks, which are twelve regional institutions that are found in the biggest area cities around America. They offer physical currency to member banks when demand proves to be unusually high. Several councils that advise it are a part of The Federal Reserve, as are technically the member banks throughout the country.

The FOMC component of the Federal Reserve is actually comprised of all of these seven Board of Governors members along with the presidents of the twelve regional banks. Only five of these presidents are voting members at a time. Together, they review the state of the U.S. national economy in order to determine what fiscal policies need to be pursued. When the economic growth is slowing, or a recession is occurring, they cut the national interest rates. When inflation is appearing or the economy is overheating, they raise these interest rates.

The Federal Reserve proves to be a unique entity among the major central banks. This is because it divides up the various responsibilities into some public and some private parts of the institution. The Federal Reserve furthermore serves to create the currency used for the country, the U.S. dollar. The fact that it is both a public and private institution, with so many varied and vast powers, makes it one of a kind.

Because the U.S. dollar is still the reserve currency of the world, the Federal Reserve's powers are far greater than simply managing the U.S. economy. In actual practice, they also are the custodians and managers of the world's reserve currency. This gives them considerable power and influence throughout the entire world economy, since they are able to create not only dollars for the U.S. economy, but also for other central banks use in foreign countries. As a result of this, more than half of the physically printed U.S. dollars are found outside of the United States.

# Federal Reserve Act of 1913

The Federal Reserve Act of 1913 created the Federal Reserve Bank. This proved to be the Act of Congress that set up the Federal Reserve System. This system became the Central Bank organization for the United States. As part of the act, the Federal Reserve acquired the powers to issue the nation's legal tender currency. President Woodrow Wilson actually signed this act, making it law in 1913.

The leadership of the country felt the need to create such a central bank for several reasons. The United States had operated without a central bank going back to the expiration of the Second Bank of the United Statesâ€™ charter. This meant that for about eighty years, the country had existed without any form of central bank.

In time, a number of financial panics had ensued without any central bank to intervene in them. The one that really galvanized congressional and public opinion for having a central bank proved to be the serious financial panic of 1907. As a result of these factors, a number of Americans decided that the nation required serious currency and banking reforms that could handle such panics by offering an available liquid assetsâ€™ reserve. They also figured such an institution might be capable of managing a consistent expansion and contraction of credit and currency from time to time as appropriate.

The original Federal Reserve Act plan recommended an establishment of an unusual combined public and private entity system. They suggested that minimally eight and as many as twelve regional private Federal Reserve banks should be created. All of them were to have their own boards of directors, regional boundary lines, and branches. This new entity would be led by a Federal Reserve Board comprised of seven members and made up of public officials that the President appointed and the Senate would confirm. An advisory committee known as the Federal Advisory Committee would be created, along with a brand new U.S. currency that would alone be accepted nationally, the Federal Reserve Note. In the final version of the bill, twelve regional Federal Reserve Banks were actually created. The rest of the above provisions became law and subsequently a part of the newly created Federal Reserve System.

Another important decision that Congress settled on with the Federal Reserve Act revolved around the private banks throughout the U.S. Every nationally chartered bank had to join the Federal Reserve System as a part of this act. They were made to buy stock that could not be transferred in their own areaâ€™s Federal Reserve Bank. It furthermore required that a set dollar total of reserves that did not pay interest had to be deposited to their own regional Federal Reserve Bank. Banks that are only state chartered have the choice, but not the obligation, of joining this system and being regulated by the Fed.

Finally, the act allowed the member banks to receive loans at a discounted rate from the discount windows of their own regional Federal Reserve Bank. They were promised a six percent yearly dividend on their Federal Reserve stock and provided with additional services. The act also gave the Federal Reserve Banks the authority to assume the role of U.S. government fiscal agents.

# Federal Reserve Bank

Twelve different Federal Reserve Banks make up the Federal Reserve System that functions as the central bank for the U.S. Federal reserve banks are also utilized to sub-divide up the country into the twelve Federal Reserve Districts.

Every Federal Reserve Bank bears the responsibility for individually regulating the various commercial banks that are found in such a bankâ€™s geographical district. Ensuring the continuation of the financial system and all of the member banks is among the primary responsibilities of the Federal Reserve System.

Each Federal Reserve Bank also issues its own stock shares that can only be acquired by participating member banks. The banks are required to obtain these shares by law. While the shares may not be traded, pledged as a loan security, or sold, they do pay dividends that run as high as six percent each year.

American banks are required by law to keep certain fractional reserves of their actual deposits. These are mostly held by the regional Federal Reserve Banks. Although in years past, the Federal Reserve did not pay member banks interest on these funds kept on reserve, as of 2008 Congress passed the EESA that permits them to pay the participating banks interest.

The twelve Federal Reserve Banks and districts are found geographically spread out around the nation. They include the Federal Reserve Banks of Boston, New York, Philadelphia,

Cleveland, Richmond, Atlanta, Chicago, St. Louis, Minneapolis, Kansas City, Dallas, and San Francisco.

The largest and still most important of the individual Federal Reserve Banks proves to be the Federal Reserve Bank of New York. Not only does this bank have the greatest asset base of all the twelve branches, valued at over a trillion dollars and representing four times the asset base of the next largest Federal Reserve Bank, but it also boasts the biggest gold depository on earth, valued at in excess of $25 billion. The gold kept in the New York Federal Reserve Bank vaults belongs to other nations who store it there for safe keeping. Saudi Arabia and Kuwait both keep their significant holdings here.

Among the various states that have Federal Reserve Banks headquartered there, a few of them contain more than one branch within their state. California, Missouri, and Tennessee are the ones that make this claim. Tennessee actually contains two branches from two different districts within its state boundaries. The only state that has two Federal Reserve Banks headquartered within it is Missouri. For the largest geographical areas covered by the districts, San Francisco is the largest, Kansas City is second biggest, and Minneapolis is the third largest.

# Federal Trade Commission (FTC)

The FTC Federal Trade Commission proves to be the agency responsible for protecting the American consumers. They strive to stop tricky, fraudulent, and unfair practices in business in the nationâ€™s marketplaces. They also disburse valuable information to consumers that helps them to recognize, stop, and sidestep these frauds.

The FTC accepts consumer complaints by phone, email, their website, and through the mail. They take these complaints and enter them into a database that is called the Consumer Sentinel Network. This secure online tool is utilized for investigation purposes by literally hundreds of criminal and civil agencies for law enforcement throughout the United States and overseas.

What the FTC would like to do is to stop these types of deceptive and non-competitive business dealings before they hurt consumers. They are also attempting to improve consumer opportunities so that they are better informed about and comprehend the nature of competition. The agency attempts to perform all of these tasks without putting too many burdens and restrictions on businesses activities that are legitimate.

Congress created the FTC back in 1914. Originally its mandate lay in stopping unfair means of competition in trade and business caused by the trusts. They were a part of the government's stated goal to bust up these trusts. Congress has given them more authority to monitor and fight practices that were against fair competition over the years by passing other laws.

The government enacted another law in 1938 that was broadly addressed to stop any deceptive or unfair practices and acts. They have continued to receive direction and discretion to govern a number of other laws that protect consumers over the subsequent years. Among these are the Pay Per Call Rule, the Telemarketing Sales Rule, and the Equal Credit Opportunity Act. Congress passed another law in 1975 that gave the Federal Trade Commission the ability to come up with rules that regulated trade throughout the industries.

The FTC has a vision for the American economy. They want to see one that has healthy competition between producers. They also desire to see consumers able to obtain correct information. Ultimately the government agency looks for all of this to create low priced and superior quality goods. They encourage innovation, efficiency in business, and choice for consumers.

This agency carries out its vision with three strategic goals. It starts with them protecting consumers by heading off trickery and deception in the business and consumer marketplace. They desire to keep competition going strong. In this role, they stop mergers and business dealings that they believe are against competition. They also work to increase their own performance with consistently improving and excellent managerial, individual, and organizational efforts.

All of these goals and efforts combine to make the FTC one of the government agencies that most impacts each American citizen's economic and personal life. They are the only government entity that possesses a mandate for both competition jurisdiction and consumer protection in large segments of the U.S. economy. They go after aggressive and effectual enforcement of the laws.

The FTC shares its knowledge with international, state, and federal groups and agencies. The group creates research tools at a variety of conferences, workshops, and hearings every year. They also develop and distribute easy to understand educational materials for business and consumer needs in the transforming technological and global market.

The FTC carries out its work through its Bureaus of Economics, Competition, and Consumer Protection. They receive assistance from the Office of General Counsel. Seven regional offices around the country help them to carry out their mandate.

# Financial Industry Regulatory Authority (FINRA)

The Financial Industry Regulatory Authority is a congressionally authorized independent and non profit outfit. Congress established them to safeguard the investors of America by ensuring that the stock market industry runs honestly and fairly for all participants.

FINRA is not an agency of the government, even though they have broad disciplinary and enforcement powers. The organization tirelessly works to ensure the integrity of the market and protection for investors by regulating the securities business.

FINRA carries out these duties in a variety of ways. They investigate brokerage firms to make sure they abide by the rules. The not for profit creates and then enforces these rules that govern the actions of more than 3,941 securities companies who have over 641,157 brokers on staff. FINRA also encourages transparency in markets and settles disputes. The group does all of this without taxpayers having to support them via taxes.

The authority works every day to make sure individuals selling securities are tested and licensed. They ensure all advertisements for securities utilized to sell the products are clear and truthful. FINRA holds companies to a high standard for only selling suitable investments to individuals that are appropriate to their needs. They ensure that every investor obtains full disclosure about their investment before they buy it.

The independent agency carried out 1,512 disciplinary actions on registered firms and brokers in 2015. This allowed them to collect fines of over $95 million. They mandated that $96.6 million be given back to investors who where harmed in these and other actions. The group handed over 800 different insider trading or fraud cases to other agencies like the SEC for settling or prosecuting the same year.

Ultimately FINRA's goals are to deter misconduct in the industry. They do this by enforcing rules for everyone. This is not only the rules that they create. The group also enforces the Municipal Securities Rulemaking Board's regulations and federal securities laws as well. They make the qualifying exams and require brokers to come to continuing education classes.

The organization puts hundreds of their own financial examiners in the field to check on the way these brokers carry out their business. Their main concern is for the investors and risks to the markets. They follow up on complaints filed by investors and other suspicious activities.

They also review all advertisements, brochures, websites, and communications to be certain brokers are fairly presenting their products. This amounts to approximately 100,000 different communications and advertisements they examine and approve between broker firms and their investors.

FINRA also disciplines rule breakers. They use their authority, technology, and professional experts to rapidly react to wrongs. The organization has the authority to fine brokers, suspend them, or expel them from the business.

The independent agency also possesses technology that is potent enough for them to be able to review various markets and pick up on possible fraud. They are able to gather data in such a way to keep tabs on insider trading or other practices that give broker firms advantages that are unfair. To this effect they process anywhere from 42 billion to 75 billion transactions daily to have a full picture of U.S. market trading.

The group is also involved in resolving disputes in the securitiesâ€™ business. This pertains to problems between investors and brokers. FINRA handles almost 100% of all mediations and arbitrations that are related to securities. They hear these disputes in 70 different locations. This includes one hearing center in every state, Puerto Rico, and London.

# Financial Stability Oversight Council

The Financial Stability Oversight Council is an organization that was created by the Dodd-Frank Act following the financial crisis of 2008. It possesses a clear legal mandate that provides an accountability to look for risks and respond to perceived upcoming threats to the United Statesâ€™ financial stability.

This is the first time that a single organization has held such important responsibility. The group is actually headed by the Secretary of the Treasury. It combines the various experience and knowledge of state regulators, an insurance expert who is both independent and Presidentially appointed, and federal financial regulators.

The Financial Stability Oversight Council was granted first time powers by Congress to restrain and head off dangerous risks within the financial system. This Council can select a financial firm that is not a bank and mark it for intense supervision so that the firm can not threaten to blow up the financial system and its stability. As an aid in determining what qualifies potential risk to the country's financial stability, this FSOC is allowed to obtain information and analysis from and supply information to the recently established OFR Office of Financial Research that is headquartered in the Treasury building.

Before the financial crisis erupted, the financial regulation in the United States focused exclusively on specific markets and institutions. This permitted gaps in supervision to expand amidst inconsistencies in the regulation. Standards weakened as a result. There was no one regulator responsible for watching over and dealing with the various risks to American financial stability. The threats often revolved around various financial firms which functioned at once in numerous interrelated markets. Because of this, critical portions of the financial system remained unregulated. The Dodd-Frank Act dealt with these failures by creating the Financial Stability Oversight Council.

The Financial Stability Oversight Council has many roles. It facilitates and coordinates regulation. They are tasked with sharing information and coordinating action with the agencies involved to deal with examining, making rules, developing policy, reporting, and enforcing their actions.

They are also to encourage gathering and sharing information among their various member organizations. If they are unable to gather enough information, they are to turn to the OFR to obtain information from individual companies they need to evaluate. Gathering and evaluating such information is supposed to eliminate blind spots in the financial system. By doing this they are fostering a more stable and less dangerous overall financial system in the United States.

The Financial Stability Oversight Council is also to select nonbank financial entities that need to be consolidated. Dodd-Frank identified companies that did not receive appropriate supervision and then led to the outbreak of the financial crisis back in 2008. The act provides the Financial Stability Oversight Council the authority which it needs to force supervision on such companies at entirely its own discretion.

The council also has the power to make recommendations for harsher standards for those firms they deem to be the biggest and most interconnected operations which provide increased risks to the system. This includes both banks and non bank financial organizations. As the Council learns about activities and practices that are threatening financial stability in the country, they are able to recommend tougher standards to the appropriate financial regulators.

The extensive powers of this Financial Stability Oversight Council are most clearly shown in their ability to choose to break up companies at will which they perceive to represent a clear and present danger to the nationâ€™s financial stability. They can decide if action should be followed to break up these kinds of firms which they deem to be a grave threat to the United States and its financial stability.

# Foreign Account Tax Compliance Act (FACTA)

Foreign Account Tax Compliance Act (FACTA) proves to be an American-issued and -rigorously enforced law. It requires all United Statesâ€™ citizens living either stateside or overseas to make annual report filings of any foreign bank account holdings they possess. This FACTA law came into effect back in 2010 along with the HIRE Act. The goal ostensibly was to encourage and foster greater transparency in the worldwide financial services universe. The ulterior motive lay in knowing any and all U.S. individualsâ€™ accounts which they might use to hide income or assets overseas. The ultimate goal is to maximize every last dollar in taxes form overseas-living Americans.

It was former U.S. President Barack Obama who signed the new HIRE Act into law in 2010. With this Hiring Incentives to Restore Employment Act, he was seeking to cut down the stubbornly high rate of unemployment that refused to disappear after the global financial crisis and meltdown of 2008-2009. Among the incentives they dangled in front of employers with the act was the ability to increase their business tax credits on every new staff member which a firm hired and retained for minimally a calendar year. There were still other incentive included in the bill. Companies benefited from a special payroll tax holiday advantage as well as a higher expense deduction limit on any new factory or production equipment which they purchased back in 2010.

Naturally the President and Congress required a revenue stream with which to pay for these business benefits and incentives. What they came up with was the requirement that all American tax payers report all of their assets maintained outside of the United States ever year. The idea was that in taxing such foreign-based accounts and assets, the country would boost its revenue sources enough to pay for the desperately needed corporate job stimulation programs. To provide a sufficient penalty incentive for American citizens to reveal these hidden assets, the IRS created a stiff regimen for any American resident or overseas-living U.S. citizen who chose not to report their international account assets and currency amounts which was greater than $50,000 value during the course of any tax year.

To grow the potential additional revenues by as much as possible, the government applied the new requirements not only to presumably wealthy and foreign-born individual Americans, but also to NFFE Non-Financial Foreign Entities and FFI Non-US Foreign Financial Institutions. These internationally based banks were then mandated to become compliant with the new revenue-catching law by revealing all American citizensâ€™ identities and the worth of any and all of their assets kept in their banks. Banks have to report this information to the IRS Internal Revenue Service or alternatively to the IGA FACTA Intergovernmental Agreement.

For those FFIâ€™s which elect to not comply with the Internal Revenue Service, they will summarily be banned from the United Statesâ€™ markets and banking system. They will also suffer a 30 percent deduction of any witholdable paymentsâ€™ amounts in the form of a tax penalty.

These payments relate to U.S. financial assets and income generated and kept in the banks. They include dividends, interest payments, remunerations, salaries and wages, profits, and compensations. Those NFFEâ€™s and FFIâ€™s which comply with the law have to report every year the identities of all their account holding U.S. citizens. This includes their names, addresses, and TIN tax identification numbers for every account. They also have to divulge the Americansâ€™ account numbers and balances, and all withdrawals and deposits made using the account during the calendar year.

The real goal behind FACTA is to eliminate tax evasion of American businesses and citizens who invest, earn, and operate in such a capacity as to gain taxable income overseas. It remains legal to own and operate an offshore account. It is in not properly disclosing it to the IRS that it becomes illegal. The reason is because the United States is the only major economy and jurisdiction to tax all of the assets and income from its citizens regardless of where they live, reside, and realize income in the world.

# Generally Accepted Accounting Principles (GAAP)

Generally Accepted Accounting Principles, more commonly referred to by their acronym GAAP, are the mostly American used set of accounting principles, procedures, and standards. These are utilized by companies to put together their corporate financial statements. Such GAAP proves to be a blend of the most accepted means of reporting and recording accounting data in the United States combined with the American policy board set standards.

Companies must use GAAP in order for their investors to have some common standard of consistency with financial statements they compare when considering the various companies in which to invest their money. These standards include such areas as balance sheet items classification, revenue recognition, and measurements of outstanding shares of stock.

Regulators expect that companies will obey these generally accepted accounting principles rules as they release their financial statements to routinely report their financial information. American investors should be leery of company financial statements that are not properly developed utilizing these guiding principles.

Despite this fact, these accounting procedures are merely a cohesive group of guidelines and standards. Crooked accountants are still able to distort and misrepresent the numbers while using these generally accepted procedures. Although a company may utilize the generally accepted procedures, investors should still carefully go through their financial statements with a healthy degree of skepticism.

The competing accounting standards that most of the rest of the world employs is known as the IFRS International Financial Reporting Standards. There has been a recent move to harmonize the two sets of standards in past years. Because of the global financial crisis and economic collapse of 2008 and its terrible aftermath, globalization, the SEC agreeing to accept international standards, and the Sarbanes-Oxley Act, countries like the United States have been severely pressured to close the gap between GAAP and the IFRS.

Doing so would have major ramifications on accounting throughout the U.S. It also would affect investors, corporate management teams, accountants, national accounting standard makers, and American stock markets. Bringing these two sets of standards together is impacting CFO and CPA attitudes regarding international accounting. This influences the International Accounting Standards quality as well as the various endeavors that professionals are making on converging the two sets of standards.

There are some problematic inconsistencies with international financial reporting because the financial reporting standards and rules are somewhat different from one country to another. This dilemma has become more of a challenge for those international investors who are attempting to figure out the various differences in global accounting and reporting. As they are thinking about offering substantial investments to overseas companies which are earnestly seeking capital in good faith, it makes it more challenging since companies report according to the standards of the country where they do business.

The IASB International Accounting Standards Board has been sincerely looking for a practical solution to this international complication, confusion, and conflict that inconsistency in accounting standards for financial reporting has created and continues to encourage. The principle difference with GAAP and the IFRS methods lies in the totally different approaches that either one uses regarding the standards.

Generally Accepted Accounting Practices prove to be based on a set of rules. It employs a complicated group of guidelines that set criteria and rules in any given scenario. The International Financial Reporting Standards alternatively utilizes a method based on principles. The IFRS instead starts with the goal of good financial reporting and gives guidance on the particular needs and challenges of a given scenario.

# Glass Steagall Act

Congress created and passed the Glass Steagall Act in 1933. This legislation arose because of the effects of the 1929 catastrophic stock market crash. Two congressmen came up with this solution in the Great Depression when many banks were failing. The law made separate all activities which involved commercial banking and investment banking.

Commercial banks had become heavily involved in the stock market. This activity received much of the blame for the stock market and financial crashes. Lawmakers felt that commercial banks had employed money from their depositors in speculation in the stock market.

The reasons this act came forcefully into law had to do with banksâ€™ activities. Commercial banks had bought new and unproven stocks to sell to individual customers.Â  It was the greed of banks that led to the new legislation. The goals of banking were mired in conflict of interest. Banks would make loans to corporations in which they already had an investment. These loans were not issued based on good underwriting.

They would then push these investments to their clients. Their goal was to have their customers help support these companies. Such commercial speculation insured that when the companies failed, the banks and their customers all lost huge amounts of money. Finally banks began to collapse in the thousands as a result of this poor and unregulated activity.

The act actually came about because of Senator Carter Glass. Glass had served as Treasury secretary previously. He also founded the U.S. Federal Reserve System. The failing banks motivated him to act on a bill. He became the main driving force of this legislation. His partner on the project was Henry Bascom Stegall.

Stegall served as House Banking and Currency Committee chairman. At first he would not support the bill with Glass. They added an amendment to create insurance for bank deposits. This brought Congressman Steagallâ€™s critical support of the act.

The effects of this Glass Steagall Act erected a variety of barriers in the banking industry. A new firewall of regulation arose between investment bank and commercial bank businesses. The two types of banks experienced unprecedented oversight and control over their activities. All banks received one year to choose a specialty in either investment banking or commercial banking.

Those that chose commercial banking were heavily limited in their investment banking activities. Income from securities could not exceed 10% of the commercial bank earnings. Commercial banks were permitted to underwrite bonds the government issued. The ultimate goal was to stop banks from committing their depositorsâ€™ funds to projects which were poorly underwritten and speculative.

Banks that were too big to fail at the time became significant targets for this act. JP Morgan and Company and rival financial empires were among these. Such outfits had to eliminate many services. This targeted a large and important part of their incomes.

Later on criticism of the Glass Steagall Act arose. This happened as different explanations became popular for the Great Depression. Many different individuals also saw that this act had created problems for financial services. They blamed the law for restricting financial firms to the point that they were not able to compete effectively.

Many opposed the act by the 1980s. Glass Steagall opposition grew into the 1990s. Congress finally repealed the act in 1999. The elimination of this act has been blamed for the Great Recession crisis that started in 2006.

Banks were again able to mix investment and lending activities. Close regulation of commercial banks had been largely eliminated. Because of this, banks again made many risky loans that were either liar loans or not properly documented for income.

# Home Affordable Modification Program (HAMP)

The Home Affordable Modification Program is also known by its acronym HAMP. This stands for a program created by the United States government. They founded it in order to assist those homeowners who were struggling to keep up with their mortgages. For any homeowners who have watched in dismay as their financial conditions deteriorated since they originally purchased their house, they could be able to qualify for loan modifications to make keeping the home possible and affordable.

The program actually helps participants by allowing them to reduce their monthly mortgage payments. This happens as the program approves a lower rate of interest, extends the mortgage's time frame (and term), or alters the type of mortgage to fixed rate from adjustable rate ARM. In some cases, two or even three of these changes may be approved together. The modifications can happen because the United States government backs them.

The Home Affordable Modification Program began as the Departments of Housing and Urban Development HUD combined forces with the Treasury in order to forge a new initiative that they named Making Homes Affordable. Though there were other parts to this ground breaking concept, the HAMP proved to be a key pillar of it. The government recognized in the wake of the Great Recession that many Americans were only one accident, job loss, or illness away from falling hopelessly behind on their mortgages and payments. This is why they decided to come up with their innovative program for modifying mortgages to make them more affordable for those who are in the most need of help.

Becoming eligible for this home modification assistance program requires an applicant be able to successfully meet a particular set of criteria. They must have bought and financed the house before or on January 1st of 2009. They have to be capable of proving a real financial hardship that makes them struggle to meet their monthly mortgage payments. At the same time, they have to show that they are already behind on the monthly payments or even at risk of sliding into foreclosure of their home. In order to successfully qualify, the property can not have been condemned. They may not owe more than $729,750 on the primary residence which is a single family home. Finally, applicants may not show any personal real estate fraud convictions from any time within the past ten years.

If they meet all of these exacting criteria, then interested parties are able to call their specific mortgage servicer to inquire about any additional requirements that could exist with their particular company. It is also important to inquire if the mortgage servicing company even participates with the Home Affordable Modification Program in the first place. If the provider does participate and the applicant actually meets all of the minimum requirements for participation, then the home owner will need to speak with his or her lender in order to obtain all of the necessary paperwork and forms to enroll.

These forms include first the Request for Mortgage Assistance Form, or RMA. There is also the Income Verification Form as well as the IRSâ€™ 4605T-EZ form to complete. It is important to note that the final application does not get submitted to the government, but instead to the mortgage servicer. They will require a tangible proof of financial hardship when the individual submits this application.

There are actually a number of key benefits which this Home Affordable Modification Program delivers for successful applicants. They are able to sidestep foreclosure of the home, reduce their costs for keeping the house, obtain a new start on the mortgage, and better their credit history and rating. The home loan will be made to work for the owners so that they can simply modify the mortgage instead of losing the house.

Though the program is one that has helped a number of Americans, it is not the foolproof answer to irresponsible home buying and borrowing. There have been a number of homeowners who availed themselves of the program in HAMP only to re-default a second time. Some of these have actually forfeited their homes in the foreclosure process. The program has been shown in a recently conducted study that it can help a number of the fully 20 percent of homeowners who are not saving money which they might be able to by taking advantage of either a loan modification program such as this one or through refinancing their home.

# Insider Trading

Insider trading is a generally negative phrase, though it can also refer to a legal activity. The illegal and better known version if it involves a person purchasing or selling a security when they have information that is not publicly available on the stock. The timing involved in such a trade often determines if it is legal or illegal.

If the critical information has not yet been released to the public, then it is not legally allowed. This is because the government determined to level the playing field in investing. Trading securities when investors have special knowledge is not fair to those traders who do not have the ability to access this information.

A person who tips off other individuals is also participating in illegal insider trading. This is the case if the tipster possesses valuable and relevant information that is not available to the public. Fines and jail time can be given to those who pass along illegal insider information. The responsible body for policing this type of illegal trading is the SEC Securities and Exchange Commission. They maintain and enforce rules that protect average investors from the results of illegal insider trading.

Legal insider trading happens all the time. It is not as well known as the illegal version. A legal trade from an insider occurs when company directors buy or sell shares that they fully disclose according to the rules. This occurs every week. The transactions must be electronically turned in to the SEC in a manner that is timely. Not only must they be sent in to the SEC, the company of the person involved must disclose this transaction information on their official website.

Congress passed the Securities Exchange Act of 1934 to address this issue. This first important step pertained to company stock transactions and legal disclosure. Major owners of securities and directors of the company as well had to disclose their positions, any transactions, and any time the ownership changed hands.

Several forms allow corporate insiders to legally disclose their stock affairs. Form 3 permits them to initially file that they have a company stake. Directors use Form 4 to make a disclosure on company stock transactions two days or less after the sale or purchase. They utilize Form 5 for earlier transactions or for transactions that become deferred until later.

It is not only company or corporate directors who are able to be tried and convicted for insider trading. Stock brokers and their clients can also be accused of this crime. Martha Stewart is a classic example of a brokerage client who the courts found guilty for placing insider trades back in 2003.

Martha Stewart received a tip from her Merrill Lynch stockbroker Peter Bacanovic concerning her shares of ImClone, a bio-pharmaceutical company. She used this information to sell her shares. Her broker had obtained this information that the Chief Executive Officer of ImClone Samuel Waksal liquidated all of his position in the corporation.

Waksal learned that the Food and Drug Administration was not going to approve his company's cancer drug Erbitux. After the two sales occurred, the FDA officially and publicly rejected the ImClone treatment drug. This caused a major selloff in the company stock of 16% in a single trading day. Stewart had saved a stock loss of $45,673 by selling out early.

The problem was that her sale had been based on the tip that CEO Waksal had sold all of his shares. This had not been publicly disclosed. Waksal became convicted and received a seven year jail sentence. Martha Steward was also convicted and forced to serve out five months in jail. She also received a number of months of house arrest and then probation.

# Internal Revenue Service (IRS)

The Internal Revenue Service is an agency of the United States government. It is an entity that falls under the Department of the Treasury. The IRS' purpose is to collect incomes taxes from businesses and working individuals. Workers generally pay in their incomes taxes to the IRS once a year. There are cases where groups pay taxes quarterly, as with businesses and independent contractors who make more than pre-determined amounts. In practice employers withhold most individuals' taxes are from their paychecks.

For most individuals and small businesses, annual tax payments are due every year on April 15th. They pay these for the preceding year. Submitting these payments and forms is known as filing taxes with the IRS. The agency also permits extensions for filing if the requests are turned in ahead of the due date. Estimated payments have to come with the request for extension.

The Internal Revenue Service figures up taxes for individuals and businesses on a sliding scale. Individuals and entities that earn higher amounts are subsequently placed into higher tax brackets. The more individuals earn, the higher amount they will be required to pay to the IRS.

Any person who earns a yearly salary or who is paid wages by the hour will have taxes estimated and deducted directly from every payroll. This creates a situation where too much or too little money may be deducted throughout the year. Individuals who overpay will receive a refund. Those who underpay will have to make a payment to cover the additional tax if the appropriate amount did not come out of checks during the year.

Income taxes in the U.S. depend on the amount of net income. This is the income that remains once deductions have been calculated and subtracted from the total gross income. Individuals in the poverty bracket are not expected to pay any income taxes. Those people who earn $50,000 will pay around 20% of their net incomes. Over $100,000 earners are more likely to pay near 25% of net income earned. Sometimes those earning millions of dollars per year are able to use tax shelters, business write offs, and accounting strategies to receive substantial tax breaks and actually pay a lower percentage of their net income in taxes. This is why the middle class in America bears the greatest taxation burden.

The IRS was not the original Federal taxing authority in the United States. President Lincoln began its original predecessor the Bureau of Internal Revenue in 1862 with Congressional approval. They set this agency up to collect a new income tax to assist in paying for the Civil War. This tax was intended and enacted to be temporary at the time.

While the first income tax did become repealed in 1872, the government reinstated it again in 1894. Supreme Court legal challenges kept the income tax in a quasi legal state until the 16th Amendment came into force in 1913 and allowed income taxes to be permanent. Eventually the Bureau of Internal Revenue evolved into the Internal Revenue Service.

The IRS website offers consumers and businesses all of their forms in a convenient, downloadable format. It also features instructional pages to properly complete these tax forms. A frequently asked questions page helps individuals with general queries. For people who need assistance in filing, there are a variety of software programs available that will ask questions and prepare the relevant tax forms for individuals. These programs then file the forms online with the IRS. Another option is to hire and pay a CPA certified public accountant to complete and file their tax forms.

# International Accounting Standards Board (IASB)

The International Accounting Standards Board is an independent and private entity which arose back in 2001. The group was originally created to replace the former International Accounting Standards Committee. The IFRS Foundation maintains all oversight of the IASB.

Under their auspices, the IASB creates, publishes, and approves the International Financial Reporting Standards for the global accounting community. There are presently 14 members of the IASB. The IASB group is headquartered in London, Great Britain.

The constitution of the IFRS foundation gives the IASB full control over all technical and operating issues. This includes pursuing and developing the technical agenda after consulting with the public and the appropriate trustees of the foundation. They also approve and deliver interpretations that the IFRS Interpretations Committee recommends. Finally, they prepare and publish the International Financial Reporting Standards and all accompanying related drafts as laid out in the constitution of the IFRC Foundation.

The IASB itself was originally organized under the auspices of the IFRS Foundation. The foundation itself proves to be a non profit company incorporated in Delaware in the United States on March 8, 2001. The IFRS Foundation oversees all of the tasks that the IASB pursues as well as its strategy and structure. At the same time, the IFRS maintains the responsibility for fund raising for the IASB.

Another governing agency within the IFRS Foundation is the DPOC Due Process Oversight Committee. This trustee committee bears responsibility for the function of overseeing the IASB, as per the foundationâ€™s constitution. The last governing board is the Monitoring Board. It monitors the trustees of the IFRS foundation. It also participates in nominating the Trustees as well as approving all final appointments that the board makes to the Trustees.

There are several technical groups within the framework of the organization of the IFRS Foundation. The International Accounting Standards Board itself is among these. It bears the sole responsibility for setting all International Financial Reporting Standards since 2001.

There is also the IFRS Interpretations Committee. Their job is to create interpretations that the IASB actually approves. It also engages in tasks as requested by the IASB since 2001. Finally there are the various working groups. These different task forces are for particular projects that meet a necessary agenda of the group.

There are also numerous advisory groups within the IFRS Foundation that carry out important functions for the IASB. The ASAF Accounting Standards Advisory Forum gives advice regarding the activities for setting technical standards by the IASB. The IFRS Advisory Council provides advice to both the IFRS foundation and the IASB.

There are also a variety of specific policy committees that serve advisory roles to the IASB and the IFRS foundation. These include the Capital Markets Advisory Committee from 2003, the Effects Analyses Consultative Group of 2012, the Emerging Economies Group from 2011, the Financial Crisis Advisory Group that merged with FASB in 2008, the Global Preparers Forum, the IFRS Taxonomy Consultative Group from 2014, the Joint Transition Resource Group for Revenue Recognition of 2014, and the SME Implementation Group from 2010.

One of the important tasks of the IASB has been to help with the project to converge the differing GAAP and IFRS standards. In order to simplify the understanding of different countries' accounting and financial statements, the group is trying to bring the standards into some sort of harmony. This will especially help out investors who must read and compare the financial statements and reports of various international companies.

# International Bank Account Number (IBAN)

IBAN is an acronym which stands for the International Bank Account Number. This standardized numbering system for identifying bank accounts around the world with precision was first conceived of and implemented by the banks of Europe. They wanted to make simpler the means of transacting between bank accounts of financial institutions based in different countries.

This internationally agreed to system for identifying the world's banks and bank accounts was critically needed for banking across international borders. European banks found it necessary to come up with a way to effectively process the cross border transactions. They wanted to dramatically lower the dangers of errors in transcription and subsequent transmission problems which sometimes resulted.

It was the ECBS European Committee for Banking Standards that first adopted the IBAN concept. It later evolved into a global standard under the auspices of ISO 13616:1997. This standard became updated with ISO directive 13616:2007 that now utilizes SWIFT as the official registrar. The system originally arose as a means of facilitating payments made throughout the European Union. It has now been put into place by the majority of European nations along with many countries throughout the globe, especially in the states of the Caribbean and Middle East. Sixty-nine different nations utilized the IBAN account numbering system as of February 2016. More sign up all the time.

The IBAN account number is made up of several components. The two letter national code comes first. This is followed up by the two check digits which enable an integrity check of the IBAN number to be sure it is correct. Finally come as many as thirty alphanumeric characters which are also called the BBAN, or Basic Bank Account Number. Each national banking association decides which BBAN will become the standard for their own national bank accounts. In general, the remaining thirty characters include such information as the domestic bank account number, branch location identifier, and additional routing information.

While the IBAN concept has taken hold effectively throughout the continent of Europe, it is not a universal global standard yet, though it is the closest thing to one. The practice of working with such standardized account numbers as these is growing and gaining in popularity in other countries of the world. This is proven by the fact that nearly forty non- European countries now employ the International Bank Account Number system for themselves on only the twentieth anniversary of the concept being introduced originally.

Before the rise of the IBAN, every country utilized its own national standard to identify bank accounts within their own borders. This proved to be confusing in Europe, particularly as the borders between the 27 different EU countries began to blur thanks to the EU. Free movement of people, capital, and goods meant that money was being drawn from and transferred back and forth between the banks and bank accounts of different European states on an increasingly common basis. Sometimes important and even critical routing information was simply missing from transfers and payments.

SWIFTâ€™s routing information does not require transaction specific formats which identify both account numbers and transaction types specifically. This is because they leave the transaction partners to agree on these. SWIFT codes also lack check digits, meaning transcription errors can not be detected nor can banks validate the routing data before they submit the payments without these two digits. Continuous costly routing errors were creating delays on payments and transfers as the receiving and sending banks were also working with intermediary banks for routing.

The ISO International Organization for Standardization overcame these problems in 1997 by creating the IBAN in association with the European Committee for Banking Standards. Because the ECBS simplified and better standardized the original format proposed by the ISO, an update was issued with ISO 13616:2003 and then again in ISO 13616-1:2007.

As of 2017, the United States' banks do not employ IBANs themselves. Instead, they utilize either Fedwire identifiers for the banks or the ABA Routing Number.

# International Financial Reporting Standards (IFRS)

The International Financial Reporting Standards prove to be the principally used set of accounting regulations in the world. Their main rival is the United States' based GAAP Generally Accepted Accounting Procedures. These IFRS turn out to be a single collection of accounting standards. They were created and are maintained still by the IASB International Accounting Standards Board based in London.

The IASB developed these IFRS standards with the goal of them being effectively utilized on a consistent basis throughout the globe. They were written with developed, developing, and emerging market economies and nations all in mind. These standards provide both investors and other consumers of business financial statements with the necessary tools to make like comparisons between various companies. Thanks to the IFRS, investors can effectively compare and contrast the financial performances of various publicly traded corporations on a consistent basis against their global peers.

This is a high standard for the IFRS. It of course requires more and more countries sign on to these accounting standards in order for the objective to be effectively and eventually met. This vision of a single set of worldwide accounting standards is well supported by numerous globally active organizations. Among these are the International Monetary Fund, the World Bank, the G20, the Basel Committee, the IFAC, and the IOSCO.

Thanks to the tireless efforts of the IASB and the IFRS foundation along with the support of these other active international organizations, the IFRS account standards have now been made law in over 100 countries. These include all of the 27 core countries in the European Union plus Great Britain as well as over two thirds of the member nations comprising the G20. This makes sense as the G20 and other critical worldwide bodies have always encouraged the important task of the IASB and its goals of achieving a universally recognized set of international accounting standards that everyone can rely on and understand.

Since the year 2001, the International Accounting Standards Board has created and continued to improve and promote the International Financial Reporting Standards. The IASB turns out to be the body that sets the standards for the IFRS Foundation. This foundation is an organization that serves the public good. It has been well recognized for the award winning examples of its organizational transparency as well as the participation of all of its stakeholders and other participants.

The 150 members strong staff based in London hail from around 30 individual countries. The IASB operates under the auspices of a 14 member Board of Directors that is appointed and monitored by 22 different trustees coming from around the globe. These trustees themselves are further accountable to a public authority monitoring board. This way all of the various members of the leadership at the IASB are accountable to someone else.

The work of the IASB via the IFRS allows international accountants to more consistently deliver a standard means of detailing the financial performances of companies and other financial entities. This benefits investors, companies, and regulators. The standards of accounting that the IASB creates and the IFRS represents give the preparers of financial statements a complete set of principles and rules to follow when they are compiling the financial accounts of these organizations. This makes for an international standardization throughout the global markets.

It all works because the various corporations traded on public stock exchanges are required by law to prepare and produce financial statements that follow the appropriate IFRS accounting standards as do their business rivals and peers. The IFRS foundation maintains an online database of profiles on 143 countries and jurisdictions to show whether or not they accept and utilize these standards.

# IRA Custodian

An IRA custodian is commonly represented by some form of a financial institution. This would likely be a brokerage or a bank. These Individual Retirement Accountsâ€™ custodians have the job of protecting your assets in your IRA.

Per the rules of the Internal Revenue Service, such IRA custodians have to be financial institutions that are approved. People can not choose to perform the role of an IRA custodian. In order for institutions that are not financial in nature to perform the responsibilities of such IRA custodians, they have to receive a special approval issued to them by the Internal Revenue Service.

These IRA Custodians actually carry out the transactions that the clients request of them. They also file any and all reports, maintain all required records of anything done on the account as a custodian, and send out statements and notices for taxes, either of which may be mandated by law or the agreement for custodianship.

They sometimes will disburse the assets found in the IRA as per the wishes of the client, as well as file all necessary and relevant paper work with this action. One thing that IRA custodians do not have to do is to offer legal or investment advice to you, the IRA holder. This means that you have to provide the custodian of your IRA with clear and accurate instructions which follow the code established by the IRS.

IRA custodians can be responsible for overseeing a great range of investment securities and financial instruments. While IRS rules restrict IRA money being invested into collectibles like rare coins and artworks, or even life insurance, the custodian is able to work with various different investments like franchises, real estate, tax liens, and mortgages.

Still, a great number of financial institutions acting as IRA custodians will choose to restrict the kinds of investments that they will allow to be held in one of their IRAâ€™s under custodianship. It is important for owners of IRAâ€™s who wish to have their funds placed into investments that are not traditional for IRAâ€™s, such as real estate or franchises, to seek out and choose an IRA custodian who will allow and work with these kinds of investments. This is the particular reason that a real estate management firm might choose to attain IRS certification in order to obtain the permission for overseeing real estate investment IRAâ€™s.

Much of the time, IRA customers will just deposit their retirement money and assets into their account that the custodian holds and will supply them with overall guidelines for their investments. The IRS mandates fiduciary responsibility for IRA custodians. They have to place clientsâ€™ interests first. This translates to practical requirements, such as not being allowed to put the IRA money into investments and projects that come with a great amount of risk, unless they have the customerâ€™s expressed consent.

IRA custodians are also involved with self directed IRAâ€™s. Self directed IRAâ€™s contain investments that are actively managed directly by the customer. The custodian only performs the actions that the customer requests in these cases.

# Keogh Plan

Keogh Plans are like 401(k) plans intended for small businesses. They are distinguished from them by having higher limits than the 401(k)s do. These tax deferred pension plans can be established by businesses that are not incorporated or individuals who are self employed.

These types of plans can be one of three types. There are money purchase plans preferred by those who are high income earners. Profit sharing plans provide yearly flexibility that is dependent on the company profits. Defined benefit plans feature higher yearly minimums.

Keogh Plans are also referred to as HR(10) plans. They are permitted to invest in the same investments as IRAs and 401(k)s. This includes stocks and bonds, annuities, and certificates of deposit. The reasons these plans are so popular for sole proprietors and small business owners has to do with their higher contribution limits. A downside to them revolves around their greater maintenance costs and more burdensome administration than SEP Simplified Employee Pension plans feature.

These Keogh Plans derive their name from the creator of the concept Eugene Keogh. He put together the 1962 Self Employed Individuals Tax Retirement Act which became named for him. The plans received a name change after the Economic Growth and Tax Relief Reconciliation Act passed in 2001. This act so altered these plans that the IRS code dropped the reference name of Keogh.

They simply call them HR(10) plans now. These retirement accounts are still utilized, but have lost many followers to the solo 401(k) and the SEP IRA. The HR(10) plans still find a good fit with professionals who are highly compensated as with lawyers or dentists who are self employed. Otherwise these plans generally do not serve retirement savers better than the competing plans.

The HR(10) plans come in two different principal breakdowns. These are defined contribution and defined benefit plans. With defined contribution plans, self employed persons can decide the amount of contribution they will make every year. This can be done either through money purchase or profit sharing plans.

Money purchase requires that the profits percentage to go in the Keogh be decided at the beginning of the year. If the employed person makes profits, these contributions must be made without changes or a penalty will be assessed by the IRS. The amounts owners contribute to their profit sharing plans may be changed every year. As much as 25% of income can be deducted and contributed every year. The limit on this amount is $53,000 for 2015 and 2016.

Defined benefit plans operate much as traditional pensions would. Business owners determine a pension goal for themselves then fund it. As much as $210,000 may be contributed in a year (up to 100% of all compensation) for the years 2015 and 2016. Business owners make all contributions in both types of Keogh plans as pre-tax. This means they these contributions come out of the taxable salary before taxes are figured.

Keoghs plans are also similar to typical 401(k)s in the way that invested monies are able to be tax deferred until retirement. This may start as early as 59 Â½ years old but can not be delayed until any later than 70 years of age. Any withdrawals taken before these years are federally and potentially state taxed as regular income and also penalized at 10%. Exceptions to the penalty rules exist if certain physical or financial health issues come up for the account owner before retirement.

In order to maintain a Keogh Plan, a great amount of paperwork has to be filed each year. This includes the Form 5500 from the IRS. It requires a financial professional or tax accountantâ€™s help.

# Land Law

Land law represents the type of law discipline that pertains to the various inherent rights of individuals to utilize (or restrict others from) owned land. There are many jurisdictions of the world that employ the words real property or real estate to describe such privately, corporately, or government owned land. Land utilization agreements such as renting prove to be a critical intersecting point where land law and contract law meet.

Water rights and mineral rights to a piece of property are closely connected to and interrelated with land law. Such land rights turn out to be so important that this form of law always develops one way or another, regardless of whether or not a country, kingdom, or empire exists to enforce it. A classic example of this phenomenon is the American West and its claim clubs. These institutions came about on their own as a means for land owners to enforce the rules which surrounded staking claims and minesâ€™ ownership.

When people occupy land without owning it, this is called squatting. This problem was not limited to the old American West, but is in fact universally practiced by the poor or disenfranchised throughout the world. Practically all nations and territories of the world maintain some form of a system for land registration. With this system there is also a process for land claims utilized in order to work out any disputes surrounding land ownership and access.

International land law recognizes the territorial land rights of indigenous peoples. Besides this, countryâ€™s legal systems also acknowledge such land rights, calling them aboriginal title in many regions. In societies which still utilize customary law, land ownership is primarily exercised by customary land holding traditions.

Land rights also pertain to the inalienable abilities for individuals to freely purchase, use, and hold land according to their wishes. Naturally this assumes that their various endeavors on the property do not interfere with the rights of other members of society.

This should never be confused with the concepts of land access. Land access means that individuals have the rights to use a piece of property economically, as with farming or mining activities. Such access is considered to be far less secure than ownership of the land itself, since a person only using the property can be evicted from it at the whim of the land owner.

Land law also deals with the statutes which a nation sets out regarding the ownership of land. This can be difficult to reconcile in some countries as they have the more traditional customary land ideas such as group or individual land rights as part of their culture instead of legal understandings. This is why the various laws between land rights and land ownership have to be harmonious to prevent bitter disputes, fighting, and indigenous territorial standoffs.

Around the world, a growing focus on such land rights and the way these intersect with traditional laws on the land has emerged. Land ownership represents an important and often necessary for survival (in many cultures) source for food, water, resources, shelter, financial security, and even capital. This is why the United Nations Global Land Tool organization links landlessness in rural areas with both poverty and malnutrition.

It led to the Millennium Development Goal 7D which works to better the lives and livelihoods of around 100 million individual slum dwellers. This project is working to promote land rights and land ownership for poor people the world over in hopes that this will finally lead them to a higher quality of life and more stable and secure existence.

# Leasehold Estate

A Leasehold Estate relates to an official and legal interest that permits a company or individuals to assume temporary ownership of the land of another individual or company. They are able to use this land for business purposes, agricultural applications, or even as a dwelling. Property could include timber land, mineral land, oil land, farm land, or business and/or residence property. With such leasehold estates, landlords possess the title of the property at the same time as the tenant holds the rights to utilize said property. These estates range wildly in the format for the agreement and how it is set up, the amount of time the status exists, and the kind of property which is being leased.

A Leasehold Estate can be established orally or as a written agreement. Those agreements which are intended to endure over a year might have to be composed in a written document per the laws of the relevant state which has jurisdiction. These agreements provide either explicit or implicit permission for all the receiving end parties, who are called the lessees, to assume control of the said property of the other party, who is referred to as the lessor.

There are other various kinds of property agreements which exist. What separates leasehold agreements from these competing formats, such as purchase agreements, is the actual termination date. Every party which is involved with a leasehold agreement comprehends that the agreed upon ownership interests will eventually conclude. This is to say that they are not intended to last in perpetuity. Another distinctive feature of such estates lies with the lessee's right to possess the said property in question. Various other kinds of property agreements, like licenses or easements, actually provide the holder with the permanent rights to utilize the property as they see fit.

Leasehold Estates are quite specific. They comprise both land and any property on the land in question at a given address. Land in this sense of the word does not simply mean the physical land, but also includes any buildings which lie on the property. It also applies to any and all natural resources which occupy the land in question. These estates could also include other forms of personal property, like machinery or fixtures which are so permanently a part of the land that they become considered to be part and parcel of the property. Such fixtures could comprise things like fencing, lighting, wells, or windmills.

Estates are types of personal property. Applicable state laws commonly govern the legal definition of personal property. This means that they could supersede clauses within the Leasehold Estate agreement. An example of this is found in the state of California. The leasehold which pertains to agricultural purposes may not be extended past a maximum time frame of 51 years total.

This is why such leasehold agreements are established with a pre-determined and limited number of years in mind. This is articulated in the tenancy of years. Such a specified length of lease is determined by both lessor and lessee. The only exception is when state laws set the time span directly. It is possible to terminate such a leasehold tenancy ahead of the articulated time. The lessee must decide to surrender his or her possession of the property at the same time as the lessor agrees to resume control over his property and rights.

Four different classifications of these Leasehold Estates exist. They are fixed term, periodic, at will, and at sufferance. Fixed term tenancy refers to the number of years of the tenancy. It is states as an interest which is established to endure a particular amount of time.

Periodic tenancy relates to a set out amount of time, as with week to week, month to month, or even year to year. The leasehold can be ended by either tenant or landlord simply giving a notice to vacate the property. Usually a 30 days notice in writing must be provided to the owner of the property.

Tenancy at will refers to the lack of structure with these kinds of leasehold agreements. No date is given for the end of tenancy in such a form of leasehold estate. Tenancy at sufferance happens as a tenant decides to overstay the date of termination as spelled out in the applicable agreement. Landlords in these cases possess the legal rights to simply evict the tenant if they wish.

# Legal Tender

Legal tender proves to be official forms of payment that the nation's government recognizes for paying either private or public debts or for meeting any number of financial obligations. In nearly all nations, national currency is the one and only legal tender. Creditors have no choice but to receive this currency for repaying of debts owed to them. It is only the appropriately endowed national institutions which are permitted to issue such legal tender. In the United States, this means the U.S. Treasury. In Canada, it refers to the Royal Canadian Mint.

Any type of payment which must be taken for a debt is legal tender. The laws of the land determine which payments are such currencies. This term mostly pertains to money in cash form like coins and bills.

It does not include credit cards, bank cards, checks, or lines of credit. Laws which pertain to legal tender are the bedrock in the forming of a countryâ€™s fiscal policy for a great number of states.

In the days of the American federalist debates, individuals who sought to restrict the powers of the new central government attempted to force rules restricting the creation of a national central bank and to ensure that the national government could not issue currency. Such positions as those espoused by the anti-federalists were mostly defeated. The U.S. Constitution does in fact forbid individual states from issuing their own currencies, meaning they obtained at least a partial state-level victory.

Following the American war for independence, the fledgling nation utilized a wide range of foreign silver and gold coins in trade. Throughout the American Civil War, these policies had to be altered because of the enormous levels of government debt issued and assumed. Because of these expenditures, the American government chose to start producing paper bills for money. With its landmark ruling in 1965, the U.S. Supreme Court affirmed that all American government issued money, including coins and bills, was legal tender. This meant that it had to be taken in payment of debts by every party within the U.S. They similarly ruled that foreign-issued money is not acceptable for forms of payments.

This Supreme Court ruling did not completely settle the issue once and for all. In 2002, the long simmering topic on the issue of currency rose to the forefront of policy debate once again. It was the introducing of the Legal Tender Modernization Act within the U.S. House of Representatives that set it off once again. Besides various other provisos, the act insisted on the termination in circulation of the penny.

Those in favor of the bill under discussion argued that pennies were worthless as a currency since they could not be utilized in most purchases or with vending machines. They cost significantly more than their face value to make and circulate and depend on heavy metal polluting industries in mining both zinc and copper. Despite its public interest, this bill never moved forward into the Congress.

Rather it died a slow death for lack of interest and sponsors following the termination of that yearâ€™s lawmaking session.

Among the great debates for the early years of the 21st century, the Europeans adopting the Euro took monetary center stage. A great number of nations had centuryâ€™s long association with their proprietary and historical national currencies. The switch over to such a common currency format angered the fearful nationalists living within Europe. Around 20 nations eventually joined this new Euro zone and replaced their beloved old currencies with the euro. Most significantly, the U.K., Sweden, and Denmark refused to join and gained exemptions from the common currency requirements and mandate, electing to hold on to their own national currencies instead.

# Lender of Last Resort

Lender of Last Resort refers to an official central financial institution which provides emergency loans to commercial and savings banks as well as other financial institutions which are suffering from extreme financial hardship or are believed to be nearing collapse. Generally such a lender turns out to be a national central bank. Within the U.S., it is the Federal Reserve which functions as the last case lender to those institutions which find themselves without any other way to borrow funds quickly. Their inability to gain access to funds and credit could lead to a devastating consequence for the greater economy in general. This is why the central banks will provide credit extensions on an expedited basis to those financial institutions which are undergoing extreme financial stress and so in consequence cannot get funds from anywhere else.

The principal job of such a Lender of Last Resort is to maintain the financial system stability and the banking system integrity through safeguarding the deposited funds of individuals and businesses. This is critical to foster confidence in the financial system and to prevent wholesale panic from taking hold of depositors who might otherwise cause runs on the banks by attempting to draw out all of their funds at once. Such an action would create an illiquidity event for the bank and force them to close their doors.

It has been over a century and a half since central banks made it their missions to head off great depressions through being the effective Lenders of Last Resort when financial crises erupted. The action does deliver the liquidity funds with a penalty interest rate. As open market operations take over the funding facility, the interest rate drops for safe assets as collateral. The process also includes direct support to the market.

Commercial banks do not enjoy borrowing from the Lender of Last Resort at any time. It would be a sure fire warning that the bank was undergoing financial stress or even experiencing a crisis of liquidity and a crisis of confidence would next follow. This is the reason that critics of this type of arrangement feel that it tempts banks into taking on a higher level of risk than they should in a form of moral hazard. This could happen because they believe that consequences for engaging in risky financial behavior will not be so severe.

The alternatives to a trustworthy central banking institution not functioning as a Lender of Last Resort can be serious. Bank runs are what result in times of financial crisis when the customers of banks begin to show concern over the solvency of their home financial institution. These customers can be seized with sudden panic and descend en masse on the bank demanding to withdraw all of their funds when confidence in the individual bank or the banking system as a whole erupts.

Banks only maintain s tiny percentage of their deposited funds on hand in their vaults. This is how a bank run can result in the liquidity of a bank rapidly disappearing. Literally these panicked customer actions can set into motion a self-fulfilling prophecy which leads to the bank failing as a result of insolvency.

This actually occurred in 1929 and throughout the 1930s. Bank runs led to catastrophic and widespread bank failure throughout the United States after the 1929 stock market crashes. This snowballed into the Great Depression which gripped the country and developed world economies for the next roughly fifteen years. The American federal government responded too late with tough new legislation which mandated severe reserve requirements on the banks. It required by law that they keep a specific minimum percentage of their deposits as available cash reserves.

# Lien

A lien is a claim on one individual's property by another person or entity. The party that holds the lien is able to recover the property if a debtor will not follow through with making payments. There are also other circumstances in which liens would allow the lien holder to take the property. Mortgages on houses or buildings prove to be one kind these. Vehicle loans for a business or individual represent other types that are put on the value of the vehicle. When the obligation is paid off, the lien becomes discharged.

Before individuals are able to receive their money after the sale of an asset like a car or house, the lien must be paid off first. With a vehicle, this means that the lender will not send out the title until they receive complete repayment of the principal.

The majority of liens allow for the individuals or businesses to utilize the property as they are paying it. There are scenarios where the lender or creditor physically holds the property while the borrower is making payments. These are a part of bankruptcy procedures as well because they are secured loans with debt repayment rules that have to be addressed in a case.

While there are a number of different types of liens, the most typical one is on a vehicle. Individuals buy a car from the dealer. The bank loans the money and secures the loan. They do this by placing a vehicle lien which allows them to hold on to the automobile's title. The lender files a UCC-1 form to record this. So long as the debtor continues to make payments, the loan will be paid off finally. The bank would then release to the individual the title.

If the individuals stop making their payments, the bank is able to take possession of the vehicle back while still holding the title. If the vehicle owners choose to sell the automobile when they still owe principal, they must clear the bank loan in order to obtain the title. Without the title, a person can not sell the vehicle.

There are a variety of different types of liens in the world. Consensual ones are those which individuals voluntarily accept when they buy something. Non consensual ones are also known as statutory. These come from a court process where an entity places a lien on assets because bills have not been paid. Three of these are fairly common.

A tax lien occurs when individuals do not pay local, state, or federal income taxes. These are put on the offender's property. A judgment lien comes as a result of a case in a small claims court. When a court gives a judgment to one party, the offending party might refuse to pay. In this case the court will place a judgment lien on the offender's property.

A mechanic or contractor lien happens when a contractor performs a job for a home owner. If the owner refuses to pay, the contractor can ask a court to place a lien on the property in question. This would have to be paid off along with other security interests before the property owner is able to sell.

# Limited Liability Company (LLC)

A limited liability company is often referred to by its acronym LLC. These business setups combine the best in both worlds of proprietorships and corporations. They offer the sole proprietorship or partnerships' advantages of pass through taxation. At the same time, an LLC provides the same limited liability for the owners which a corporation receives.

With a limited liability company, the owners will file their business losses or profits with their individual tax returns. This is because an LLC is not considered to be its own taxable structure. When lawsuits against the company are involved, it is only business assets that are at risk of seizure.

Creditors and lawsuit parties are not usually able to get to the LLC owners' personal assets, like cars or houses. This is not absolute protection. If the owners of the LLC engage in unethical, illegal, or irresponsible behavior, then they can forfeit this level of security.

Setting up a limited liability company is harder than establishing either a sole proprietorship or partnership. Once this hurdle is cleared, it is much easier to run the LLC than it is a corporation. Officers of corporations are not completely protected from actions they undertake in the business.

LLC owners must be careful not to behave like the entity is a mere extension of their own individual activities. Should the owners not act as if the LLC is its own separate business concern, then courts can determine that the business LLC does not really exist. In these cases, the judge could decide that individuals are masquerading their business affairs and conducing business as a personal venture. They can became liable then for these actions if this determination is made.

Taxes are another major reason that individuals opt to set up a limited liability company. As pass through entities, the income from their business passes on through the entity directly to the members of the LLC. This means that they must report all financial gains or losses from the enterprise directly on their own tax returns. They do not have to file separate business tax returns. The IRS does require that LLC owners make an estimated quarterly tax payment four times per year.

LLCs which are owned by more than one individual do have to file the informational return Form 1065 every year with the IRS. This form clearly states every owner's share of the limited liability company profits or losses. The IRS goes over these to be certain that the owners are all appropriately reporting their share of the earnings.

Limited liability company management is specific in how it has to be conducted. There are two forms of this. Member management involves an equal participation of the owners in the operating of the business. This is the way that the majority of smaller LLC owners run them.

The alternative form of management is called manager management. In this type of business operation, the collective owners of the LLC must choose someone to handle the daily responsibilities of managing the company. This could be an owner or several of the owners. It could also be someone who is not a part of the LLC ownership who professionally manages the business on their behalf. In this arrangement, the owners who are not managing are only tasked with sharing in the profits or losses of the business. This is often the case with family members or friends who invest in a limited liability company.

# Maastricht Treaty

The Maastricht Treaty is the main treaty of the European Union. It was originally known as the TEU Treaty on European Union. This agreement was signed in Maastricht, the Netherlands on February 7, 1992. Members of the European Community debated it in their individual countries and then signed it. The treaty came about as an effort to fully integrate Europe into a closer political and economic union.

The treaty established the European Union. It also set the groundwork for creating the euro, the single currency of the EU. The Maastricht Treaty was subsequently amended by several other agreements. These included the Amsterdam, Nice, and Lisbon treaties.

This treaty represented a significant milestone in the process of integrating Europe. It modified other previously signed agreements like the treaties of Paris and Rome, as well as the Single European Act. These earlier arrangements had economic goals for the community. The original stated objective had been to create a common market for trading and investment.

With the Maastricht Treaty, the Europeans signed on to a spelled out vision of political union for the first time. After the treaty came into effect, the European project no longer went under the name of European Economic Community or EEC. Instead, it became known as the EU or European Union. Article 2 in this treaty called for â€œthe process of creating an ever closer union among the peoples of Europe.â€▯

This Maastricht Treaty had a structural base of three pillars. The central pillar referred to the community dimension. It set out arrangements that pertained to common community policies, citizenship in the EU, and economic and monetary union. These were laid out in the Euratom, the ECSC, and the EC treaties. This pillar led to the eventual creation of the European Central Bank and the euro.

The second pillar concerned the CFSP Common foreign and security policy. Under this idea, the countries of the European Union would create a foreign minister for the EU to represent their single voice and policy objectives overseas. They also began working to come up with a common defensive policy with the intention of eventually creating an EU military force. This pillar also pertains to immigration and border control issues. It has suffered a serious challenge since the European refugee crisis has brought more than a million mostly Syrian and Iraqi refugees across the external borders of the E.U.

The third pillar of the Maastricht Treaty is the idea that there would be police and judicial cooperation. This pertained to criminal issues and concerns. It established a European Court of Justice whose decisions supersede those of the national country high courts.

The Maastricht Treaty also laid the grounds for the creation of the European Commission and the European Parliament. These bodies govern many budgetary and even political affairs within the block.

The Maastricht Treaty set in motion the discontent that led to the Brexit vote and the United Kingdomâ€™s decision to leave the EU. The pillars on common security and judicial cooperation turned out to major sore points with the British people. On the one hand, they despised the loss of control over their immigration policy and borders.

On the other they did not like the fact that they had also lost judicial control. A number of high profile court cases decided in the highest British court were subsequently overturned by the European Court of Justice. This all helped to explain why the majority of the British voted against the ever further political union which article two of the treaty established.

# Margin Call

Margin Call refers to a demand from a broker that the account holding investor (who is utilizing margin) deposit additional funds or securities in order to restore the margin account to a minimum preset maintenance margin level. This could occur with a stock, futures, or commodities margin account. Such margin calls happen as the account value falls to a ratio which that specific brokerage deems unacceptable. Many brokerage houses use their own unique formulas to determine the amount at which they will issue such a call for more funds or securities.

Investors get into this unpleasant position when one or many of their securities they have purchased (utilizing money they borrowed from the brokerage) drops to a specified value point. That is when the call goes out from the broker for more money to restore the account to an acceptable minimum value. Investors will have two choices. They could comply with the request for additional funds and make an urgent deposit. Otherwise, they could sell off some or all of the positions in the account to reduce the need for minimum margin maintenance or raise the account equity position. The third choice of completely disregarding or ignoring the margin call would result in the broker force-selling positions to reduce this maintenance amount required.

Margin calls would not be necessary at all if investors did not buy securities, futures, or commodities with a combination of their own cash plus money they borrow off of the broker. This is why many experts recommend not utilizing such margin accounts unless an investor is a both seasoned and experienced trader.

Investors have equity in these margin-purchased investments. This amount equals the securities market value less the funds they originally borrowed to complete the purchase in the first place. If and when this equity of the account holder drops to lower than the brokerage-set percentage requirement of maintenance margin, then such a margin call becomes issued. Such maintenance margins do vary somewhat significantly from one broker to the next.

The constant is the Federal minimum maintenance margin requirements. These are set at a lowest common requirement of 25 percent, regardless of who the responsible broker is. The brokers can choose to utilize a higher margin maintenance level than this amount, but they can not ever reduce their own limit to less than the 25 percent set by the Feds. Brokers can decide to change their maintenance level higher or lower than their present set one with little to no advance warning or notice, so long as they do not drop it below the government-mandated minimum amount. Raising their margin maintenance requirements may also result in creating a margin call.

Looking at a tangible example helps to clarify the concept and make it more understandable. Investors might purchase $50,000 worth of stocks via a combination of $25,000 of their own funds and through borrowing the balance $25,000 off of the brokerage firm. Assume that this particular broker chooses to utilize the government-set minimum of 25 percent maintenance margin. The investor has no choice but to honor this.

When the investors open the trade, at that point the equity positions of the investments prove to be $25,000 (or $50,000 minus the $25,000 borrowed). This makes the investor equity percentage an even 50 percent (using the $25,000 equity divided by the $50,000 original securities market value). This is twice the required minimum 25 percent margin maintenance.

Yet a week later, our investors suffer a drastic decline in the value of their securities, which precipitously drop to $30,000. The investors’ equity is now down to a mere $5,000 (or $30,000 minus the $25,000 borrowed). Yet the brokerage (and government regulations which are the same in this scenario) requires that they keep a minimally $7,500 worth of equity for the account to remain margin-eligible (which is 25 percent of the borrowed amount of $30,000).

It means that there is presently a $2,500 deficit ($7,500 requirement minus the $5,000 actual market value). The broker will then issue a margin call for $2,500 in additional cash to be deposited immediately. Should the investors refuse or take their time, then the broker is legally bound and permitted to sell off some of the securities to reach the minimum $7,500 in account equity value.

# Marine Salvage

Marine salvage operates as a special part of the law that has to do with the many international treaties as well as conventions that pertain to recovering goods and vessels which disappear in the sea. There are many reasons why ships and good could simply vanish in the ocean or sea. Among these is a breakdown of navigational equipment, unexpected bad weather, piracy, or forced sinking of the ship. Those who work in this salvage industry try to recover lost goods at a profit.

There are many different rules and laws pertaining to such salvage rights at sea. This depends in which jurisdiction the wreck or lost goods are discovered. It is why there are two main kinds of salvage which the various operators work under, pure salvage and contract salvage.

Pure salvage operators do not work with a contract. They are more like modern day treasure hunters. They cause the most problems as the original owners try to regain control over their property once it has been liberated from the depths. Such issues as the legal rights’ owners hang over the odds of making money in this business. Professional salvage operators must have a full understanding of the law which governs the recovery of ships and goods in the waters where they operate. Otherwise, they will be unable to secure the rights to gain from any rescued goods, ships, or other valuable equipment.

The other types of salvage workers operate as contract salvage professionals. They attempt to earn a set percentage or finder's fee from the recovery of property which has effectively been lost at sea. The efforts at recovery are contracted directly between the original owner of the property and the company performing the salvage. This means that there is far less chance of a disagreement breaking out between the two parties.

In practice, it also releases both of the parties from needing a thorough comprehension of the laws of marine salvage of the governing authority which has jurisdiction over the territorial waters in question. The only thing the salvage operation really needs to have a handle on pertains to the laws which govern the operation of international laws in the sea region.

The world's earliest known internationally accepted marine laws originated in Rhodes, a (modern day) Greek island off the coast of Turkey. This independent maritime power promoted a set of international conventions that were accepted throughout the Hellenistic and Roman worlds eventually. The two historical literatures of the Roman Empire and the Byzantine Empire reference and reprint the Rhodian Laws.

This historical precedent for a common "law of the sea" is important because the admiralty laws which internationally influential nations like Great Britain, Italy, and the United States use were co-opted by these same imperial powers. This means they became the internationally accepted standards for the modern world. Such admiralty laws have to do with the business dealings and understandings which are instrumental in those operations of the sea and salvage. They also pertain to the international laws of the sea as well.

It is interesting that not only professional divers take part in the range of marine salvage operations around the world. Novice divers also take a hand in such salvage projects. Regardless of their status personally or professionally, the same international laws mandate that they must honor the jurisdictional and commonly accepted rules. This means that private divers hunting for sunken treasure off of Mexicoâ€™s coast will have to abide by the identical maritime laws which professional divers working the international deep seas will.

It is true that a great number of the marine salvage laws are identical in the majority of the countries in the world today. This interesting fact resulted from the near universal adaptation of a range of international conventions. Still, it is true that every legal jurisdiction has its own variations on the common standard of where, when, and how salvage operators can realize profits in their pure salvage endeavors.

# Money Laundering

Money laundering refers to the methods for taking income from corruption and crime and turning them into legal assets. Many countries and jurisdictions have re-defined the term to focus on financial or business crime, often used to support drug dealing empires or terrorism financing. The phrase can also refer to improperly utilizing the financial system for a variety of reasons. In these cases, it might involve digital currencies, traditional currency, credit cards, and even securities.

In recent years money laundering has become associated with international sanction avoidance and financing of terrorist acts. The pursuit of this focuses on the source of money while that of terrorism financing is worried about the destination of this money.

Throughout history, countries, kingdoms, and rules created regulations designed to seize wealth from their citizens. This eventually caused the formation of tax evasion and offshore banking. Though these are not crimes in all countries, the ones that do penalize and pursue it consider it to be a form of money laundering.

In the early years of the 1900s, wealth began to be seized as a means of stopping crime. This began in earnest during the American Prohibition of the 1930s. Law enforcement agencies and the government became concerned with tracking down and seizing money involved in illegal alcohol sales. Organized crime had obtained an enormous boost because of the major new source of funds illegal alcohol vending provided.

The emphasis for fighting money laundering shifted in the 1980s to drug dealers and empires in the American led war on drugs. Governments and law enforcement became concerned with seizing the financial rewards from drug related crime as they pursued the drug empire founders, managers, and dealers. These laws required individuals to demonstrate that their seized funds were from legitimate sources in order to get them back.

The most recent focus of this illegal activities pursuit centered around terrorism empires that began with the 9/11 attacks in 2001. The Patriot Act in America and comparable legislation passed around the developed world gave a new motivation for such rules which would help fight terrorism and its financing.

The G7 Group of Seven wealthy nations created its Financial Action Task Force on Money Laundering to pressure other governments around the globe. They wanted greater observation and monitoring for financial transactions with information sharing between nations. This resulted in improved monitoring systems for financial transactions and stronger anti-laundering laws from 2002.

These regulations have created a far heavier burden for international banks. Enforcement of perceived money laundering breaches has led to severe investigations and steep fines against major international financial institutions. British banking giant HSBC received a hefty $1.9 billion fine from the U.S. in December of 2012. French bank BNP Paribas reeled from a steep $8.9 billion fine from the U.S. government in July of 2014.

A number of nations have also instituted stricter rules on the amount of currency which is allowed to be physically carried across borders.

Governments have set up central transaction reporting systems to make all of the financial institutions report every electronic financial transaction. The American Department of the Treasury established its Office of Terrorism and Financial Intelligence to seek out and exploit weaknesses in the networks of money laundering operations through national and international financial systems.

# Money Market Funds

Money market funds are investment vehicles with a unique objective of keeping a consistent NAV net asset value of $1 each share while they provide interest for their investing share holders. To accomplish this, the portfolio of a money market fund is made up of securities that are short term in nature with maturities which are under a year. These securities typically are liquid debt and money instruments that are of the highest quality. Investors can easily buy money market fund shares by going through banks, brokerage firms, or mutual funds directly.

The ultimate goal of these money market funds is to give their investors a safe haven investment for assets which are both readily accessible and equivalent to cash. In essence they are mutual funds. Among their most common characteristics are that they offer low returns and provide low risk as an investment.

Because these funds offer comparatively lower returns than many other investments, financial advisors recommend that investors not remain in these vehicles as a long term selection. Their returns will not provide sufficient appreciation on capital in order to achieve the investors' objectives over a longer time frame. Employer provided retirement plans will often sweep employees' unallocated dollars into these funds until they give orders as to where to invest them specifically.

The pros to money market funds can be significant. They offer more than simply high liquidity and lower risk. A number of investors find them appealing because there are not any fund entrance or exit fees (or loads) as with many mutual funds. A variety of them will offer investors gains which have tax advantages. These come from investments they make in state and federally tax exempt municipal securities. Other investments which these funds could hold include T-bills and other shorter time frame government debt issues, corporate commercial paper, and CDs certificates of deposit.

There are also some downsides to money market funds besides their low returns. Though they are supposed to be stable and consistent in their values, they are not insured by the FDIC Federal Deposit Insurance Corporation. This means that in the rare cases where such funds break the buck, investors can suffer losses of principal. Competing investments like CDs, savings accounts, and money market deposits accounts provide similar returns but do offer this government backed guarantee of principal. This does not stop investors from regarding money market funds as extremely safe. The funds are carefully regulated by the Investment Company Act of 1940.

The government changed the rules on such money market funds regarding their net asset values and in what they could invest in 2014. After that year, the funds were not permitted to set their NAV permanently at $1 any longer. They did this because of the three times in the history of such funds where the $1 share price had been broken (as of 2016). It had created â€œbank runsâ€ on the assets of the money market funds in 2008 when it occurred most recently in the Financial Crisis.

The American SEC Securities and Exchange Commission decided to prevent this from happening again by changing the fund management rules to provide them with more resilience and better stability. Such new restrictions more strictly limited the assets these funds were allowed to hold. The SEC also introduced triggers that would suspend redemptions and charge liquidity fees to prevent chaos in the markets. The fund managers had to start utilizing a floating NAV which created risk where it was not perceived to exist previously. Individual investors were not impacted by the floating NAV share rule since the funds are designated as retail funds and are exempt from this rule.

# Money Purchase Plan

Money Purchase Plans are another type of retirement vehicle that some traditional for profit companies offer their employees. In these plans, employees and their employers both make contributions. These contributions from the employers are figured from a yearly earnings percentage.

The plans are different from Profit Sharing Plans in which the annual basis of profitability determines how large the contributions are. Money Purchase Plansâ€™ annual earnings percentages assigned for contributions stay the same ever year as set out in the originals terms of the retirement benefit plan. These plans do not enjoy a great deal of attention from the media. Despite this they are still a critical employer provided retirement vehicle that offers significant tax advantages for employees.

These plans are classified as defined contribution plans much like 401(k)s, even though the employer contributions are mandatory. Employees enjoy account control over the investments as much as the specific plan investment rules permit. Account owners also carry full responsibility for determining when any money is distributed or transferred.

The beauty of these Money Purchase Plans is that every contribution made to them is fully tax deductible while all gains in the account are tax deferred. This means the accounts are funded with pretax dollars. None of the money in the account will become taxable until it is distributed at retirement. The maximum contributions to the accounts in a year from employer and employee are $53,000 for 2016.

There are some downsides to the Money Purchase Plans. A significant one is that the retirement accounts require substantial administration costs for these types of accounts. This comes out of the account returns and earnings on investments. Besides this, account holders are unable to obtain loans from these types of plans. Most other defined contribution plans do allow for such loans to be taken. Rollovers can also be hard to accomplish with these types of plans. The level of difficulty depends on the individual guidelines of a specific plan.

It is critical for anyone considering a rollover to investigate the particular documents of the plan. The IRS does not limit rollovers from these plans. It is instead the specifics of the plans themselves that make it difficult for those who are still working for the company and under the official retirement age to transfer them. When the plan allows for them, rollovers proceed as with any other qualified retirement vehicle. They can be transferred into an individual IRA or rolled into another employer 401(k) plan.

Any individuals who attempt to take cash distributions before they reach the government set retirement age of 59 Â½ will suffer substantial penalties. Besides becoming fully taxable, these funds will be subjected to the 10% early withdrawal IRS penalty. Because of the stiff penalties, direct rollovers are more sensible than indirect ones.

When individuals begin indirect rollovers, they receive a check distribution. The 60 day clock to complete the rollover then begins ticking. There are also withholding requirements when these types of indirect rollovers are attempted. Early distribution penalties can result from not completing these rollovers according to the strict IRS timetable.

Investment choices are a weak point of these Money Purchase Plans. Legally they are allowed to invest in individual government and corporate bonds and stocks, mutual funds, options, and exchange traded fund shares. The plan provider may limit these choices further as they see fit.

This means that these accounts may not invest in physical gold bullion holdings directly as with self directed or precious metals IRAs. They can participate in paper gold investments such as gold mining company stocks or mutual funds that own them. They may also purchase gold mining ETFs or gold ETFs like GLD.

# Monopoly

Monopolies refer to markets where a single producer or supplier controls all or nearly all of the market. This means that they have the ability to set prices for the good or service they produce. For there to be a true monopoly, there can not be any near substitutes for the product in question. The term monopoly has also come to represent the company which dominates the market of the good or service. Monopolist is another better name for the supplier who controls the market.

When a monopoly exists, there is no competition in the price of the good or service. The monopolist is able to set the price. They will usually choose to make it as high as the market will bear.

Monopolies usually occur because there are particular factors that prevent other companies from competing effectively against the monopolist. These factors are called barriers to entry. There are a number of different barriers to entry which can cause a monopoly to arise.

Sometimes a company exclusively owns a critical resource that companies need to produce the product. This can help it to become a monopoly. Exclusive knowledge of a process to make something would also count as sole ownership of a critical resource. This is what makes pharmaceutical companies monopolies in various types of medicine which they develop and first release.

Government protected ideas can also create monopolies. This can exist in the form of copyrights and patents. In these protections, the government guarantees these companies a minimum period of time to produce the goods or services without any competition. This creates a temporary monopoly until the intellectual property protection expires.

Markets where a good or service is new typically see these types of monopolies. Governments justify copyrights and patents as the means to encourage invention and innovation. Without this temporary protection, many companies would not invest resources needed to create new inventions and products.

A related monopoly is a government franchise. Governments create these types of monopolies when they give the exclusive ability to operate in an industry to a single business. This could happen with a business that is owned by the government or a private company. Train operators and mail delivery companies like the postal service are good examples of this type of government franchise.

Natural monopolies sometimes arise on their own without government help or intervention. This is most often the case when the costs are lower for a single company to service the whole market. Numerous smaller companies competing against each other could actually raise costs and prices in these instances.

Some companies have limitless economies of scale. This means that they are so large and powerful in an industry that no new players could compete with their prices. This could be because the costs to enter the industry are so high that no one will bother. They also represent natural monopolies. There are a number of technology infrastructure companies in this position. Some of the more common industries where these types of natural monopolies occur include telephone operators, Internet service, and cable television providers.

It is not always clear if a company possess a monopoly in a given industry. Some people consider certain brands to be monopolies because of how popular they are. This is true even when they do not control all of the product market share.

The Coca Cola Company has a monopoly on producing the soft drink Coke. This is not the only soft drink on the market, but there is no exact substitute for it. Even though rivals Pepsi Cola and Dr Pepper Snapple Group control a large share of the soft drink market, neither of them produces Coke. This is why the debate for monopolies continues to rage on about what constitutes a close substitute. Anti-monopoly regulators constantly wrestle with the question.

# National Bank Act

The National Bank Act refers to three different congressionally passed acts which set up a regime of national banks for the disparate state banks across the United States. These three Federal Banking Acts enabled the U.S. National Banking System to arise. The idea was to foster the creation of a nationwide currency which would be backed up by U.S. Treasury securities held by banks.

The Office of the Comptroller of the Currency under the umbrella of the U.S. Department of the Treasury wanted to be the sole issuer of American currency. To this effect, Treasury authorized the Comptroller of the Currency to start examining and regulating the nationally chartered U.S. banks. These series of acts were responsible for determining the system of national banks in place today and supporting a cohesive banking policy for the United States as a whole.

The first such effort to create a central bank since the First and Second Banks of the United States had failed began with the National Bank Act of 1863. This became the model which was used in the Federal Reserve Act of 1913 eventually. This first act permitted national banks to be created, gave the Federal government permission to sell securities and war bands, and established a plan for creating a unified national currency backed up by government securities.

The Federal government itself directly chartered these subsequent national banks which became subjected to tighter regulation than other banks were at the time. The national banks had to maintain larger capital requirements and could not loan out in excess of 10 percent of their total deposits. The government discovered they could discourage the competition by levying a burdensome tax on the state banks. It only took until 1865 for the majority of the state banks to apply for national charters or to fail altogether.

In 1864, the Federal government waded into the realm of active supervision of all commercial banks. They did this using the National Bank Act of 1864, which was itself based on a law from

New York State. This important act created the Office of the Comptroller of the Currency. This office carried the responsibility for chartering, supervising, and examining every national bank.

A year later Congress added still more to this new legislation in the form of the Banking Act of 1865. This July 13, 1866 passed legislation expanded the law to more than simply mandating a 10 percent tax on all of their own state bank proprietary notes. It extended the tax from state banks, national banking associations, and state banking associations so that individuals who utilized such proprietary state bank notes would also be subjected to an additional 10 percent tax.

The act became challenged and subsequently strengthened as a result of the court case known as *Veazie* Bank versus *Fenno*, supra. Thanks to the Chief Justices of the Supreme Court electing to rule with Congress on the matter, all final resistance offered by the state banks to the National Bank Acts of 1865-1866 collapsed.

The 10 percent taxed proved to be so onerous that the majority of state banks chose to change their charters for national ones in order to sidestep the heavy handed tax. This led to the decline for a few years of state banks. In the 1870â€™s and 1880â€™s, state banks saw a resurgence once again as state bank created checks allowed them to get around the failing profitability and importance of their own proprietary bank notes.

# Nonprofit Organizations

Nonprofit Organizations represent entities whose reason for being is to provide help or value to members or the community at large. These are also called not for profit organizations as well as non-business entities. There are many reasons why an agency would incorporate as a not for profit. They are often interested in promoting points of view or social and charitable causes. Such outfits utilize excess revenues they obtain in order to promote their mission and purpose. They do not ever distribute the so-called profits to stakeholders in the form of dividend payouts. This unique feature of nonprofits is called the non-distribution limitation.

When entities elect to become a Nonprofit Organization, there will typically be tax status ramifications involved. This is the case as not for profits generally seek out tax exemption because of their charitable or socially oriented nature. It is important to note that not all NPOs are charitable organizations, even though many individuals equate the two types of organizations. It is true that charities comprise the most visible component of the category, yet many other kinds of nonprofit organizations also exist.

Founders typically design other kinds of not for profits to serve their communities or members. Among the ones which serve their communities are organizations that concentrate on delivering services to the general community on a local, national, or global scale. These could be those that provide human development and aid, human service projects and programs, health and education services, medical research benefits, and others.

Member serving nonprofit organizations include such entities as cooperatives, mutual societies, credit and trade unions, industry associations, retired servicemenâ€™s clubs, sports clubs, and advocacy or lobby groups. All of these kinds of not for profit organizations actually benefit a certain group of individuals.

With many nonprofits, they are both member-serving and community-serving at the same time. Any grassroots-based support group for cancer victims would be such an example. It serves its members who have cancer by supporting them directly. It also benefits the community at large by providing much needed services to citizens who are also members of the general public.

Though the nonprofit organizations are allowed to create additional revenues beyond their expenses, they have to keep such profit surpluses and use them for ongoing future operations, plans, or expansion efforts. They can not distribute them to any board member or director, organization participant, or beneficiary of the group.

Not for profits have one thing in common with their for profit cousins. They both have boards of directors which exercise control over their respective organizations. Both will also typically have management and other staff which receive compensation for their efforts. Some NPOs utilize executives and volunteers who are not paid or who work for a token compensation. There are jurisdictions and nations that require a nominal fee be paid to directors and managers so that they can form a legally binding contract between organization and executive or board member.

It is interesting to remember that because an organization receives the nonprofit designation, this does not signify that it will not try to turn profits. Instead it means that the entity will not have any owners who benefit from the revenues and/or profits earned. In many cases, the amounts of surplus revenues that NPOs are able to generate, keep, and even deploy are restricted by government laws and regulations within their jurisdictions.

While many nonprofit organizations are service or charitably inclined, others organize and function like a trust or a cooperative. Supporting organizations are much like NPOs. They work as a foundation yet are more complex in their administration requirements. These supporting organizations also obtain a more advantageous tax treatment and commit to restrictions on the various public charities which they support. Such an organizationâ€™s goals are not to amass wealth, but instead are to provide help for and meaning to the peoples they support.

# OCC

The OCC is the acronym for Office of the Comptroller of the Currency. This independent bureau falls under the United States Department of the Treasury. The U.S. President appoints an individual to serve as Comptroller of the agency for a term of five years. The American Senate must approve this appointment. The Comptroller serves as one of the directors of the Neighbor Works and the FDIC Federal Deposit Insurance Corporation.

The OCC has its headquarters in Washington, D.C. They also maintain four district offices throughout the U.S. as well as London office to monitor the national banksâ€™ international activities. The United States Congress created the agency with its 1863 National Currency Act. The group celebrated its 150 year anniversary back in 2013.

There are important responsibilities that the OCC has regarding banks. It charters, supervises, and regulates every national bank and federal savings association. Besides this, it also manages the foreign banksâ€™ federal agencies and branches. It has a mission to make certain that all of these financial institutions run according to sound, safe practices and abide by all relevant regulations and laws. It also ensures that there is sufficient access to financial products and services and that customers are treated fairly.

This government agency operates as a foremost financial supervisor. Its vision is to improve the value of financial institutions by offering supervision that is both proactive and detects risks. It works to ensure a healthy and well rounded banking system that helps the economy as a whole and businesses, consumers, and communities. The group is frequently sought out for its expertise and knowledge.

One of the main functions of the bank examiners who work for the OCC is to go on site to national financial institutions and hold on location reviews. They continue their supervision after this as well. The examiners study the funds management, investment and loan portfolios, earnings, capital, liquidity, and market risk for all of these organizations. Any national financial institution that has under $10 billion of assets falls under their enforcement of consumer banking laws. In pursuit of this, they examine external and internal audits and internal controls along with compliance to the laws. The examiners also check on the ability of the bank managements to identify and manage their own risk.

Where these federal thrifts and national banks are concerned, the OCC has substantial powers. This starts with examining the institutions. They can then deny or approve applications the banks put in for new charters, capital, branches, and other forms of change to their banking or company structure.

There are a number of actions this supervisor can take regarding national financial institutions. They can remove offending directors and officers at these banks. They may also deliver financial penalties and cease and desist orders when banks will not change their unsound or illegal practices. The agency prefers to negotiate changes to such practices first.

The bureau has tremendous powers in implementing the banking laws. They may create regulations and rules. They also provide legal interpretations of them. Finally they issue binding decisions that govern bank lending, investments, and other activities.

Congress does not provide the OCC with a budget. The agency derives all of its revenues from several activities. They receive assessments from the national financial institutions. Banks must pay the agency to conduct examinations that they undergo. Financial institutions also pay fees for having their applications processed. Finally the bureau has revenues that come in from their investments which are mostly U.S. Treasuries.

# Office of Financial Research (OFR)

OFR is an abbreviation and stands for the Office of Financial Research. This government organization that has its headquarter in the Treasury Building works to supply information in support of the Financial Stability Oversight Council.

The OFR strives to encourage financial stability throughout the United States. They do this by scanning throughout the American financial system in order to find, measure, and consider risks. They also engage in gathering critical research and then compile and homogenize the financial data so that it can be easily referenced, understood, and compared.

The Office of Financial Research says about itself that its job revolves around illuminating the darkest parts of the financial system. As they do this, they are looking to see where the risks to the system are heading. They then determine the level of threat such risks pose to the system and the economy. Finally, they deliver financial analysis, data, and insight on these threats along with an available policy toolsâ€™ evaluation in order to effectively address and diffuse the threats.

Congress created this Office of Financial Research back in 2010 under the Dodd-Frank Wall Street Reform and Consumer Protection Act. They established this new organization in order to provide material support to the all important new super regulatory entity the Financial Stability Oversight Council.

The OFR was also to deliver useful information on the risks to the system to the member organizations of the Council as well as to any interested and concerned members of the public. The Director of the OFR is both appointed at the discretion of the President and must be confirmed by a majority vote of the Senate. In 2016, this Director was Richard Berner. The group was created to work around two offices of a Data Center and a Research and Analysis Center.

The mission of the Office of Financial Research is to encourage American financial system stability via providing high quality financial standards, data, and analysis of the information on behalf of the Financial Stability Oversight Council, its various member organizations, and the general public. To this effect, they maintain the vision of a financial system that is efficient, effective, stable, and transparent.

Every year, the Office of Financial Research produces several publications. Two of these that have become annual productions are the Annual Report to Congress on Human Capital Planning and the Annual Report to Congress. The Dodd-Frank Act itself requires that the OFR produces, compiles, and presents this general annual report once a year before Congress.

Every general annual report must include a complete analysis of the various threats to the American financial system and overall stability, the progress in their endeavors to meet the mission of the

OFR, and the critical discoveries regarding threats from their research and analyzing of the whole United Statesâ€™ financial system.

The 2015 Office of Financial Research Annual Report to Congress is the fourth such yearly report since the office became established under the requirements of the Dodd-Frank Act. This particular report reviewed and analyzed the possible threats to American financial stability, reported on their important discoveries of risk, detailed their progress in meeting the OFR overall mission, and laid out the agenda of The Office for 2016.

The 2015 report stated that the various threats to United Statesâ€™ financial stability increased slightly from the prior yearâ€™s report. They still consider the risks to be in the moderate to medium range. They did not change their threat assessment after the Federal Reserve FOMC raised the short term interest rates. A major portion of the 2016 agenda for the OFR is to affect a new programmatic approach in their work. They are striving to concentrate their initial efforts on the core areas of eight programs.

# Office of Price Administration

The Office of Price Administration was a Federal agency created under the Office for Emergency Management within the U.S. Federal government. It was established by Executive Order number 8875 back on August 28th of 1941. The purposes of this OPA were initially to help keep a reign on the prices of rents and essential goods following the beginning of the American involvement in the Second World War.

It was then-President Franklin D. Roosevelt who dusted off the thirty year old Advisory Commission to World War I Council on National Defense beginning on May 29th of 1940. His goal was to involve both the divisions of Price Stabilization and Consumer Protection. These he merged together into the Office of Price Administration and Civilian Supply, known by its acronym OPACS under the auspices of the Office for Emergency Management utilizing

Executive Order number 8734 on April 11th of 1941. As a result of this move, he transferred civil supply functions over to the Office of Production Management.

President Roosevelt's Office of Price Administration was intended to nip any wartime inflation in the bud before it appeared. His organization decreed a general maximum price rule which made any prices being charged as of March 1942 the maximum ceiling prices for the vast majority of commodities. At the same time, the OPA similarly imposed ceilings on all residential rents which consumers were forced to pay. Such regulations became modified and expanded as necessary under various administrators of the OPA, most especially Leon Henderson from 1941-1942, Prentiss H. Brown in 1943, and Chester B. Bowles from 1943-1946. By the time they had finished these tasks, nearly 90 percent of all retail food prices had been frozen through the end of the Second World War.

Despite these humanitarian aims and endeavors though, the prices kept creeping up steadily. The Office of Price Administration then initiated yet more attempts to force price and rent controls compliance on businesses and landlords. By the end of the war, the OPA was able to say with some satisfaction that it had mostly succeeded in maintaining generally stable prices throughout the second half of the war years for Americans.

The Office of Price Administration had a second function during the war. This was to carefully ration hard to find consumer goods during the time of war. Rationing commenced with cars, tires, gasoline, sugar, coffee, fuel oil, meats, and even processed foods. By the conclusion of the war, the rationing gradually became abandoned. Price controls became abolished little by little. Ultimately the government disbanded the entire agency by 1947.

The majority of the Office of Price Administration functions then transferred over into the newly created OTC Office of Temporary Controls under Executive Order number 9809 on December 12th of 1946. The Financial Reporting Division became a part of the Federal Trade Commission at this point.

Eventually the OPA became entirely abolished as of May 29th of 1947. The March 14th of 1947 dated General Liquidation Order issued by the OPA Administrator was responsible for this closing up action. More important function of the ex-agency continued to be performed, albeit under the auspices of succeeding agencies.

Sugar and refined sugar products were still distributed under the Department of Agriculture’s Sugar Rationing Administration thanks to the Sugar Control Extension Act of March 31st 1947. The Reconstruction Finance Corporation picked up the food subsidies from the war beginning on May 4th of 1947. The Office of the Housing Expediter assumed the rent controls policy beginning on May 4th of 1947. Any violations of price became litigated by the Department of Justice as of June 1st of 1947. Price controls on rice were assumed by the general Department of Agriculture as of May 4th of 1947 per Executive Order number 9841. Any other remaining OPA functions were assumed by the Department of Commerce’s Division of Liquidation as of June 1st of 1947.

A number of important and famous individuals worked for the Office of Price Administration during the war. Among these were future President Richard Nixon, legal scholar William Prosser, and economist John Kenneth Galbraith.

# Orderly Liquidation Authority

As part of the Dodd-Frank Act that Congress passed following the Financial Crisis and Great Recession of 2008, they accepted that there are financial firms that will ultimately fail. This is despite the fact that the new regulatory and supervisory framework scrutinizes banks and non banking financial entities more carefully than ever before now.

In the crisis and the years that followed, many policymakers decided that the U.S. Bankruptcy code and process did not quickly and effectively wind down institutions which were systemically important as they became insolvent.

The FDIC had the role of seizing such failing banks in order to resolve them. Their method for doing this has been seen as the best way to stop runs on banks and eliminate financial panics in the process. The FDIC maintains full discretion on which claims that are not deposits to pay and according to the priority that it sees fit. The FDIC generally subordinates debtors and creditors to the U.S. government and its interests.

Congress decided that a new way of winding down these failing institutions was in order to help regulators mitigate risks to the system. Because of this increasingly prevalent view in Washington, D.C. the Dodd-Frank Act set up a new mechanism mostly following the FDIC's existing process for resolving failing institutions. This new Orderly Liquidation Authority is designed to help liquidate financial firms that are systemically important and fail.

All entities that fall under the new regulation provided by the Financial Stability Oversight Council and the Federal Reserve will be resolved under this new mechanism. This includes not only companies who pose a systemic risk. It also covers financial entities whose failure can lead to negative consequences for the remainder of the United States' financial system. The Orderly Liquidation Authority is also known as simply the Liquidation Authority.

For the remainder of financial companies, the standard United States' Bankruptcy Code and judicial process continues to apply. Only in the cases where financial company failure threatens risk to the entire system as determined by the judgment of the Financial Stability Oversight Council will the Orderly Liquidation Authority mechanism supersede the traditional bankruptcy process.

Where the new Liquidation Authority takes precedence over the traditional bankruptcy rules and process, the FDIC is able to utilize this mechanism in order to seize a failing financial entity and move forward to liquidate it. This way, the company and its various creditors will not ponderously and slowly engage in typical restructuring agreements that the U.S. Bankruptcy Code envisions.

Because of these provisions contained in the Dodd-Frank legislation and now enforced by the Financial Stability Oversight Council, financial firms that may fail and threaten the system as a whole will be treated differently than other non-systemically important financial firms. This means that rating agencies, lenders, and various counterparties to financial firms should remember that there will be different results from companies wound down under the mechanism of the Liquidation Authority versus that of the standard United Statesâ€™ Bankruptcy Code.

In order for financial firms to be handled by the Orderly Liquidation Authority, the Treasury Secretary as head of the Financial Stability Oversight Council must intentionally designate these companies to be â€œcovered financial companies.â€ The secretary must first decide that the company will default or be at a substantial risk of default and that it also presents a risk to the financial system as a whole.

This authority gives the federal government the ability to put any financial entity under the auspices of the Liquidation Authority as they deem fit. Insurance companies that become insolvent will continue to fall under the authority of state regulators. Insured thrifts and banks will still be dealt with by the FDIC and its present system for winding down failed institutions.

# Pension Benefit Guaranty Corporation (PBGC)

Pension Benefit Guaranty Corporation is also referred to many times by its government given acronym the PBGC. This federal agency arose as a result of the ERISA Employee Retirement Income Security Act of 1974. Its mission is to safeguard the benefits of pensions provided by private sector benefit plans that are defined. These plans commonly promise to pay out a fixed amount per month when retirement begins.

Should a plan end in the event of plan termination, and there not be enough money to pay out all of the promised benefits, then the insurance program of the Pension Benefit Guaranty Corporation will pay out the pension plan-provided benefit to the limits which the law establishes. This means that the majority of plan participants will actually still get the full benefit which they had already earned and been promised before termination of the plan occurred.

Some people have wondered where the money for the PBGC comes from so that they can cover failed plan benefits this way. The answer is that those firms whose plans the Pension Benefit Guaranty Corporation protects are required to pay insurance premiums for the insurance. PBGC similarly has investments as well as seized assets that they assume when they become trustee of a terminated pension plan. They also have assets from recoveries of firms which used to manage the plans. They do not derive any of this benefit-covering money from the general tax base. Even if a given employer does not pay its insurance premiums properly into the fund, the defined benefits pension plan will still be insured.

Employers may close out these defined benefit plans in what the PBGC calls a standard termination. They are only allowed to do this once they have demonstrated that the plan is sufficiently capitalized to pay out all owed benefits to the plan participants. To do this, the plan will be required to do one of two things. They might buy an annuity off of an insurance company. This annuity will pay out the promised lifelong benefits upon retirement of the participants.

Alternatively, they may provide one time single large payments that amount to the full benefit value amount. The PBGC provided guarantee of the plan will then cease to exist once the employer either buys this annuity or provides the beneficiaries of the plan with the one time, single payment.

Should the plan lack the money needed to cover all promised pension benefits to the participants of the plan while the employing firm finds itself in financial trouble, then the employers are able to request a distress termination from the PBGC fund. The plan will only be terminated under these scenarios when the employing firm proves to either a bankruptcy court or the PBGC itself that they will not be able to continue operating the firm if the plan does not become terminated. Once such an application request is approved, the PBGC typically becomes trustee and administrator of the plan. They would then pay out the promised plan benefits to the extent allowed by law.

The law similarly allows the Pension Benefit Guaranty Corporation to act alone in order to close out a pension plan where necessary to safeguard the participants' interests or that of the insurance program of the PBGC itself. As a standard procedural example, they will terminate any plan that is sure to be incapable of paying out the promised benefits when they become due.

The PBGC covers the overwhelming majority of defined benefit plans which private sector businesses provide. The lion's share pledge to pay out a set benefit (typically in a once per month distribution) upon commencement of the beneficiaries' retirement. Some pledge to deliver a single-value lump sum payment for their benefit. It is important to know that the PBGC will never insure any defined contribution plans that do not pledge to deliver a guaranteed benefit amount.

PBGC insures defined benefit plans offered by private-sector employers. Most promise to pay a specified benefit, usually a monthly amount, at retirement. Others, including cash-balance plans, may state the promised benefit as a single value. PBGC does not insure defined contribution plans, which are retirement plans that do not promise specific benefit amounts, such as profit-sharing or 401(k) plans.

PBGC does not commonly insure any plans that lawyers and doctors offer if they have under 25 active participants. They also do not cover the plans provided by local, state, or Federal governments. Finally, church group pension plans will not be covered.

# Ponzi Scheme

Ponzi Schemes prove to be frauds surrounding investments that are related to the pay out of returns to investors in the scheme that are covered using contributions from new investors. The individuals who run Ponzi schemes are able to attract newer investors through boasting of tremendous opportunities that will guarantee terrific investment returns, typically with little to no risk.

With a great number of these Ponzi Schemes, the managers of the scheme concentrate their efforts on constantly bringing in new sums of money in order to be capable of giving out the payments that they promised investors from earlier time periods. Besides this, they utilize the new money for their own personal expenses. Rarely does any energy actually go into real investment opportunities and strategies.

Ponzi schemes always fail at some point in time. This eventually happens since there are no real earnings to distribute. Because of this problem, Ponzi schemes need constant money flowing into them from newer investors in order to survive. As attracting newer investors becomes more challenging, or if a great number of currently involved investors request their money back, then the Ponzi Scheme will likely fall apart.

Ponzi Schemes actually earned their name from a famed early con artist Charles Ponzi. He became famous after he tricked literally thousands of well to do New Englanders into pouring their money into his speculation in postage stamps in the 1920â€™s. The allure of his scheme proved to be hard to resist, since bank accounts were paying only five percent annual returns while he offered investors incredible returns of fifty percent in only ninety days. In the early days, Charles Ponzi really did purchase a small quantity of international mail coupons to support his investment scheme. Before long, he decided to employ the money that came in to cash out earlier investors.

The most successful Ponzi Scheme of all time proved to be the one run by Bernie Madoff. Madoff ran an over thirty year, over thirty billion dollar investment scheme that tricked thousands of investors out of their money. Madoff proved to have a different angle on his Ponzi scheme in that he did not offer his investors who were short term amazing returns. Rather than this, he sent out fake account statements that constantly demonstrated moderate but always positive gains, no matter how turbulent the market proved to be.

Bernie Madoff is presently undergoing a one hundred and fifty year sentence in federal prison for his activities. His investment advisory company began back in 1960 and did not come down until the end of 2008. All during the years that his scheme ran, he served as Vice Chairman of the National Association of Securities Dealers, and even as a member of the board of governors and chairman for the NASDAQ stock market.

The Securities Exchange Commission is ultimately responsible for discovering and prosecuting Ponzi Schemes. They typically utilize emergency actions to freeze assets while they break up the schemes. In 2009 as an example, the SEC actually pursued sixty different Ponzi schemes, the highest profile one of which turned out to be Robert Allen Stanford's $8 billion Ponzi scheme.

# Power of Attorney

A power of attorney is an agreement in writing that grants another individual the authority to make some choices if the grantor is not available. This person who receives the power does not have to be an attorney. Attorneys are typically only involved in drafting up or potentially witnessing such an agreement. The phrase comes from an individual receiving status as an agent or attorney in fact.

When people implement such a power of attorney they do not lose the ability to make their own decisions. Instead they are allowing another individual to act for them in matters specified within the written text. This can be very helpful if people are out of the country or in the hospital as an example. Someone else with this authority would be able to cash checks at the bank or pay bills on their behalf. It is simply a matter of sharing power with another person. The agent is only carrying out the grantor's wishes, not actually making choices for them, so long as they are coherent and mentally capable.

People who will be out of town for an extended period of time might find these arrangements particularly useful. With a power of attorney, the agent could carry out major decisions such as selling cars or other personal assets. The Internet has eliminated the need for some of these functions as computers and mobile devices make it possible for people to buy and sell stocks and handle many financial transactions from anywhere they have an online connection. There are still cases where a transaction will require an in person agent to handle them.

There is also a special kind of power of attorney that is used by individuals who lose their ability to handle decisions for their personal financial affairs. This is known as a durable power of attorney. In this case, the word durable refers to the ability of the agent to make the choices on the grantorâ€™s behalf when he or she can not mentally do them. This type of arrangement grants the agent the legal authority and responsibility to make the best possible physical and financial decisions for the grantor.

It means that the agent is able to spend the individualâ€™s money as appropriate, cash checks, deposit checks, and even withdraw money from the personal bank accounts. The agent further gains the authority to sign contracts, sell personal property, take legal actions, and file and follow up on insurance claims.

When people decide to enter a durable power of attorney arrangement, a notary public or lawyer should witness the document before they sign and execute it. If such individuals need to have a durable agreement established and are not mentally able to do it, courts can do this for them as they deem necessary.

Agents who become appointed to this position are expected to keep correct and segregated records on each transaction they perform. The records must also be easily available at all times. When the individual dies, his or her power of attorney becomes null and void. The will is responsible for the dispensation of the deceased personâ€™s estate.

Powers of attorney can be rescinded. If individuals feel unhappy in the ways that their agent is managing their personal affairs, they can simply revoke the authority back at any point. It is always wise for people to choose an individual to be agent whom they know and implicitly trust.

# Price Gouging

Price gouging involves businesses charging higher prices than those that are considered to be fair or normal. It is most often done when there are crises or natural disasters strike. This gouging could also result from temporary boosts in demand that are not matched by supply. If suppliersâ€™ expenses rises, this is not considered to be a form of gouging when they pass it along to customers.

Because price gouging is usually considered to be unethical, it is generally treated as strictly illegal in a great number of places. Interestingly though, this gouging originates from what many economists call an efficient market outcome.

As demand goes up for a given product, this signifies that consumers will and are able to pay more to purchase an additional quantity of the good at the fair market price. Increases in a goodâ€™s demand generally lead to short term product shortages. Suppliers are tempted when they see extended lines of people forming (to purchase their product) to both raise their prices and to increase the amount of their product that is available. Suppliers who are retailers will attempt to bring in more product into their stores. Supply and demand return to balance at a higher price in many examples.

When demand increases, everyone can not have the amount that they want for the initial market price. This means that if the price does not go up, shortages will occur. It is because the supplier needs an incentive to provide a greater amount of the goods in question. As supply and demand return to balance, all people who are capable of paying the market price can obtain as much as they need.

The supply and demand balance proves to be efficient economically. The goods go to all individuals who want the product for a greater price than they cost to make. Companies can maximize their profits as well. With shortages, there is no set way that the goods become rationed. Though usually this is on a first come, first serve basis, it might be resolved through bribes to the owner of the store. Such a bribe would amount to raising the price anyway.

It is critical to realize that in times of excessive demand, everyone can not obtain their full demand for the product at the original price. Higher prices will generally increase the amount of good supplied so that those who wish most to have them can. This should not be confused with price gouging per se.

There are many critics of price gouging, including most governments. These critic argue that short term supply can not be adequately resolved by higher prices. Demand increase in cases like natural disasters do not allow for suppliers to provide more of the product. They only lead to increases in the price or shortages. This is because supplies in these cases are limited to the inventory a store has on hand.

The critics say that such short term shortages and accompanying price gauging only leads to suppliers realizing excessive profits at the consumerâ€™s expense. Though higher prices are often illegal in such cases, these prices serve a purpose. They distribute the goods more efficiently than prices which prove to be artificially low will since they lead to shortages.

As a classic example, when there is an increased demand, higher prices will reduce hoarding by the people who arrive first at the store. This means that there should be more of the demanded good remaining for others who arrive later and are willing to pay more than the original price.

# Promissory Note

Promissory notes are negotiable instruments that are called notes payable in accounting circles. In such promissory notes, an issuer writes an unlimited promise that he or she will pay a certain amount of money to the payee. This can be set up either on demand of the payee, or at a pre arranged future point in time. Specific terms are always arranged for the repayment of the debt in the promissory note.

Promissory notes are somewhat like IOUâ€™s and yet quite different. Unlike an IOU that only agrees that there is a debt in question, promissory notes are made up of a particular promise to pay the debt. In conversational vernacular, loan contract, loan agreement, or loan are often utilized in place of promissory note, even though such terms do not mean the same things legally. While a promissory note does provide proof of a loan in existence, it is not the loan contract. A loan contract instead has all of the conditions and terms of the particular loan arrangement within it.

Promissory notes contain a variety of term elements in them. Among these are the amount of principal, the rate of interest, the parties involved, the repayment terms, the date, and the date of maturity. From time to time, provisions may be included pertaining to the payeeâ€™s rights should the issuer default. These rights could include the ability to foreclose on the issuerâ€™s assets.

A particular type of promissory note is a Demand Promissory note. This specific kind does not come with an exact date of maturity. Instead, it is due when the lender demands repayment. Generally, in these cases lenders only allow several days advance notice before the payment must be made.

Within the U.S., the Article 3 of the Uniform Commercial Code regulates most promissory notes. These negotiable forms of promissory notes are heavily used along with other documents in mortgages that involve financing purchases of real estate properties. When people make loans in between each other, the making and signing of promissory notes are commonly critical for the purposes of record keeping and paying taxes. Businesses also receive capital via the use of promissory notes that are sometimes referred to as commercial papers. These promissory notes became a finance source for the creditors of the firm receiving money.

Promissory notes have functioned like currency that proved to be privately issued in the past. Because of this, such promissory notes that are bearer negotiable have mostly been made illegal, since they represent an alternative to the officially sanctioned currency. Promissory notes go back to well before the 1500â€™s in Western Europe. Tradition claims that the very first one ever signed existed in Milan in 1325. Reference is made to some being issued between Barcelona and Genoa back in 1384, even though we no longer have the promissory notes themselves. The first one that we still have dates back to 1553 where Ginaldo Giovanni Battista Stroxxi issued one that he created in Medina del Campo, Spain against the city of Besancon.

# Property Tax

A Property Tax refers to a type of tax levied by a government in their jurisdiction on the personal or real estate property of an individual or business. The government will assess the value of the property for the purpose of taxing it. The authorities will then determine how much taxes the owners owe by multiplying the propertyâ€™s fair market value times the then current tax rate.

What makes property taxes so frustrating to so many different people is that the amount which the tax is based on may be changed at will over time when the governing authorities choose to reassess the value of a property entirely at their own discretion and according to their time table. Usually the property tax does not increase alongside the value of the property or house. Instead the tax value usually remains based on the propertyâ€™s value based on the point and value when the owner originally purchased it.

This is not the case when the owner engages in significant improvements. When the owners choose to construct additions to homes or instead to do major remodeling activities, this will often times lead to a reassessment of the value of the property in question. Such a reassessment will generally raise the tax amounts levied.

The laws on the subject are different by every jurisdiction and according to each governing authority. In other words, tax assessment laws that pertain to a given property may not be the same as those on a comparable property lying in another city or state.

Most property taxes become due once per year. It is possible for the yearly amounts due to be divided up into quarterly or otherwise periodic installments. Commercial property owners often pay according to this time table. Where homes are concerned, this can be assessed and paid in monthly installments. This is often simply added on to mortgage payments every month.

The property tax has other names as well. It is sometimes called Realty Tax since it is commonly assessed on real estate. Sometimes they call it ad valorem tax. This means that the tax rate will be set by the value of the land itself. Conversely, there are various other types of taxes. One of these is personal property tax. It is commonly charged and levied differently than by taxes assessed on real property. Such possessions as campers, motorcycles, boats, and cars are affected by it.

It is not usually federal governments which assess such property taxes. Rather local governments like counties, cities, and states gather much if not most of their operating income from these taxes. Such revenues as those generated by property taxes they will commonly deploy to pay for the administration costs of government as well as the costs associated with hiring, training, equipping, and maintaining the critical first responder personnel and vehicles. This includes such necessary services as paramedics, firefighters, and police. Local courts will also be paid for with these revenues, along with such important community services as libraries, civic centers, schools and community parks. School districts in fact gain a huge part of this property tax revenue each and every year.

The states also commonly garner some share of this property taxes revenue. The ability to assess and collect this type of property tax resides with the states alongside the local governments within the U.S. The Federal Government does not have such property taxing rights or tax collecting powers.

# Proportional Taxes

Proportional Taxes are a type of income tax system. In this taxation system, the identical percentage of taxes is applied to all taxpayers in an economy. It does not matter how much or how little they earn. This type of tax simply levies the same rate on all high income, middle income, and low income workers as well as businesses.

This stands in direct contrast to a more widely utilized progressive tax system. In this competing type of tax plan, those taxpayers who enjoy greater income levels pay at higher income tax rates than the unfortunate bottom income earning citizens. Proportional taxes are also often known as the flat tax since it is a one tax plan fits all sizes means of collecting revenues for a government.

Besides proportional taxes and progressive taxes, there are also regressive taxes. A regressive tax takes a larger share of income from the lower classes than they can afford. Sometimes flat taxes are considered to be regressive in nature. The difference between these three types of tax structures comes down to the way the tax addresses the tax base (of a business income or household income) as the income level is significantly different.

In these proportional taxes systems, every tax payer, regardless of income level or job, will pay the identical percentage of their earnings in taxes. If this given proportional rate is set up at 20 percent, then the earner at $10,000 gives $2,000 of income to the taxing authorities, while the worker making $50,000 will pay in $10,000. At the same time, the higher earner with $1 million in annual income will pay the same rate for a grand total of tax payment amounting to $200,000. This system is so much simpler and eliminates the needs for large, wasteful, and bureaucratic taxing agencies.

Sales taxes are another example of proportional taxes. This is the case because every consumer, regardless of the amount of money which he or she makes, will pay the sales tax at the identical fixed sales tax rate. It is almost a given that sales taxes will be proportional. Since all goods and services are affected by them, a government can not simply alter the rate based on a person's actual income. Buying a good does not factor in the income of the buyer in the transaction, and so far there is no known way to change this to a more progressive form of tax.

Many economists and analysts consider these proportional taxes to be a form of regressive tax by accident. Since the rate never goes up regardless of how high the income of the person in question goes, the higher burden remains on the lower income earners. They can least afford to pay the flat rate tax, while a high income earner has the ability to pay his or her elevated but still same percentage share. With the same example from above, the earner who garners $10,000 only has $8,000 left on which to live after paying his or her share of taxes. The worker bringing down $50,000 gets to keep fully $40,000 after taxes. The million dollar stunner holds on to $800,000 after paying his or her share. The percentage of the tax is the same in every scenario.

Many people call this the epitome of truly fair. The problem is that the low income earner suffers from a severe after-tax hangover effect because the burden makes it impossible for him or her to live on what remains. This is how the critics of such a flat tax are able to insist that higher income people should be forced to pony up a larger percentage in income taxes than the poorer workers who outnumber them so vastly anymore.

Those in favor of proportional taxes insist that they are more fair since they encourage workers to go for greater earnings without punishing their results with higher income tax brackets and rates, as a progressive tax system inherently would. They argue that when everyone receives the same treatment, this is the ideal definition of the concept of fair. Proportional tax systems have the additional advantage of being simple for everyone to grasp and to practice. This is because there is no room for debate on the tax rate in question for any business, individual, or family.

# Protective Tariff

A protective tariff is a choice by a national government to create a financial barrier or tax on the imports of one or more nation's imports into the country. In many cases, such tariffs are not intended to raise additional national revenue as much as they are to artificially increase the prices of said imports. This helps to protect the sales and production of domestic goods and services so that they will continue to be manufactured and sold successfully in the host nation. Some critics argue that these types of tariffs are a real threat to free trade. Others argue that they provide two important benefits.

The first benefit is to trap domestic spending within the national economy rather than bleed it out to a foreign competing company and country. The second benefit lies in stopping cheap imports from crushing local business and industry. The import of oranges is a classic example of such a protective tariff. Not every place is able to grow citrus. South American countries are ideally situated and acclimated to grow huge amounts of citrus fruits to export.

While a nation may produce its own oranges but might instead simply import them from South American countries at a cheaper price than growing them internally, they could decide to apply a protective tariff to the price of foreign oranges and other citrus produce. Such a tariff is guaranteed to raise the price of the potentially imported oranges in order to level the playing field for domestic citrus producers. The tariff will make sure that these foreign oranges are similar to or more expensive than the prices of the locally grown variants.

Such a protective tariff proves to be a true tax on goods which a country chooses to import. These taxes make the prices of the foreign imports higher than the prices for typically more expensive goods and services. A piece or cloth might cost $5 in the United States and similarly $5 in Great Britain. If the American government wanted to encourage domestically-produced cloth over British manufactured cloth, they would need to set up a tariff on British cloth so that the cost was higher than locally produced cloth. They might add a $1 per piece tariff to the British cloth with a 20 percent rate. The ultimate goal of such a protective tariff is to protect the native industry from its foreign competition.

The very first American to suggest utilizing these protective tariffs to encourage American industrializing proved to be founding father and Treasury Secretary Alexander Hamilton. He wrote the important â€œReport on Manufacturersâ€ to further this agenda. Hamilton believed that imposing a tariff on textile imports would help American industrial efforts to build up manufacturing facilities in order to one day compete effectively with the dominant in the world British companies.

Following the War of 1812, inexpensive British products began to flood the American markets. This undercut and even threatened to destroy the young industries in the U.S. Congress complied with Hamiltonâ€™s wishes and established tariffs in 1816 so that they could deter British goods from dominating in the country. They followed this up with another tariff in 1824. The much debated Tariff of Abominations of 1828 culminated these early efforts. It was President John Quincy Adams who approved the final Tariff of Abominations following the majority vote approval of the House of Representatives.

The goal of this 1828 tariff actually lay in protecting both Western and Northern agricultural products from foreign competitors. The setting of this kicked off a national debate regarding how constitutional it was to slap tariffs on foreign imports unless the goal was to raise revenues from duties. Included in the case in question were molasses, iron, flax, distilled spirits, and various other completed goods.

Critics of these policies claim that tariffs are unethical. They argue that the expenses involved with shipping would be the only equitable cost to add on to a final good's price. Applying such protective tariffs threatens fair and free trade they correctly claim.

# Public Company Accounting Oversight Board (PCAOB)

The Public Company Accounting Oversight Board turns out to be another regulatory group that Congress established to provide oversight on the auditing of public companies. This not for profit corporation is not a government agency. It does provide protection to the public and investors who are interested in the independent, accurate, and revealing audit reports that this group encourages. Besides this, the PCAOB oversees dealers and brokers' audits in order to foster protection for investors. This includes oversight of compliance reports that federal security laws require from public corporations.

This accounting oversight board arose as a result of the Sabanes-Oxley Act of 2002. It mandated that the firms which audit public companies in the United States endure independent and external oversight for the first time ever. Before Congress passed this 2002 regulatory law, auditors were completely self regulating.

The PCAOB Board and chairman of this board are made up of five members who receive appointments to five year terms each from the SEC Securities and Exchange Commission. They select these individuals after consulting first with both the Secretary of the U.S. Treasury and the Federal Reserve System Chairman of the Board of Governors. Given this SEC appointing role, it is not surprising that the SEC also maintains oversight responsibilities for the PCAOB. As part of this oversight, they must approve the Board's various standards, budget, and rules before they become final.

The SOX Act became amended by the Dodd-Frank Act. It created the necessary funding for all PCAOB pursued activities. This money mostly comes from the accounting support fees assessed annually on all publicly traded companies. These fees are actually figured from their average monthly market capitalization. Brokers and dealers are instead levied fees which are dependent on their quarterly average tentative net capital.

The mission of the PCAOB lies in providing oversight of public companiesâ€™ audits. This ensures that they prepare and deliver reliable, honest, and unbiased audit reports for the benefit of both the interested investors and members of the public. Along with this oversight role, the PCAOB monitors the broker dealers and their audits to encourage protecting investors from fraud. This includes monitoring their federal securities law required compliance reports filing.

PCAOB has a particular vision they seek to fulfill. Their overriding goal is to prove themselves a model for regulatory organizations everywhere. They seek to reduce the numbers of audit failures throughout the public securities markets in the United States, to improve the overall quality of audits, and to foster the publicâ€™s trust of auditing as a profession and the process of financial reporting itself. They aim to do this while utilizing cost efficient and cutting edged tools.

The PCAOB maintains two special advisory groups as part of its mandate. The first of these is the PCAOB Investor Advisor Group, also known by its acronym IAG. It presents advice and viewpoints to the general board pertaining to investor concerns and regarding work related matters and important policy issues. The board is able to count on the IAG to deliver it expert and quality insight and advice for carrying out its important mandate to safeguard investors as outlined in the Sarbanes-Oxley Act.

The board also relies on its Standing Advisory Group, refereed to by its acronym SAG. The SAG advises the board regarding standards of professional practice and continuing developments within the world of auditing. Among the members of the Standing Advisory Group are investors, auditors, executives of publicly traded companies, and other individuals. This SAG group holds meetings between two and three times each year. They are chaired by the Chief Auditor and Director of Professional Standards of the PCAOB.

# Regressive Taxes

Regressive taxes are those which exact a greater percentage in income off of the lower income wage earners than they do from the fortunate higher income earners. This stands in direct contrast to aÂ progressive tax that instead grabs a bigger percentage of taxes from the higher and highest income wage earners. A regressive tax is typically one which is equally applied to all residents in whatever their situation may be. It does not matter what the financial condition of the payer turns out to be.

The problem with a regressive tax is that it most harshly impacts those who can least afford to bear it, the lower income segment of society. The higher income individuals do not mind such taxes, as they can most easily afford to pay the flat rate percentages which are common in regressive taxes. It might actually be fairer for all people to pay in the identical tax rate, yet this proves to be most unjust in some scenarios. The majority of developed nationsâ€™ tax systems actually utilize a more progressive schedule which over taxes the higher income persons more than the lower wage earners.

Some other kinds of tax are more equally levied. There are many examples of real world regressive taxes. Among these are sales taxes, property taxes, and user fee taxes.

Sales taxes are nearly always equally levied on all consumers in a given economy. Their ability to pay is not a factor so much as is the amount of money which they spend on taxed items. The tax is equitable as a flat rate for all consumers, yet it remains a fact that those lower income earners are most dramatically impacted and even materially harmed by it.

Take the case of two separate individuals who both buy $200 in groceries every week. They will each pay $14 in sales tax on their grocery bills. The first person in this example makes $2,000 every week, translating to a sales tax rate for the groceries of .35 percent of all income. The other worker only brings home $320 each week. This amounts to a grocery sales tax of a whopping 2.2 percent of actual income. While the literal tax rate may be the same in the two scenarios, the individual with the significantly lesser income is paying a far greater share of his or her income on the regressive sales tax.

Property taxes are another classic example of regressive taxes in theory. Assuming two property owners reside in the same taxing jurisdiction and own similar properties with identical values, they will both pay the identical dollars in property taxes to the local taxing administration. This is the case no matter how much they make. The lower wage earner would pay a substantially greater share of his or her income on the property taxes in this case. One caveat is that different wage earners do not usually have identically valued properties. The poorer people and families typically live in cheaper homes, which help to index property taxes to relevant income. This is why property taxes are not purely regressive in practice.

User fees taxes are those which the government assesses in a regressive tax form. These might cover admissions to government-owned and -operated state parks, national parks, and museums. They might also include tolls on bridges and roads and drivers’™ license and identification cards fees. As an example, when two families go to the Grand Canyon National Park, they each pay the same $30 fee for admission to the nature park. The higher income family is actually paying in a significantly lower percentage of total income than is the poorer family. The fee may be identical literally, yet it represents a substantially greater burden for the family which has the lesser income.

# Regulatory Compliance

Regulatory Compliance refers to companies choosing to incorporate standards that meet certain government requirements. It could also be thought of as the specific set of regulations which a firm has to observe when it meets the given requirements. Because of the ever growing burdens of regulations, companies are increasingly finding they must become more transparent operationally.

This is why they find the need to adopt a universal set of controls for compliance. The idea is to measure up to all government mandated requirements while avoiding any wasted resources or duplicated activities in the process. Even when done effectively and efficiently, this level of compliance is often both costly and burdensome for businesses and other organizations to meet.

There are a number of organizations that produce a set of standards to make such Regulatory Compliance simpler. ISO is the International Organization for Standardization. They create such internationally observed standards as the ISO/IEC 27002. Another group which develops the electro-technology arena international standards is the IEC International Electro-technical Commission. There are other specialized compliance issuers in various countries and industries. One of these is the ASME American Society of Mechanical Engineers. The SEC Securities Exchange Commission issues and enforces standards of regulation compliance for publically traded stock companies. The CFTC Commodities and Futures Trading Commission handle the compliance for the commodities trading industry.

There have been numerous triggers for greater amounts of Regulatory Compliance over the past several decades. Many of these revolved around corporate failures and scandals which could have been easily prevented had more regulation been part of their various industries. A classic example of this is the Enron failure from 2001. Thanks to this and the WorldCom scandal, the United States Congress enacted the Sarbanes-Oxley Act for setting standards for greater compliance and regulation for upper level corporate management reporting accurate and truthful financial statements. The Consumer Protection Act and Dodd-Frank Wall Street Reform Act also followed after a need for still more regulation compliance became evident in events like the Global Financial Crisis and subprime mortgage meltdown from 2007-2009.

In the United States, Regulatory Compliance generally revolves around regulations and laws. Such legal statutes come with civil and/or criminal penalties for violating the relevant regulations. There are a number of agencies within the United States government which handle and enforce the issues of regulation compliance. Among these are the OFAC Office of Foreign Assets Control, the U.S. Small Business Administration, and the OSHA Department of Labor, Occupational Health and Safety Administration.

OFAC is the agency which deals with Regulatory Compliance for trade and economic sanctions. They operate under the Department of the Treasury's Terrorism and Financial Intelligence division. The goal of this regulatory agency is to handle and enforce U.S. foreign policy- and national security policy-based trade sanctions and economic embargoes. They target foreign organizations, countries, and individuals who are on the Treasury Department list.

The U.S. government maintains many Regulatory Compliance statues pertaining to businesses. The Small Business Administration offers its services to help small companies with information and access to various government services under its Business.USA.gov website.

The United States OSHA is a congressionally created agency for enforcing healthy and safe working conditions for all people in the country. They erect and enforce various standards pertaining to education, outreach, training, and assistance. This agency is responsible for Regulatory Compliance in the areas of recordkeeping, agriculture, maritime law, and construction.

Such laws are not the same in every country however. As an example, the United Kingdom has its own laws for Regulatory Compliance. These are among the most similar to the United States' own laws in many ways. Among the compliance acts and frameworks for organizations and businesses in Great Britain are those created by the Data Protection Act of 1998 and the Freedom of Information Act 2000. Their FRC Financial Reporting Council lays out standards for appropriate practices of company leadership pertaining to accountability and effectiveness for the shareholders. They issue the UK Corporate Governance Code, which is most like the United States Sarbanes-Oxley Act.

# Repayment Penalty

A repayment penalty is commonly associated with paying back a loan before the end of its term. If you are contemplating paying off your loan balance in advance of its due date, then you should be aware that a number of loans come with these repayment penalties for liquidating the balance early. Different types of loans utilize different names for these same fees. Repayment penalties can also be called redemption charges, early redemption fees, prepayment penalties, or financial penalties.

The fees associated with repayment penalties vary depending on the loan in question. These repayment penalties are commonly stated as a percentage of the balance that is outstanding when prepayment is offered. Alternatively, they might be figured up as a certain number of months of interest charges. In general, when they are figured up using months of interest, they are comprised of one to two months' interest in fees. The sooner in the loan's life that you choose to repay the loan, the greater amount of charge you can expect to pay. This is because the anticipated interest portion of the loan comprises a great part of the repayment earlier in the loan's time frame. Early repayment penalties might increase the total cost of your loan significantly.

If you wish to avoid a repayment penalty in paying off your loan in advance of the term's end, then you will have to be aware of the loans that come with these fees and the ones that do not. Even if you change a currently existing loan into a loan for debt consolidation, you will have to cover the early repayment penalty if one is in the terms. The only way to avoid early repayment penalties is by selecting loans that specifically do not have ones attached to them. It is ironic that some of the least expensive loans out there do not include repayment penalties for early pay off actions.

Another factor of repayment penalties involves a gradual disappearance of the provision over time. With many mortgages, these repayment penalties gradually go down over the years of the mortgage. After the fifth year, the majority of repayment penalties no longer even apply. In many cases, repayments of as much as twenty percent of the original balance are permitted in a given year without you having to be penalized.

Besides this, there are different kinds of penalties for repayments. Penalties that only apply to your refinancing of the mortgage are called soft penalties. Penalties that include the sale of the house and a refinancing are known as hard penalties.

# Required Minimum Distribution (RMD)

The Required Minimum Distribution is a concept that pertains to retirement accounts and IRS rules which govern their distributions. Many individuals are not aware that they can not simply choose to hold retirement money in their retirement vehicle forever. They must begin accepting withdrawals from their traditional IRA, SEP IRA, Simple IRA, or other type of retirement plan and account after they turn age 70 Â½. The notable exception to this rule is for Roth IRAs, which do not mandate disbursements while the owner is still alive.

The required minimum distribution is literally the minimum legal dollar amount that account holders have to take out of the retirement account every year. Naturally most people choose to withdraw a larger amount than this required minimum. Withdrawals that are received must be detailed in the individualsâ€™ taxable income. The exception to this is for any income that had been previously taxed as with Roth IRA contributions or any earnings which accrued on a tax free basis. This relates to distributions from Roth IRA accounts.

Figuring out the actual amount of the RMD is not so easy. The simplest way to do it is to work with the IRS published Uniform Lifetime Table. In this method, people figure their RMD in any given year by taking the balance from the end of the prior calendar year and dividing this amount by a distribution period taken from the Uniform Lifetime Table. There is also a different table to be utilized if the owner of the accountâ€™s spouse is the only beneficiary and he or she is at least ten years younger than the owner.

The IRS provides worksheets on their website to help account holders figure up the mandated minimum amount. They also provide several tables to help with this. As mentioned, the Uniform Lifetime Table is for every IRA account owner who is figuring up his or her own withdrawal. The Joint Life and Last Survivor Expectancy Table is for those whose spouse is at least ten years younger and who is the only beneficiary.

The initial date for the first RMD on an IRA is figured out by taking the April 1st of the year that comes after the calendar year in which the account holder turns 70 Â½. With a 401(k), 403(b), profit sharing plan, or similar defined contribution plan, either this same April 1st deadline applies or the April 1st that follows the calendar year in which the owner actually retires.

The individual turns 70 Â½ on the calendar date which falls 6 months following his or her 70th birthday. The plan terms themselves govern whether the individuals can wait until the year in which they actually retire to take the initial RMD. Other plans will require distributions begin on the April 1st following the year of turning 70 Â½ whether or not the person has retired.

Once account holders have received the first RMD, they must take their subsequent ones on or before December 31st. It is possible to avoid having the first and second RMDâ€™s included in a single tax year. In the year individuals turn 70 Â½ they can simply go ahead and take that first RMD by the end of the year to avoid the double distribution taxation in one calendar year.

People who do not take their full minimum required distribution will suffer an IRS penalty. Any amount which they do not take as the law requires will suffer a 50% excise tax that will be levied on it. This failure to take the RMD must be reported on a Form 5329, Additional Taxes on Qualified Plans.

# Reserve Requirement

The reserve requirement proves to be the quantity of funds which banks are required to hold on hand each and every night. This is expressed as a percentage of the bank's total demand deposits. A country's central bank is responsible for setting out the effective percentage rate.

Within the United States, it is up to the Federal Reserve's Board of Governors to determine the member banks' reserve requirements. Such a requirement is applicable for commercial banks, savings and loan associations, savings banks, credit unions, Edge corporations, U.S. based branches or agencies of foreign banks, and agreement corporations.

The banks are allowed to keep their cash physically within their proprietary on-site vaults or keep them deposited with their area Federal Reserve Bank. When banks lack sufficient cash to fulfill their reserve requirements, they are able to borrow cash from other banks with extra to spare. They could also obtain a loan from the discount window of the Federal Reserve alternatively. Money which banks lend or borrow from one another in order to meet their own requirements is called the Federal funds.

Among the many tools which the Fed counts at its disposal, the reserve requirement is the underlying basis for all of them. They are able to employ this to precisely control cash liquidity within the economy. Smaller reserve requirements prove to be expansionary types of monetary policy. This is because they permit a greater amount of money to flow through the banking system into the real economy. Higher reserve requirements conversely are contractionary. They soak up money from the pool of available liquidity and tamp down on economic activities.

It is also true that the greater a reserve requirement is, the smaller the profits will be for a bank deploying its customers' money. Higher requirements are particularly challenging for smaller banks. This is because they begin with a smaller pool from which to lend out money. Because of this reality on the ground, small banks are usually exempted from such onerous requirements. Smaller banks are those which have fewer deposits than $12.4 million.

The Fed does not often actually change the reserve requirement. This is because it is expensive to do so. Banks are forced to rectify their policies to compensate when this is done. Because of this, the board avoids changing the requirements on its member banks. It is far easier for them to tweak the amounts of deposits which are subjected to the various reserve requirements every year.

For example, since October 12, 2012, the Federal Reserve has mandated that every bank possessing greater than $79.5 million in deposits must keep a minimum reserve amount of 10 percent of total deposits. Those banks which count under $79.5 million but still greater than $12.4 million only have to keep three percent of deposits on hand. Again those banks with fewer than $12.4 million in deposits fall under the pre-determined exemption amount. They enjoy a zero percent reserve requirement.

The Federal Reserve does raise the levels of deposits which are subject to its various ratios each year. This provides the banks with an incentive to become larger. From June 30 to June 30, the Fed is able to raise its low reserve tranche and accompanying exemption amount by 80 percent of the amount that deposits increase in the previous year.

Deposits which are considered for these reserve requirements include a number of different types. These are automatic transfer service accounts, demand deposits, NOW accounts, telephone or authorized transfer accounts, share draft accounts, ineligible bankersâ€™ acceptance, and affiliate-issued obligations which mature in seven or fewer days. Banks are only required to accept the net amount. They are not expected to cover any amounts owed to them by other banks or any cash that remains outstanding. As of December 27, 1990, deposits do not comprise Euro-currency liabilities or non personal time deposits.

# Restricted Stock

Restricted Stock refers to those company stock shares which prove to be unregistered. These are typically issued out to affiliates of the corporation such as the directors, board, company insiders, and company executives. Because this stock class is non-transferable, it can only be traded as those SEC special regulations set out. This stock class is often referred to as letter stock or Section 1244 stock. It commonly becomes available for sale under the guidelines of certain vesting schedule provisions which transpire over a few years' time in most cases.

Companies have two different types of such awards they can make in reward for faithful service which goes above and beyond the call of corporate performance and duty. These are restricted shares of stock and restricted stock units. The difference is that the units could be offered either as cash or stock shares. This will always be spelled out in the award letter or agreement. The units which are converted to stock do so at a typical one for one ratio. The underlying shares do not actually become issued until the unit fully vests. This means that the voting rights on the shares underlying the units will not yet be available. Units are also not paid dividends as they are not yet physical shares of stock. There are plans though which credit the dividend equivalents for the underlying stock to the account in any case. Taxes become due on such awards only when they fully vest.

It was actually in the years of the middle 2000s that such restricted stock shares grew in popularity and practice with companies. Corporations were made to expense out stock option grants. Insiders of the company receive restricted stock following merger and acquisition transactions, affiliate ownership, or underwriting activity to keep them from advance selling shares which could negatively impact the firm. When executives choose to leave the company, they could forfeit all shares of their non-vested restricted stock. Failing to attain set standards of performance or to measure up to corporate and personal goals are other reasons for inadvertently forfeiting their stock shares. If they run afoul of the Securities and Exchange

Commission and its stringent trading restrictions, they might similarly lose their promised shares.

This matters enormously since the SEC's regulations which govern all restricted stock trading and transactions are contained within the SEC Rule 144. It lays out very clearly and specifically the ways and means for registering and publically trading any stock shares that are restricted as well as the limits placed upon volume and holding periods.

Restricted stock is also taxed under the Internal Revenue Service codes which are laid out in Section 1244 of their IRS Code. The computations and regulations are quite complicated. Holders of such stock which is restricted will have to pay capital gains or losses tax which is figured up based on the difference from the value of the underlying shares at the time of vesting and the date where the holder sells the shares. Such restricted stock shares become taxed in the year in which they vest as ordinary income. In other words, the share awards are treated as compensation. Those amounts which holders must declare to the government as income are the fair market value of the vesting date less the original exercise price of the underlying shares.

Those restricted stock share awards can be forfeited by the recipient if he or she were to leave the company earlier than their vesting. This would happen regardless of whether the separation was voluntary or involuntary in the end. Any taxes which were prepaid to the IRS on shares that had not yet vested would be non-refundable, making the matter more complicated still.

# Right of First Refusal

Right of First Refusal refers to a right, but not an obligation, to enact a transaction regarding an asset with another party ahead of any competitors. It is similar to possessing a particular call option on the asset in question. Such a contractual right will typically be negotiated after a party to a transaction wishes to first see how its business will go. The participant could easily decide it is better to have the option to become involved in the asset or opportunity later on instead of having to commit to and pay for it in advance.

There are some significant advantages and benefits to having a Right of First Refusal. It represents a true insurance policy for the contract holder to not lose the possibility of later acquiring the valuable asset which may help to build up the business. It is always helpful to consider a concrete example to better understand this. The commercial tenant of a building might wish to lease or re-lease their office space. It might be willing to purchase the space if the alternative was to be thrown out in favor of a new tenant. This is a good instance when a tenant would want to obtain a first right of refusal as part of the lease contract.

At the same time, such a Right of First Refusal is an inconvenience for the owner of the office building and property. This is because it restricts the capability of seeking out buyers for the building or selling it off. The landlord for the building in this example will discover how hard it is to entice buyers for the property when they learn that the present tenant has the right to match any offer which they decide to make on the property. Yet for building owners, getting the right tenant can be worth providing the first right of refusal incentive in order to secure the lease deal.

There are many cases in the business world where such Rights of First Refusal are in evidence. This is especially the case with joint venture scenarios. Joint venture partners will usually have a true Right of First Refusal to buy out their partnersâ€™ interests in the venture when the partners wish to exit the business. Private companies also have common scenarios with their stockholder agreements that permit the pre-existing stake holders to buy out the ones who wish for an exit event before any new stock holders are created.

There are a wide range of other cases where these Rights of First Refusal apply in business and entertainment. This goes well beyond the world of corporate deals and boardrooms or even partnerships. In avenues as wide ranging as sports, real estate, or even arts and entertainment they are quite common elements of the business models and contract traditions. There are countless examples of this to consider.

With Real Estate, buyers of land may obtain a first right of refusal from a property holder on the future sale of any adjacent land next to that which they are acquiring. In this case, the property holder would have to offer the original buyer the opportunity to add to their existing holdings by purchasing the adjacent property.

In entertainment, large publishing houses sometimes require a new author to provide them with a Right of First Refusal on additional books they may write and seek to have published. The author would likely have to go along with this, as the publisher could simply refuse to take a chance on the unknown author if he or she is unwilling to accommodate the company. Publishers who put up significant resources into new authors look for this financial incentive of having sequels or additional hit books to help justify their risk.

On the one hand, this likely guarantees the author will have subsequent books published by the same publishing house (unless the first book is a commercial failure). At the same time, the author may not be able to accept a more lucrative competing offer from a rival publishing house. This is because the original publisher will likely not have to meet competitorsâ€™ offers as part of the first right of refusal clause.

# Risk-Weighted Assets

Risk-Weighted Assets refer to those which are utilized to decide on much capital financial institutions like banks must hold in order to decrease the chances of becoming insolvent. Regulators determine the capital amount required using a complicated risk assessment of every individual kind of asset the bank holds. As a simple example, the loans which have been secured by only letters of credit will be deemed to be far riskier than those loans which are instead backed up by tangible collateral. These would similarly require a greater amount of additional capital than the ones with real collateral.

The concept of Risk-Weighted Assets is relatively new and only dates back to the aftermath of the Global Financial Crisis. At this time following the worldwide financial meltdown from 2007-2009, the banking industry faced stark and rigorous new regulation as a drastic change following the crisis.

The government regulators, spurred on by Congress with their Dodd-Frank banking reform act, came out with massive new and complex capital requirements for the financial institutions in the United States, Great Britain, and Europe especially. As a direct result of this historical phenomenon, today's banks must hold far greater capital cushion levels than ever before. The dilemma for them is that the accounting rules surrounding these new regulations are extremely complex. Few investors nowadays are able to understand them really, yet they are critically important for investors in banks to grasp.

The central pillar of the revised and still fairly-new calculations is the Risk-Weighted Assets. It would be next to impossible to work out the numbers here, but it is instructive and helpful to concentrate on the general meaning of the idea and to show some examples of how it works generally in practice. Investors can not understand a bank's balance sheet any longer without having some command of the topic.

Because the 2007-2009 financial crisis occurred mainly as a result of the banks and other financial institutions choosing to heavily back the subprime mortgage home loans, they suffered from massively higher defaults than regulators, investors, and government officials conceived was possible. These massive consumer defaults led to enormous capital sums being lost by the banks, which were too highly leveraged at the time. This caused some of the largest of them to become insolvent. Among these were Washington Mutual Bank (the largest savings and loans institution in history), Wachovia Bank, Bear Stearns, Lehman Brothers, Merrill Lynch, and many more.

So that this problem can be avoided in the future, regulators force every bank now to combine their assets into categories which are similar by asset risk level. The idea is to stop the greedy banks from suffering devastating capital losses again as a single asset class plunges severely in value. Regulators use a few different kinds of tools in order to determine the level of risk for a given category of assets. As a huge percentage of assets the banks hold are loans, the regulators look at the loan repayment sources and the collateral value which underlies them.

For example, commercial building loans generate both principal and interest payments. They do this using income from tenants in the form of lease payments. When buildings are not completely leased out, it is possible that the property manager will be unable to service the loan payments due to a lack of enough regular income. The building itself represents collateral against the loan. The regulators will contemplate the building's value as part of the determination for Risk-Weighted Assets.

Another example surrounds United States Treasury bonds. These are backed up by the federal governments' ability to generate taxes. Since these government securities come with a higher credit rating than do the commercial building loans, the regulators will expect less capital to be carried for the bonds than they would for the commercial loans.

Regulators understood these differences in risk levels and so decided that the only sufficient way to guarantee sufficient capital for a bank is to make them vary their capital requirements according to the risk they were taking with different types of assets. This is how the risk-weighted assets came into being in the first place.

# S Corporation

S Corporation refers to the Subchapter S Corporation type of company filing which measures up to certain requirements set by the IRS Internal Revenue Service. This status provides a corporation which possesses a hundred or fewer shareholders all of the advantages of incorporation while also keeping the benefits of only being tax treated like a partnership.

One of the many benefits to this type of incorporation is that it is able to pass all of the company income straight through to the shareholders, thus avoiding the problems of double taxation which are a real issue with shareholders of public companies. There are some particular requirements that must be met to enjoy these advantages. The firm must be domiciled as a domestic corporation. It cannot possess over a hundred shareholders, and it may only count a single class of stock.

Such S Corporations can pass all of their credits, deductions, losses, and any income straight through to the various shareholders. They may then report this loss or income directly via their own personal tax returns. It allows them to pay out their taxes at generally considerably lower individual income tax rates. There are some built in gains on which the S Corporation will pay the taxes at the corporate level, but these are few and far between.

These S Corporations have to be domestically headquartered firms whose shareholders are estates, certain kinds of trusts, and individuals. A corporation, partnership, or non-resident alien can never qualify for this category of shareholder. There are also some financial institutions, domestic international sales firms, and insurance outfits that are not allowed to incorporate as an S Corporation.

There are some significant advantages to establishing an S Corporation. It builds up real creditability with employees, possible customers, investors, and suppliers as it proves the owner is seriously committed to the firm. Employees may also be shareholders in the company, which allows them to enjoy company salaries while also receiving any corporate dividends and distributions which are tax-free as compared to the investment in the company. This is certainly beneficial for morale.

Paying out distributions in the form of dividends or salaries allows the owners to lower the self-employment tax liability at the same time as it creates wage and expense deductions for the firm. Since this S Corporation will not pay any federal taxes at company level, such losses can be utilized to offset other forms of income for the tax returns of the shareholders. It is always helpful to save money on the onerous American corporate income taxes, particularly for new firms. It is another benefit to these companies that the various interests within the corporation can be easily transferred without creating tax liability events and consequences. Complicated accounting rules do not create restrictions nor does the company have to adjust the basis of property either.

Yet there are also a few downsides to establishing a company as an S Corporation. The IRS closely examines any and all distribution payments made to shareholders in the forms of either dividends or salaries to make sure that they are really employees working in the firm. If wages become characterized as dividends, then the company will lose its compensation paid deduction. Should dividends be characterized as wages, then the company will pay a greater amount of employment taxes. It is also easy for mistakes to be made in the areas of notification, consent, election, filing requirements, or stock ownership requirements that lead to the S Corporation being untimely terminated. There is considerable money and time investment in such a corporate structuring as well.

The owner will have to begin by filling in and filing articles of incorporation to the Secretary of State, get a registered agent on board for the company, and pay any relevant fees and costs involved. Owners often have to pay yearly reporting fees and franchise taxes along with ongoing types of fees. These may be inexpensive, but they can still be deducted under the cost of doing business category. Even if the investors possess non-voting shares of stock in this form of corporate structuring, they will still get distribution and dividend rights.

# Sale And Leaseback

A Sale And Leaseback is also known as a simply leaseback. This arrangement involves an asset seller who first sells the asset or property in question then immediately leases it back exactly as it is from the buyer. These types of deals are fleshed out and contracted immediately following the asset in questionâ€™s sale. The precise amount in payments and the specific time period to be covered are both set at this point. It amounts to the asset seller personally becoming the lessee while the buyer becomes the actual lessor under such an arrangement.

Many owners of small to medium sized enterprises (SMEs) find that they require a great deal of fresh capital in order to expand their operations. There are a number of different ways in which they can come up with such capital. Two of the more popular and better known ones are surrendering equity in order to obtain funds or taking on debt either as bonds or secured loans.

With equity, it does not have to be repaid to the provider. The cost for this is that a portion or even all of the ownership of the enterprise is surrendered. The tradeoffs for debt are that it has to be repaid one day (or in regular periodic payments). It also appears as debt on the balance sheet of the company, which may impact future opportunities for financing, debt purchases, or obtaining fresh capital via an equity offering.

Hybrid arrangements which are not either equity or debt are these Sale And Leasebacks. Instead they function more as a hybrid form of debt arrangement and product. The firm entering into the deal will not grow its debt load, yet it still manages to achieve the goal of accessing capital by selling assets. Some have referred to this as a company variation on the consumer-entered pawn shop arrangement.

Extrapolating on this example, the company in question goes down to the pawn shop and provides them with a valuable piece of property or asset. In tradeoff for this asset, the company receives an agreed upon amount of cash. The only point where this comparison breaks down concerns repurchasing the asset in question. In a sale and leaseback, no one expects that the company will attempt to repurchase the property or asset, only that they will make periodic payments in order to utilize the asset.

Consider the following example. The fictitious company Johnny Appleseed Orchards requires more funding to pay its increasing numbers of contractors and employees. It is unable to obtain funding from banks thanks to a downturn in the lending market brought on by the Great Recession and Financial Crash of 2007. The company decides it will sell half of its orchard acreage to an investment company which wishes to become involved in realizing an income stream from the sale of produce. The acreage is instantly leased back to the owner-operators of Johnny Appleseed. This benefits them if the cost to lease back the acreage is less than the interest rate and total interest payments on higher interest loans they would otherwise be forced to seek.

The most typical type of a sale and leaseback occurs with builders and those firms that have many expensive and fixed assets. This is useful when they require cash which is tied up in their costly assets to utilize for other capital needs or investments, yet they still require use of the equipment or assets so that they can continue to run their business.

Such sale and leasebacks and their arrangements also give the seller of the asset some beneficial tax deductions. The lessor gains the advantages of a stable payment and guaranteed lease arrangement which continues for a predetermined and contractually pre-set amount of time.

Such sale and leaseback deals do come with a whole different set of regulations for accounting purposes than do debt arrangements. Despite this, they are not called financing in most of the cases. This keeps them as off-balance sheet arrangements. Some analysts will therefore add on capitalized leases such as these to the category of longer term debt. They do this especially as they are attempting to gain the bigger picture view of the firm in question's aggregate debt obligations.

# Sales Tax

Sales Tax refers to a government imposed tax on consumption of both services and goods. Traditional sales taxes are collected at the appropriate points of sale. The retailers gather the money which they then pass on to the appropriate governmental agency. Businesses are also liable to pay such sales taxes to the relevant jurisdiction (state or local government) if they have what is known as a nexus in that jurisdiction. This could be an employee, physical office location, presence of some other type, or an affiliate. The laws of the jurisdiction in question determine which of these criteria apply in determining business residence.

Conventional forms of sales taxes only become charged to or are payable by the final seller of a service or a good. Since the overwhelming numbers of goods in today's economies go through a range of manufacturing points and stages, they become a part and parcel of many different entities' operations. This means that great quantities of paper work must be kept and filed in order to determine the end seller who will be finally liable for the sales taxes owed.

As an example to better understand the dilemma this poses, consider a sheep farmer. The farmer sells his wool to a firm which makes yarn. The yarn maker would be responsible for the sales tax unless it is able to gain a resale certificate from the responsible governmental agency. This certificate must declare that the yarn maker is not the final user. Next, the yarn maker will sell its yarn products to a clothing manufacturer. This manufacturer also has to get such a resale certificate. The clothing maker then sells its wooly sweater to an outlet store. It is this outlet store that must charge sales tax to its customers besides the price of the sweater.

The various jurisdictions all charge their own sales tax rates. This can be confusing as they are also overlapping on one another. In some localities, the state, the county, and even the municipality (city or town) will all levy their individual sales tax amounts.

The nexus point raises an often-confusing set of issues for many businesses. They are only resident to a particular jurisdiction (state or locality) if the government there defines the nexus in a way that will call them resident for business purposes. Such a nexus is defined usually by the criteria of physical presence. Such a presence may not only be limited to maintaining a warehouse, factory, or office though.

It could mean that a company which has an employee who lives in the state will be considered to have a nexus. Partner websites (which direct traffic over to a business’™ websites in exchange for cash payments), or affiliates, can also be considered to be part of a nexus. This illustrates the difficulties encountered between sales tax collection and the sprawling and growing arena of e-commerce. Bigger states like New York have enacted what they call “Amazon laws.” These make all internet retailers selling goods to customers in their states pay the sales tax, regardless of whether or not they maintain a physical presence in the state. The laws were named for the giant Internet retailers like Amazon.com.

Sales taxes usually work on a percentage basis of the goods’™ prices. As an example, states could collect a five percent sales tax, while the county gets two percent, and the city one percent. This would mean the residents in that given city of the county would have to pay a total sales tax of eight percent.

Many necessary items can be exempt from these taxes to help the lower income earners. This includes food as well as sometimes clothing items which cost under $200 in total. Other taxes specially levied on only certain products are called excise taxes. Many of these the states refer to as “sin taxes.” In essence, this kind of excise tax would cover cigarettes and alcohol, which have been historically labeled by the churches as sins. New York State levies a $4.35 excise (and “sin”) tax on every pack of cigarettes, as of 2016.

# Sarbanes-Oxley Act of 2002

The Sarbanes-Oxley Act of 2002 is also properly called the Public Company Accounting Reform and Investor Protection Act of 2002. It is more typically referred to by its abbreviation SarbOx or even SOX. Congress passed this much needed reforming federal law of the United States because of a variety of significant accounting and corporate scandals that successively rocked the nation. Among these were Enron, WorldCom, and Tyco International. Such scandals eroded the already low public trust Americans held in both accounting and reporting procedures.

The law became named after its two sponsors the democratic Senator Paul Sarbanes of Maryland and the republican Representative Michael Oxley of Ohio. The vote on the act proved to be nearly unanimous as the Senate passed it 99 â€" 0 while the House approved it 423 â€" 3. The legislation proved to be far reaching. As such it created improved or new standards for every publicly traded U.S. company management, board, and public accounting company.

Congress was also hoping to safeguard investors from fraudulent accounting practices that corporations had been increasingly engaging in over the years. The SOX decreed strict major structural changes that were intended to step up corporate financial disclosures and stop accounting fraud.

The numerous early 2000s years accounting scandals prompted Congress to act to improve the deteriorating situation. The failures at Enron, WorldCom, and Tyco had severely shattered investorsâ€™ confidence in public financial statements. These led to a massive overhaul of the standards that regulated reporting in the industry.

The act itself is comprised of 11 sections or titles. These run the whole spectrum and range from criminal penalties to the responsibilities of Corporate Boards. The SEC Securities and Exchange Commission is charged with implementing the new rulings and requirements for compliance with the provisions in the new and improved corporate governance law.

Some observers felt the new legislation turned out to be important and helpful. Others believed that it actually created more economic harm than it stopped. Still others claimed that the act itself was more modest in its scope and reach than the tough rhetoric that surrounded it proved to be.

The initial and most crucial ruling of the act set up a new semi-public agency. This Public Company Accounting Oversight Board was tasked with regulating, overseeing, inspecting, reprimanding, and disciplining any accounting firms who failed in their critical jobs as public company auditors.

The SOX Act also deals with important matters like corporate governing, auditor independence, and improved financial disclosure practices. Some analysts have called this among the most substantial changes to United States laws dealing with securities since President Franklin D. Roosevelt's New Deal in the 1930s.

These regulations and accompanying policies for enforcement, which the SarbOx laid out, changed and supplemented legislation that already existed and pertained to regulating securities. Two key provisions emerged from the SOX Act. In Section 302, a mandate was established requiring upper level management to personally certify and sign off on the accuracy of the financial statement as reported.

Section 404 provided a new requirement regarding internal controls and methods for reporting that auditors and corporate management were required to establish. The controls had to be determined to be sufficient enough to ensure accuracy. Publicly traded companies were less than pleased by this section. It implied costly changes would be required from companies which would have to create and build the necessary internal controls from the ground up. This proved to be expensive to implement.

# SARSEP

SARSEP is an acronym that means Salary Reduction Simplified Employee Pension Plan. The government offered this advantageous retirement vehicle to those small businesses which possessed fewer than 26 employees. With this SARSEP, employees receive their own SEP IRA account in their specific individual name. They and their employers can both make contributions to the accounts.

These accounts are interesting primarily because they were stopped in January of 1997. In 1996, Congress passed the Small Business Protection Act which eliminated the SARSEP accounts. They became replaced by Simple IRA plans on a going forward basis. Those SARSEPs that already existed have been grandfathered in to the system. They continue to function unchanged as before.

Employees may make contributions to their accounts by using pre tax reductions from their salaries. Employers also may contribute as they so desire. Their total is limited to the lesser amount of either $53,000 or 25% of the total salary of the employee. Employees are limited to an annual contribution amount of $18,000 (or $24,000 if they are 50 years or older).

Besides this, net profits limit the total amount of all contributions that can be made to the account. These may not be greater than 18.6% of the company's net profits for 2016 per the SEP IRA self employed rules. All of this means that SARSEPs are SEP IRA collections held by an employer. The individual accounts of employees are governed by the IRS rules for SEP IRAs.

The IRS does allow transfers or rollovers to be made from SARSEPs. Employees can do these without incurring tax penalties by moving the money to another account that is also qualified. Both plans in question have to permit rollovers from other retirement savings vehicles. Individuals may also choose to move a part of the account value or the whole account balance in an SEP rollover.

Anyone who receives distributions before reaching the minimum retirement age of 59 ½ will be penalized with the 10% early withdrawal penalty. To avoid these problems by accident, direct rollovers make more sense than indirect rollovers. With an indirect rollover, there are requirements for withholding. Accidental early distributions still incur penalties if the rollover is not completed within 60 days.

SARSEP accounts are unusual retirement vehicles. They may hold precious metals and a variety of other non traditional investments within them. These include individual stocks and bonds, mutual funds, options, ETFs, CDs, real estate holdings, and physical precious metals bullion. This makes these SEPs more versatile than the traditional and other types of IRAs. They permit investment choices from regular IRAs as well as hard commodities and land. This makes SARSEPs one of the only ways to possess actual gold, silver, palladium, or platinum in a retirement account.

Per the IRS, legally these types of accounts can hold all of these different kinds of assets. The only exception to this ability comes down to the particular contract of the individual accounts. The SEP IRA custodian may not make all of these types of investments available to their account holders.

Also choices for such investments can be limited by the written employer account agreement. This is why it is critical to read these agreements and to talk with the account custodian before making investment choices. In the event that physical precious metals are not permitted by the custodian or employer, paper gold is still an option. This includes Gold ETFs or gold miner ETF shares, as well as gold mining company stocks.

# Securities Exchange Act of 1933

The Securities Exchange Act of 1933 became sponsored and passed because of the devastating stock market crash which happened on and following Black Monday in 1929. The administration and Congress had two principle goals with this piece of legislation. These were to make certain a greater amount of transparency would exist with financial statements so that investors could engage in better informed choices on their investments. The other goal was to create laws which would crack down on fraud and misrepresentation of securities within the various securities markets.

This Securities Exchange Act of 1933 turned out to be the original piece of significant legislation that dealt with securities and their sales. Before this law became enacted, it was state laws which governed securities' sales principally. The laws dealt with the desperate need to have more effective and consistent disclosures from firms. It mandated that corporations must register their operations with the SEC Securities and Exchange Commission. This registration guaranteed that the corporations would deliver appropriate information to both possible investors and the SEC via both a registration statement and an official prospectus.

It was the Securities Exchange Act of 1933 which mandated that all investors deserve appropriate, fair, and free information on any securities the corporations are providing for sale to the public. Thanks to this act, before companies could launch an Initial Public Offering, they were required to provide information on the deal which was being freely disseminated to investors. Such a prospectus became not only required. It had to be shared with investors by the Securities and Exchange Commission on their own website.

This prospectus was required to deliver certain basic minimum information. Among this was a company business’ and properties’ description. They also had to offer a full description detailing the security which they were offering to investors. They had to divulge any and all relevant information concerning the management that operates the corporation. Finally, they had to provide certified financial statements which independent third party accountants signed off on before they could be released to the public domain.

Besides this, the Securities Exchange Act of 1933 was intended to outlaw any misrepresenting or deceiving throughout the process of securities sales. The framers of the act wanted to ensure that securities sales fraud could be not only reduced but eliminated.

This Securities Exchange Act of 1933 had an important legacy and set critical precedents for the financial world and American securities markets alike. As the first national laws which regulated and ruled on the stock markets, it seized this regulatory authority from the fifty states. The power of oversight for financial markets permanently evolved up to the federal government level. Most importantly, this act developed a universally acknowledged and clear body of regulations which helped to safeguard investors from fraudulent practices.

Today this act is generally referenced by the nickname the “Truth in Securities” law. Sometimes financial advisors and regulators will refer to it as â€œThe Securities Actâ€ or the â€œ1933 Act.â€ It was then-President Franklin D. Roosevelt who signed this important legislation into law. As such, it is often deemed to be part and parcel of the legendary New Deal package crafted personally by President Roosevelt.

There have been a range of important amendments to the Securities Exchange Act of 1933 which Congress passed into law over the years since the legislation became effective. Among these amendments which updated the regulations were those passed in 1934, 1954, 1959, 1960, 1970, 1980, 1982, 1987, 1996, 1998, 2000, 2010, and in 2012.

# Securities Exchange Act of 1934

The Securities Exchange Act of 1934 is also known by its acronym of SEA. This piece of legislation was crafted in order to regulate transactions in securities which trade on the secondary market after they are already issued. The goal of this is to guarantee a higher level of financial transparency, better accuracy of trades, and a lower degree of manipulation and outright fraud.

This The Securities Exchange Act of 1934 laid the grounds for the SEC Securities Exchange Commission creation. In this way, the SEC became the SEAâ€™s regulatory body. Thanks to the act, the Securities Exchange Commission gained the authority to regulate securities like over the counter issues, stocks, and bonds. Thy also have regulatory oversight on the markets as a whole and the behavior of all financial professionals which includes dealers, brokers, and financial advisors. The SEC also reviews the financial reports of the various publically trading corporations, which they mandate be released.

Every company which chooses to be exchange listed has to adhere to the rules and regulations which The Securities Exchange Act of 1934 spells out for everyone. The principle requirements are disclosure, registration of all stock exchange listed securities, audit and margin requirements, and proxy solicitations. The reason for such requirements as these are to make sure that the playing field is level and fair. They also want to instill confidence in investors who participate in the various stock exchange markets.

It was then-President Franklin D. Roosevelt and his administration which arranged for The Securities Exchange Act of 1934 to come to Congress. They launched it as their official response to the generally accepted idea that poor financial market practices had been the primary perpetrator in the Black Monday stock market collapse of 1929. This act actually was not the first such legislation on the topic. The Securities Exchange Act of 1933 preceded it by a year. The 1933 piece of legislation mandated that all corporations had to publically disclose important and regulated financial information. This covered distribution and sales of stock shares. The 1934 act was more concerned with the behaviors of professionals in the financial advising and brokering industries.

The Roosevelt administration was not content with these two acts where regulation was concerned. They sponsored the Trust Indenture Act of 1934, the Public Utility Holding Company Act of 1935, The Investment Advisers Act of 1940, and finally the Investment Company Act of 1940. The numerous acts of legislation were passed in the wake of a devastated financial environment where the securities sales had little effective regulation. At the time, corporations could become controlled by a handful of investors while the public had no knowledge of these facts at all.

Thanks to this Securities Exchange Act of 1934, the SEC obtained broad and vast powers to oversee and police all corners of the securities business. To this effect, it is headed by five commissioners who lead the five divisions. The President of the United States appoints these commissioners. The divisions of the SEC are Division of Trading and Markets, Division of Corporation Finance, Division of Investment Management, Division of Economic and Risk Analysis, and Division of Enforcement.

They have both the authority and are the mandate to head up investigations into possible violations of The Securities Exchange Act of 1934. This covers a wide range of illegal and unscrupulous activities. Included in these are stealing the funds of clients, insider trading, selling unregistered stocks, manipulating the prices of the markets, and releasing falsified information or breaking the broker customer trust.

Besides this, the SEC is tasked with enforcing all corporate reporting they mandate for any company which possesses greater than $10 million of assets if their shares are owned by over 500 stake holders. The SEC has two tools for dealing with any and all matters which pertain to their areas of responsibility. They may settle any issue without it going to trial by dealing directly with the parties in question. They might also file a federal court case to resolve the problems.

# Self Directed IRA

Self directed IRAs prove to be special kinds of individual retirement accounts. They are different from traditional IRAs because they provide the account holder with a significantly greater variety of investment choices and control over decisions on the account. With these types of IRAs, the owner or an investment advisor makes a variety of investment decisions. They then deliver these instructions to an IRA custodian who executes them.

Federal law allows these types of IRAs to invest in a tremendous range of investment vehicles. It is IRS section 408 that restricts the few categories that are not allowed. The IRS forbids investments of IRA funds in life insurance and collectibles such as rugs, art, gems, etc. It does allow a wide range of investment choices that cover most anything else.

Self directed IRAs may purchase real estate, mortgages and trust deeds, energy investments, gold and other precious metals in bullion form, privately held stock, privately owned LLCs and Limited Partnerships, and corporate debt or promissory notes. When accounts such as these are opened primarily to purchase precious metals bullion, they are typically known by the name of their primary metal in which they invest.

These Precious Metals IRAs can be called Gold IRAs, Silver IRAs, Platinum IRAs, and Palladium IRAs. Such self directed IRAs can even purchase franchises such as Subway or Timothy Horton. All of these different investment choices allow for superior and broad based asset diversification of investors' retirement funds.

These types of IRAs also provide all of the usual benefits which are commonly associated with Traditional IRAs. Money saved in these plans is contributed on a tax free or tax deferred basis. No taxes will be paid on either the money deposited, or the gains made on these investments within the account, until they are withdrawn at retirement or under early withdrawal rules and limitations. Self directed IRAs are still subject to the same yearly maximum contribution limits of $5,500 in 2016. They allow for larger contributions of $6,500 to be made as catch up once the account holders reach age 50.

Early withdrawals from these IRAs as with traditional ones are penalized. It is often more advantageous to take a loan against the value of the IRA rather than suffer the financial consequences of early withdrawal. When loans are taken, there is no penalty. A repayment plan is established to put the borrowed funds back in the account in installments. Loans can be approved for a variety of expenses, such as home purchase, educational needs, or health care related expenses.

When an actual early withdrawal is taken, two penalties are assessed. First the money in the account is taxed as ordinarily earned income. Next a 10% penalty is levied by the IRS on all monies which the owner early withdraws.

These types of IRAs do have some limitations. The custodian must physically hold all assets in the account. This means that the account owners are not allowed to keep their real estate or mortgage deeds, stock certificates, or precious metals bullion at home in a safe. There have been offers made by some companies to help investors become their own IRA custodian by forming a special LLC company. This is a gray area which the IRS has not yet come down on with a hard ruling. In the future, they are likely to rule that investors absolutely can not be a custodian for their own gold, silver, platinum, or palladium bullion using either a safe deposit box or a home based safe.

The IRS requires that owners of these accounts begin taking distributions no later than at age 70. They can start withdrawing them as retirement funds at 59 Â½ if they wish to begin using the money earlier.

# SEP IRA

SEP IRAs are special simplified employee pensions that permit employers to contribute money to the retirement plans of their employees. If individuals are self employed, they may also set up and fund one of these accounts for their own benefit. These plans compare favorably to the more popular and utilized 401(k) plan. SEPs offer greater contribution amount limits. They are also much less complicated to establish and maintain than are the 401(k)s.

Any type of employer is allowed to create an SEP IRA. This means that businesses which are not incorporated, partnerships, and sole proprietorships can all work with and utilize them. Even self employed individuals who are employed elsewhere as well (with retirement plans at their other workplace) can make their own SEP.

SEP IRAs offer several advantages to owners and contributors. They provide significant tax benefits for employees and employers. Employer contributions give tax deductions to the employer during the tax year in which they make the contribution. Self employed individuals also can take this tax deduction for themselves. SEPs are also popular because they do not require any annual paperwork to be filed with the IRS. The paperwork that creates these accounts also offers the plus of being simple and minimal.

Individuals can make contributions for SEP IRAs in the year after the contribution applies. Deadlines for these contributions may also be stretched to the tax return due date. As far as establishing these accounts goes, deadlines are for the tax return due date and any extension that the IRS grants on the taxes.

In general, these accounts have to be opened and all contributions should be made by the April 15th that comes after the year in which the income was attained. Any taxpayers who take an extension on their tax returns to October 15th would receive a similar grace period for opening and funding the SEP IRA.

The contribution amounts for SEPs are quite flexible. No set percentage has to be contributed as with some of the rival retirement accounts like Keoghs. One could contribute nothing or as much as 25% of his or her income for the year (on as high as a $265,000 income amount). The full contribution for a single individual is not allowed to be greater than $53,000 in the year 2016. This amount contrasts with the typical standard IRA contribution limits of $5,500 for the year 2016.

The SEP limits are also substantially higher than the contribution limits on 401(k)s that come in at $18,000 for 2016 or at $24,000 for those who are at least 50 years old. SEPs do not have any provisions for catch up, as with other forms of IRAs or 401(k)s. Thanks to the higher contribution limits for every given year, this does not usually present a problem for those who are behind on their retirement accounts and want to put in more.

Employers are required to treat all employee contributions equally. This means that they must give the same contribution percentage for each employee who has made at least $600 in the year, who is 21 years or older, and who has worked for the company minimally three out of five prior years.

The only point where contributions to SEP IRAs get complicated centers on maximum contribution amounts. The 25% of income limit mentioned earlier is not figured out of gross revenue, but from net profits. Besides this, deductions on the half of self employment tax have to be first taken off of the net profit number before the limit for maximum contributions can be accurately determined off of the net profits.

# Sherman Clayton Antitrust Acts

The Sherman Act and Clayton Act are two pieces of legislation which Congress designed to combat abusive trusts and monopolies. Over the years they have been utilized to break up certain large monopolistic enterprises. Their passage also led to the creation of the anti-trust division in the Department of Justice.

In 1890 Congress passed its Sherman Antitrust Act. Though it has been supplemented by other subsequent acts, analysts still consider it to be the most significant. The government felt that the act became necessary because of trusts and monopolies that were taking over major industries in the decades that followed the Civil War.

Trusts proved to be understandings where stockholders of a few companies would transfer over their shares to a group of trustees. The trustees would then give these stockholders certificates that provided shares of earnings from the companies that would then be jointly managed. This is how trusts became monopolies in a variety of significant industries. Among these were steel, railroads, sugar, tobacco, and meatpacking.

Trusts were bad for the economy and smaller competitors because of the means they utilized to eliminate their competition. They would undercut competitors' prices temporarily, make clients purchase products they did not want to get the ones they did, force their customers to agree to long term contracts, and buy out competitors. When none of these methods worked they would send out intimidators and use violence as necessary.

Farmers and other small businesses complaining about high costs of transport they had to pay for rail caused enough of a stir for Congress to take action. The public had become tired of the economic power that the big corporations had amassed and with the trusts. Sherman turned out to be a commerce regulation expert. As such he acted as main author for the Sherman Antitrust Act.

This measure proved to be the first such effort by Congress to outlaw trusts and monopolies of all kinds. A few states had passed their own laws, but these only applied to commerce passing within their own borders. This act used Congressâ€™ constitutionally held powers to regulate commerce between states. It found almost no opposition in Congress. Only 1 member voted against it in the Senate and none in the House. President Benjamin Harrison signed it to make it the first such national antitrust law. The act granted the Federal government the authority it needed to dissolve these trusts.

Enforcing the law turned out to be another matter. The Supreme Court ruled against the government on the attempted enforcement of it against The American Sugar Refining Company in 1895. President William McKinley enacted an era of busting up trusts in 1898 by setting up the U.S. Industrial Commission. President Theodore Roosevelt at last managed to build on their report to break up the trusts. Subsequent action led to the breaking up of Standard Oil Company, among the most famous and powerful trusts of all time.

The Sherman act still needed more strengthening, so Congress acted again in 1914. This time they passed the Clayton Antitrust Act. This act laid out specifically illegal actions that monopolies were doing. It made it illegal for competitors to buy each other out without approval. Companies could not arbitrarily charge different prices to their customers. Board members could not sit on multiple companiesâ€™ boards of directors. At the same time, Congress established the Federal Trade Commission to look into antitrust law violation and to stop practices that were not fair and competitive.

The Sherman Act most successfully applied to breaking up AT&T in 1984. The government attempted to use it against Microsoft for abusive anticompetitive practices in the late 1990s. A number of observers believe they failed to utilize the victory and sufficiently correct Microsoft.

# Simple IRA

Among the stable of various types of IRAs American savers for retirement can take advantage of is a less common plan called the SIMPLE IRA. These kinds are a combination of traditional IRAs and employer offered plans like 401(k)s. The word SIMPLE in this case is actually an acronym that stands for Savings Incentive Match Plan for Employees. This is the most common name for the employer offered tax deferred retirement savings account.

SIMPLE IRAs were created to help smaller employers who have 100 or less employees. The idea was for them to offer their workers retirement plans. The IRS knew that the bigger packages of benefits all too often involved long and difficult opening procedures with mountains of complicated paperwork. Smaller employers simply did not have the time or resource capacity to complete and maintain these types of plans.

Among the advantages of SIMPLE IRAs is that they are not governed by ERISA, the Employee Retirement Income Security Act. This means that they are able to sidestep substantial expenses and significant amounts of paperwork in establishing them. The contributions to these kinds of IRA accounts are also fairly straightforward. Employers must make specific minimum amount contributions to the accounts of the employees.

They can accomplish this by establishing a match program at a minimum of 3% of their employee contributions. Alternatively they might set a 2% of his or her salary flat rate and offer it to every employee who participates.

When employees become part of a company SIMPLE plan, they are basically establishing a traditional IRA via their employing company. A significant disadvantage to these types of IRAs centers on their lower contribution limits. These are less than comparable 401(k) plans or other plans which employers sponsor. The limits amount to $12,500 for a single year in tax years 2015 and 2016.

Rolling over from these types of IRAs is also more complicated. They can not be started without a waiting period first being observed. Once employees start their participation with the plans, they can not do a rollover for generally two years on from their participation dates. The only exception to this rule pertains to transfers between SIMPLE IRAs.

These can be done at any time since they are considered to be a tax free transfer from one trustee to another. In the even of any other type of transfer within the two years waiting period, these are deemed as distributions by the IRS. While most penalties for tax deferred plans are set at 10% withdrawal penalties, these particular IRAs carry a more punishing 25% withdrawal tax penalty.

After the conclusion of the two year time frame, individuals may then move their funds from the SIMPLE plan to a different kind of IRA. The only restriction is that they can not move them to a Roth IRA which is funded with pre-taxed dollars. The current SIMPLE plan as well as the new plan must also allow for the transfer to occur.

As with any kind of retirement plan, early withdrawal penalties apply. If any withdrawals occur before the official retirement age of 59 Â½ is attained, the early withdrawal penalties of up to 25% will be assessed against the account withdrawals.

When rollovers are done, direct rollovers are much preferred to indirect rollovers. If account holders pursue indirect rollovers there are tax withholding requirements. It is also possible that the account owner will inadvertently fail to complete the transfer in time or at all and then suffer from the substantial early withdrawal tax penalties of up to 25%.

# Social Security

Social Security in the United States refers to the federal governmentâ€™s OASDI Old Age, Survivors, and Disability Insurance program. President Franklin Roosevelt created the first such program and signed the Social Security Act legislation in 1935. The present day law has been amended to include other social insurance and social welfare schemes.

The Social Security program is mostly bankrolled using payroll taxes which are referred to as the FICA Federal Insurance Contributions Act tax. The other legislation on it pertains to self employed people. SECA Self Employed Contributions Act Tax collects their contributions. The Internal Revenue Service collects all of these tax deposits and delivers them to the two Social Security Trust Funds. These are the Federal Disability Insurance Trust Fund and the Federal Old Age and Survivors Insurance Trust Fund. All income paid by salaries to a maximum amount set by law contributes to the payroll tax for these programs. Income that people earn above this limit does not incur additional taxes for the programs. This maximum level of taxable earnings in 2016 amounted to $118,500.

The program provides a basis for economic security for 59 million Americans who are retired, disabled, or the family members of those who are deceased or disabled workers. This number amounts to about one in six Americans who receive money from the program. Of this amount approximately 39 million beneficiaries are retired while the rest are survivors of deceased or disabled workers or disabled people themselves. Around 163 million individual Americans pay these taxes so that the others can receive their monthly benefits. This amounts to around a quarter of families collecting income from the programs.

Social Security proves to be a program based on a pay as you go system. Today's workers contribute taxes into the program so that money can go directly out in the form of monthly income to the recipients. This makes it different from prefunded company pension plans. Prefunded programs collect money in advance of retirement benefits being paid. This way it can be distributed to the workers of today when they retire.

Both workers and employers make contributions to the program. Workers give 6.2 percent of income up to the cap. Employers similarly pay an amount that is matching to arrive at the joint contribution of 12.4 percent of all earnings. Those persons who are self employed must pay for both employer and employee share.

Social Security's finances have a bleak outlook. The Office of the Chief Actuary of Social Security comes up with a "best estimate" on when the fund will run out of money to pay benefits. If Congress makes no changes to the law, then in 2020 the benefits spending will actually surpass the revenues for payroll taxes along with the interest on the funds' securities.

At this point, the fund will start cashing in its Treasury securities it obtained as IOU's for loaning money to other branches of the Federal government. In order for the government to pay these IOU's, they will have to obtain money from one or more of a few different sources. Other spending will have to decrease, taxes will have to rise, or the Treasury will have to borrow additional money by selling more securities. This last choice would increase the already high Federal debt.

By 2034, all the assets of the trust fund would have been completely exhausted. This means that all Treasuries the fund has would have been redeemed. By this point, the combined workers and employers taxes would be enough to cover 79 percent of currently promised benefits to recipients. The last year of the 75 years projection shows that by 2089, the payroll taxes would be sufficient to cover around 74 percent of currently promised benefits.

# Standard Deduction

A Standard Deduction refers to the minimum amount of income which will not be subjected to taxes. This deduction may also be utilized to decrease the AGI adjusted gross income of the tax payer in question. Such standard deductions are only allowed to be employed in cases where the tax paying individual elects to skip the itemized deductions for figuring up income which is taxable.

Standard deductions are ultimately dependent on a number of personal factors that are particular to the filing individual. Among these are the age, filing status (married or single), any disabilities, and ability of any other taxpayer to claim them as dependent on their tax return.

Naturally, not every tax payer will elect to go with the standard deductions. Many do however. The single most compelling reason that they choose this over the itemized deduction route has to do with the fact that the majority of tax paying individuals (in the nation) will not accrue receipts for all of their potential deductible expenses as they go through a given year.

Besides this fact, a great number of individuals decide that the governmentâ€™s standard deduction is reasonably generous. When they examine the comparisons between the two, they discover that the standard deductions will usually provide them a better reduction to their taxable income than the alternative method of figuring up the sum total of their allowable expenses and entering these instead. For one thing, such standard deduction amounts receive an adjustment for inflation every year. For another, if tax payers cannot supply evidence of such allowed expenses upon request to the Internal Revenue Service, then they may not choose to proceed with the itemized deductions method in any case.

The ultimate idea behind such standard deductions is to make certain that every tax payer will receive at least a portion of their income which will not be assessed by the federal income taxes. These standard deductions also apply to many different states which levy a state income tax. They generally permit individuals to claim some kind of deduction like this on the income tax return of the given state.

Each personâ€™s level for standard deduction varies based on the filing status that they have particular to their situation. It always helps to look at a clear and real world example to understand challenging concepts like this one. Take the tax year of 2016. Those single tax payers along with married filing separately tax payers were allowed to take the standard deduction of $6,300. For those who filed as married filing jointly, they received $12,600, exactly twice the deduction of the single filers. For those who file as the head of a household (which are single individuals that can claim at-home dwelling dependents), the deduction rises to $9,300.

There are also higher standard deductions available to those taxpayers who have blindness, are at least 65 years old, or who are both. For those who are totally or partially blind, the Internal Revenue Service gives this special adjustment. Such filers require an eye doctor-certified statement to reinforce their claim. A great number of the various states throughout the country also give these kinds of adjustments based on blindness or old age.

Though there is little doubt that it proves to be significantly simpler to just take the standard deduction than it is to go through the trouble and time to itemize specific deductions, this could cost filers tax-reducing deduction amounts. Many individuals who gave large amounts of money to churches or charities, encountered major medical costs, paid property taxes or interest on mortgage, or who suffered from uninsured losses because of natural disasters or theft will find itemizing pays off. This is why the IRS suggests individuals spend some time to work their tax deductions both ways to learn which one will provide a larger deduction. For people who utilize a good tax program like Turbo Tax, it will do it on the behalf of the filer.

# Sub-prime Borrower

A sub-prime borrower is an individual who has credit that is considered to be less than perfect. This is the opposite of a prime borrower. Bankers call prime borrowers those who possess higher and better credit scores, low debt ratios, and significant incomes which are more than enough to cover their monthly bills and expenses.

Sub-prime borrowers often are only able to obtain sub-prime loans. These types of loans received the blame for causing the 2008 mortgage crisis. Despite this fact, the loans continue to exist today. They are an important part of post crisis lending, though so far they have not caused another financial crisis or global meltdown.

Those called sub-prime borrowers have many characteristics in common. These imply that the individuals are more likely to default on their mortgage loans than other individuals. Poor credit is the first element they share. This could be because they did not receive any opportunities to create a sufficient credit history.

It might also be from problems they had with making payments in the past. The dilemma for these borrowers is that they do not have many choices other than sub-prime lenders. This often traps them in a cycle of debt from which is difficult to escape. An under 640 credit score is considered to be sub-prime, though some lenders set the defining limit lower to even 580.

The sub-prime borrowers also have problems with their monthly payments. These payments are so large that they consume a significant part of the monthly income for the borrowers. This is determined in how high the debt to income ratio proves to be. A higher DTI ratio means that the borrowers do not have enough money to cover bills if they suffer a drop in income or have unanticipated expenses arise. Loans can still be approved in some scenarios when the borrowers' present debt load is significant.

The cost for a sub-prime loan is another thing these borrowers share together. These forms of mortgage loans usually cost more since lenders do not want to assume additional risk without higher compensation. Predatory lenders have used this limited ability to receive loan approvals in order to prey on borrowers with no other choices. These higher expenses manifest in a few different ways. It might be junk application and processing fees, greater interest rates, and penalties for early prepayment which prime borrowers seldom pay.

Risk is the dominant theme for sub-prime borrowers, lenders, and loans. Because the loans have a lower chance of being paid back, the lenders exact more in fees and higher rates. These greater costs cause the loans to be riskier for the borrowers as well. Debt is difficult to retire when higher interest rates and costs come with it.

Sub-prime borrowers should try to avoid these expensive and debt trapping loans whenever they can. Staying out of such costly credit is essential for individuals to not drown in debt. This is easier said than done when people are put into the sub-prime category. There are not as many options to comparison shop for the loans. There are also fewer options for alternative kinds of loans to use for the needed financing.

If these borrowers are able to make themselves look less risky to the various lenders, it will improve their chances of escaping from these types of loans. This may mean some credit repair work needs to be done before individuals with credit challenges make applications for loans.

# Sub-prime Lender

A sub-prime lender makes loans to customers who fall into the sub-prime borrower category. These products often include loans which are normally considered to be standard. They are structured for and marketed to borrowers who possess inadequate income, lower credit scores, and a higher debt to income ratio. These borrowers can not qualify with lenders regarded as traditional.

Sub-prime lenders are often willing to issue loans to customers with special circumstances. These include those who possess less documentation of income, high LTV loan to value ratios, and sometimes a combination of the two. This type of lending is considered to be aggressive and overly risky for most traditional financial institutions.

Where mortgages are concerned, sub-prime lenders are still providing basically the same product in the form of a 5/1 ARM adjustable rate mortgage or a 30 year fixed rate mortgage. The main difference is that the rate which accompanies such a product will be considerably higher.

There are other types of mortgage loans that some observers include in this category as well. Among these are negative amortization loans, interest only loans, and non fixed interest rate mortgages. A great number of analysts consider FHA loans to be in the subprime category. This is because their highest allowable LTV is 96.5% while they accept a credit score minimum of 500.

Sub-prime lenders will also make loans for other assets and in other categories besides housing and mortgages. In fact they issue them for practically all financing needs. This includes credit cards, car loans, unsecured personal loans, and student loans.

After the financial crisis that started with sub-prime mortgages, the government enacted a number of laws protecting consumers from these predatory types of finance. It has made it more difficult to find sub-prime house loans since then. There are a great many of the original loans from before the crisis still in existence. Besides this, sub-prime lenders have found means of circumventing them and giving approval to loans that fall into this category.

Borrowers can take many actions to avoid being a victim of a sub-prime lender. Managing credit carefully is among the most important. It is free to check all credit reports for accuracy. Borrowers can fix errors. Consumers should also deal with any defaults or missed payments if they can. Rebuilding credit requires some time, but going through the process will help borrowers to be considered more prime to lenders.

There are many newer lenders these days that are considered to be legitimate. Online searches and online lenders have opened a whole new avenue to consumers trying to avoid sub-prime loans. Some of these online lenders appeal to those with poor credit and still provide acceptable rates.

There are also peer to peer lending services. They can be more flexible with borrowers than the traditional credit unions and banks often are. It is always a good idea to research any lenders which consumers consider before providing them with important personal information or paying any fees.

Borrowers who are struggling to avoid these sub-prime lenders can also look into a co-signer on a loan. It can help credit challenged borrowers to receive approval from a lender which is traditional and offers better rates. These co-signers put their own credit at stake and take a big risk in doing so.

# Sub-prime Mortgage

A sub-prime mortgage is one where the home loan that the bank or lending institution makes is offered to the category of consumers who are considered to possess the riskiest credit. Sub prime mortgages are actually sold on a different market than are prime mortgage loans. Sub prime mortgage borrowers are determined through a combination of factors, such as the credit rating of the borrower, the documentation offered for the loans, and the borrower's debt to assets ratio. Besides this, sub-prime mortgage are also deemed to be those that do not fulfill the prime mortgages' standards and guide lines offered by Fannie Mae and Freddie Mac, the two biggest issuers of mortgages within the United States.

A universally agreed upon definition for sub-prime mortgages does not exist today. In the U.S., sub-prime mortgages are commonly considered to be those where the associated borrower possesses a FICO credit rating score that is less than 640. This phrase became a part of pop culture in the credit crunch that occurred in 2007.

The original sub-prime mortgage program began in 1993. At this time, some lenders started offering sub-prime mortgages to borrowers classified as high risk, who possessed credit that was less than ideal. Traditional lenders showed wariness towards sub-prime mortgages and borrowers. They tended to shy away from people who had impaired credit histories. Sub-prime mortgage borrowers commonly have information on their credit reports that argue for greater percentages of defaults. These include too much debt, a track record of not paying debts or missing payments, recorded bankruptcies, and low amounts of experience with debt.

Around twenty-five percent of the American population is grouped into this category of sub-prime borrowers who qualify for the category of sub-prime mortgages. Because of this, proponents of sub-prime mortgages argued that they allowed a large number of people to gain access to credit who would not otherwise have experienced the opportunity to purchase and own a home. Borrowers with less than perfect credit who can demonstrate enough income are able to qualify for sub-prime mortgages. This proves to be the case even if their credit scores are lower than 640.

The lenders who participate in sub-prime mortgages take significant risks in so doing. This is because people who have a credit score of less than 620 statistically possess a significantly greater rate of defaulting on their mortgages than do those people with much higher scores over 720. Lenders compensate for the risks associated with offering sub-prime mortgages through several different means. One of these is by charging higher rates of interest. They also collect late fees for any customers who do not keep up with their payments. These greater interest rates and fees help to reward lenders who take the risks of the higher default rates, and who also incur costs for collecting and keeping up with these -mortgage accounts. As an example of their potential danger, sub-prime mortgages proved to be among the main causes of the Financial Crisis of 2007-2010.

# Tariff Programs

Tariff programs are tariff regimes that apply to imports. Tariffs prove to be taxes that governments put on goods that are imported. Every nation has its own tariff programs and amounts. There are five principle tariff types in any tariff program. These are revenue, specific, ad valorem, protective, and prohibitive.

Revenue types of tariffs are those that boost government revenues. A revenue tariff would be one set up by a country that does not grow oranges but imposes tariffs on the import of oranges. This way, that government makes money when any business chooses to import and sell oranges.

Ad valorem tariffs are those that a government places as a percent of the value of imports. An example of such a tariff is fifteen cents for each dollar value. This contrasts with specific tariffs that do not revolve around the imported goodsâ€™ estimated value. Instead, they are levied as a result of the specific quantity of the goods in question. Specific tariffs can be figured up based on the volume of the goods that are imported, on their weight, or on any other form of measurement applicable to goods.

Tariffs that are prohibitive in nature turn out to be the ones that stop a business from importing a good at all. These tariffs might be used on goods that a government does not wish brought into the country. This might be for safety, health, or moral reasons.

Protective tariffs are set by a government in order to ensure that the sale price of goods that are imported do not destroy a local industry. These are employed to protect domestic markets from foreign competition. Higher tariffs will permit local companies that may not be so efficient to compete effectively against the foreign competitors within the local domestic markets. While protective tariffs have their time and place in building up the local firms and economy, they can have unintended consequences. They might cause an item to be so costly that companies have to charge more for their related products.

A good example of this pertains to the prices of gasoline. As they rise excessively through tariffs, companies involved in shipping, like trucking companies, have no choice but to charge retail businesses higher prices for getting their products to them. The retail businesses will then respond by increasing the prices of their goods to compensate for the greater costs of transportation. They have to do this to make the same level of profit that they did in the past. The final result will be that consumers bear the brunt of the tariff by having to pay higher prices for their products and goods.

All countries employ tariff programs for one reason or another. They may not apply them evenly to every import or industry, but they will utilize them somewhere. Sometimes countries choose not to put tariffs on goods being imported. This is known as free trade in these cases. Free trade is believed by many economists to permit higher levels of economic growth. Critics say that without tariff programs, economies will be forced to rely on global markets instead of their own local markets.

# Tax Abatement

Tax abatement represents a taxation level reduction. It can be for either individual consumers or companies. There are many examples of this type of tax break. They could be in the form of a rebate, reduction in tax penalties, or an actual tax decrease. Sometimes people or firms pay too many taxes or get a tax bill that is higher than it should be. In this case, they have the right to ask for an abatement from the IRS or state taxing agency.

Among the different types of tax abatement is the property tax kind. Owners of property might feel that their property value is assessed too highly. They would be able to appeal to the area tax assessor to receive a tax abatement. Businesses that are not for profit can obtain them on their property because of their special tax exempt status.

Tax abatement on property is a major savings. Most owners of houses will be required to pay property taxes that are commonly from 1% to 3% of the value of the house every year. This annual expense does not disappear when the mortgage is completely paid. It represents part of the ongoing cost of owning a home.

There are cities that offer special programs of real estate tax abatement. Such a package assists consumers dramatically. It could help them to purchase a nicer house for the same payment. It might also allow them to be able to obtain a mortgage that they might not otherwise. This is the case if the monthly house payment drops to a level they can afford through such abatement. This type of abatement on property can also help to boost the resale value of the house if it is still in effect when the owner sells.

Some cities in the U.S. offer tax abatement's to massively lower or even completely eliminate tax payments on houses for not only years but even decades. The idea behind such a program is to bring in buyers to neighborhoods that are in poor demand. This could be part of the inner city which the city is attempting to revitalize. Cities can offer these abatement's throughout the entire limits. Others provide them for specific areas. Authorities can choose to restrict such programs to middle or low income owners of property as well. A great number of these abatement programs do not carry such an income restriction.

It is possible to purchase properties that are already under abatement. Individuals may also buy properties that are eligible and go through with the necessary improvements. They then apply for this program. It is far easier to buy a property with an abatement than to go through the hassle of bureaucracy and construction.

For abatement's on improvements to a property, there are special rules. The improvement, rehabilitation, or construction property taxes can be reduced or eliminated. This does not mean that the entire property tax is gone. The pre-improved value of the property will still have taxes owed for it in this particular case.

It is often necessary for a house to be occupied by the owner for the abatement to continue. Renting the house out would cause the special status to disappear. When an owner sells a home to another owner who will occupy it, the property tax abatement will stay with the house. Abatement periods never restart just because the property transfers ownership. If a 10 year program eliminates or reduces the taxes on a home and the seller has enjoyed seven of these years, then the new owner will have the three years left of the status.

## Tax Accountant

Tax accountants are professionals who help clients with finances. One of their main tasks is to prepare tax returns for individuals and businesses. They complete taxes for local, state, and federal levels. These agents can do this because they have great knowledge of governmental regulations and business rules. The Internal Revenue Service established tax accounting with the section Title 26 of its Internal Revenue Code.

Tax accountants also perform a variety of other functions. They help their customers minimize the amount of taxes owed. They assist them in meeting tax filings and requirements. Accountants also update their clients on any changes to the tax code that will impact their business. When there are government audits or disputes over taxes, companies turn to their tax accountants for representation to help resolve them.

Tax accountants' work schedules are different than those of many professionals. This is because much of their business is seasonal. From mid April thru end of December, they keep busy with typical work weeks. Starting in January through mid April, these professionals see their work hours go up dramatically. The first four months of the year they are doing individual and business tax returns for clients.

Becoming a tax accountant requires significant amounts of education and licensing. These professionals generally need bachelor's degrees either in accounting or a related field. Business administration is another major that individuals can take to become an accountant. It makes a good base for a master's degree in accounting. Other master's programs that help with this line of work involve taxation, auditing, business statistics and calculus, or financial planning.

The professional qualification that sets accountants above many of their peers is the CPA. To obtain the official Certified Public Accountant status they must put in another 30 educational hours and obtain experience in accounting. Finally, accountants take an exam to gain this designation. Having a CPA credential with their state board allows them to file financial reports with the Securities and Exchange Commission.

Each state has its own requirements for the CPA license. One hundred and fifty semester hours of college or university credit is usually necessary. Most states also require a candidate to demonstrate minimally two years work experience in the field.

The American Institute of Certified Public Accounts is the governing body that administers the CPA exam. After candidates have met the other educational and experience criteria they may take this. Gaining the certification is not the end of the process. CPAs are usually required to stay caught up with various continuing education courses. Otherwise they will not be allowed to keep their designation.

There are several questions that business owners should ask before hiring a tax accountant for their enterprise. It is good to know the types of clients these professionals count. Finding one that understands their business is important. Companies also need to make sure a potential accountant is available all year round.

Finally, companies should determine that their potential financial planning company has real experience dealing with the IRS. Sometimes CPAs are a more impressive designation. This does not give them the experience that an Enrolled Agent has with the IRS. The Federal Government actually certifies EAs precisely to handle taxes. Another advantage that EAs have is that many of them have been IRS agents. As such they possess real and valuable experience in performing and handling business and personal tax audits.

# Tax Bracket

A tax bracket refers to a certain income range against which the government levies a specific income tax rate. With the majority of income taxing systems in the world today, lower incomes fall under lower income rates tax brackets. At the same time, higher incomes are taxed at greater rates. The idea behind such brackets is to ensure that a progressive income tax system remains in place.

In the tax year for 2016, the Internal Revenue Service decreed there would be seven different tax brackets. Each of these offers minute variations on the theme for married filers, single filers, and head of household filers. This led to the de facto establishment of 21 real tax brackets for the tax year.

Importantly, the tax bracket thresholds did increase a little for tax year 2016. As an example, the lowest bracket proves to be under $9,325 for individual taxpayers, which was raised from $9,275 back in tax year 2015. The highest possible tax bracket for this tax year 2016 is now $418,041, itself raised from the 2015 tax bracket high of

$415,051. This changes every year, so it is important to consult the IRS.gov website for current information annually.

Those individuals whose incomes are under the minimum bracket of $9,275 have income which is taxed according to the minimum 10 percent tax rate. For everyone filing singly who earns over this amount, the first $9,275 becomes taxed at the rate of 10 percent. Earnings which exceed this on up to $37,650 are then taxed at 15 percent. From $37,650 to $91,150 the earnings become taxed at a steeper 25 percent rate. Income beyond the $91,150 is taxed at still higher rates. This means that many tax filers actually fall into several tax brackets and not only the first one.

The tax bracket should never be confused with the tax rate. Tax rates represent the actual percentage at which the given income becomes taxed. All tax brackets possess their own unique tax rates. Many people simplify and call their tax rates the bracket at which they are taxed as if they were identical. The comparison is not valid since the majority of Americans have earnings which fall into more than one tax bracket.

An example helps to make the tax bracket concept clearer. Consider an individual who earns a hefty $500,000 every year. At such a lofty level as this, the filer will have income that goes into each of the single filing tax brackets. This means the person will pay many different tax rates (seven in fact). This will depend on which part of his or her income is being considered. On all earnings which exceed $406,751 the tax rate will be a punishing 39.6 percent. On the initial $9,075, the rate will merely be the 10 percent rate of the first tax bracket. This means that the actual tax rate of such an individual will lie somewhere in the middle of the two tax rate extremes of 10 percent and 39.6 percent, making it closer to 25 to 35 percent effectively.

The opposite of such a progressive income tax system as this one is a flat tax system. In these taxing arrangements, every individual becomes taxed on all income at the identical rate. It does not matter how much people make in this type of tax setup.

Those analysts and economists in favor of the tax bracket system in particular and progressive tax systems in general argue that the people who make higher incomes can bear a heavier taxing burden and still enjoy a comfortable, high standard of living. Lower income earners will struggle to cover their basic human needs at any tax rate.

The other argument is that such a system will cushion and stabilize against losses in after tax income. The reason is because a real salary decrease becomes counterbalanced out by a drop in the effective tax rate. In this way, people who suffered a pay cut would feel the blow to their post-tax income less severely since the tax rates would drop alongside the income decline.

It is worth noting that such tax brackets do not only apply to individuals who file their income taxes. The IRS also sets the rates and brackets for trusts, companies, and corporations. They adjust both these and the personal tax brackets for the impacts of inflation from time to time.

# Tax Credits

Tax credits refer to different sums of money which taxpayers may deduct from their total tax bill that they owe the federal, state, or local government. The amount of a given tax credit will naturally depend on the type of credit involved.

Some kinds of credits accrue to businesses or individuals who operate (or live) in particular locales, industry segments, or specific classifications. These credits are different from exemptions and deductions that lower the amount of income the IRS considers to be taxable. Instead, a tax credit will actually decrease the amount of tax which the business or individual owes.

Governments often provide such tax credits to foster certain patterns of behavior and actions. This could be to lower the aggregate cost for certain taxpayers' housing, or for replacing appliances which are older with newer and more efficiently operating appliances.

Generally speaking, such tax credits prove to be more beneficial than an exemption or deduction since they diminish the amount of taxes the entity or individual must pay on a dollar for dollar basis. These other types of expenses and exemptions do lower the ultimate tax liability. Their limitation is that they only reduce this based on the marginal tax rate of the individual or business. This means that those individuals who are considered to be a member of the 15 percent tax bracket only receive 15 cents in tax savings for each marginal tax dollar deduction. On the other hand, the credit decreases such tax liabilities by a whole dollar.

These credits can be broken down into refundable, partially refundable, or nonrefundable tax credits. Refundable credits prove to be the most helpful form since they are refundable in their entirety. No matter how high (or low) the tax liability or income of particular taxpayers may be they will receive the full dollar credit amount. This is still the case even when such a refundable tax credit decreases the tax liability to under $0. In such a scenario, the taxpayers will receive a negative tax liability, which the IRS calls a refund.

Per the year 2016, the most typical refundable tax credit remains the EITC Earned Income Tax Credit. There are similarly other types of refundable tax credits which taxpayers may claim for health care insurance and coverage, for educational expenses and costs, and for raising children.

Other tax credits may be partially refundable. This means that they can reduce taxable income and also decrease the individualsâ€™ (or businessesâ€™) tax liability. In 2016, a partially refundable form of tax credit proved to be the American Opportunity Tax Credit. When taxpayers manage to lower their liabilities to below zero and still have part of the $2,500 (as of 2016) tax deduction remaining, they may apply 40 percent of what is left as a refundable credit.

The final type of such a credit is the nonrefundable tax credit. These the taxpayers may deduct directly from the liability of taxes all the way to the point where the liability then equals zero. The remaining nonrefundable tax credit can not be deployed to take refunds. These types of credits have a negative effect on lower income taxpayers, since they can not gain the full benefit from the credit amount. Such credits which are nonrefundable will only be valid for the particular reporting year too. They also expire once the return has been filed and can not carry forward to future years. Specific examples of such nonrefundable tax credits for 2016 include raising children, adoptions benefits, realizing foreign income, and paying interest on mortgage.

# Tax Deductions

Tax Deductions prove to be a legal method for reducing income which the taxing authorities consider to be taxable. They typically arise because of expenses, especially such costs as taxpayers or businesses experience in the course of producing income or earning profits. This differs from exemptions and credits as both exemptions and deductions actually reduce the amount of income which can be taxed, while the credits applied actually reduce the total tax individuals and business will have to pay.

Two categories into which tax professionals often divide tax deductions are above the line and below the line. Above the line deductions benefit all taxpayers regardless of how much income they earn. Below the line ones only provide value if they surpass the individual taxpayersâ€™ standard deductions. For 2016, this deduction turned out to be $6,400 for single taxpayers without families or dependents.

Tax deductions also differ according to business and personal types. For the United States, (as well as most business taxing jurisdictions), businesses may take both trade and business expenses off of their taxable income. These allowances vary widely from one type to another and are often restricted. In order to be permissible, said expenses have to be realized in the operations of the business on an activity the owners undertake in an effort to make profits.

Cost of goods sold is a nearly universally accepted tax deduction for most every system of income tax regardless of the jurisdiction. This reduces the gross income, and tax authorities typically consider it to be an expense. In the United States, the Internal Revenue Service permits â€œall the ordinary and necessary expenses paid or incurred during the taxable year in carrying on any trade or businessâ€ as typical business tax deductions. These will be governed by any applicable limitations, enhancements, and qualifications.

Limitations do exist with regards to these types of business deductions. This is the case even though the necessary expenses may pertain directly to the business in question. Some of these limitations apply to activities which include lobbying expenditures, key employeesâ€™ compensation packages, the use of vehicles, and entertainment related to the business. Besides this, deductions which exceed the income of one enterprise can not necessarily offset income earned in other ventures. The U.S. limits those deductions from one passive activity to being used against income from another such passive activity.

Depreciation is another key tax deduction which the U.S. permits businesses and sole proprietors. This mechanism for cost recovery happens through deductions in the form of depreciation. It applies to most any tangible asset. The IRS permits such depreciation throughout the potential useful life of the asset, which they estimate.

The government assigns most depreciation (useful life) time-frames using the nature and utilization of such assets and the type of business as their guidelines. For example, they may allow three years of depreciation for tax deductions on a laptop or desktop computer. This means that the cost of the purchase can be divided by three and each resulting third of the price may be used as a specific tax deduction for three consecutive years.

Personal deductions are the other principal type of tax deductions. These pertain to individual taxpayers. Some intrinsically personal goods, costs, or services may be deducted from taxable income, per the IRS. The standard and set allowance for taxpayers and also some of their family members or dependents which they support is determined by the Internal Revenue Service and varies most every year.

The IRS calls these personal exemptions. In the United Kingdom and other British English-speaking jurisdictions throughout the world, these are known as personal allowances. In both types of systems, such exemptions and allowances become reduced and finally eliminated for those married couples or individuals whose income surpasses preset maximum levels.

Among the types of personal exemptions (which the U.S. and many other systems allow) are property taxes and local or state income taxes paid, medical costs, primary home loan interest charges, contributions to charitable organizations, contributions to either health savings or retirement savings plans, and some educational costs or interest paid on education-related student loans. The U.S. and Britain also allow payments to other individuals to become deducible in many cases, such as with child support or alimony.

# Tax Evasion

Tax Evasion refers to the illegal actions undertaken by an individual, company, or other organization on an often international scale to get out of paying their fair tax burden in their home tax jurisdiction. Individuals who get caught evading their taxes often suffer from criminal charges and penalties that can even include several years in real and served out jail time. The Internal Revenue Service in the United States classifies such tax avoidance as a serious federal offense under its national tax code.

The idea behind tax evasion covers both an illegal underpayment of owed taxes as well as the illegal non-paying of taxes in their entirely. The way that such individuals become caught when they do not at all submit their tax forms to the IRS is through the IRS Internal Revenue Serviceâ€™ s ability to figure out that their taxes are owed in utilizing the third party submitted base information including 1099s and W-2s from the employer of the individual in question. Such parties will not usually be convicted of deliberate tax evasion unless they are able to successfully and conclusively determine that it was done willfully and deliberately.

Deliberately not paying correct federally owed taxes though is a very serious matter. In fact it often ends with criminal charges being filed by the IRS or another national taxing authority in other developed nations. For such charges to actually be filed, the agency must first ascertain conclusively that the tax avoidance was done intentionally by the offending taxpayer. This means that the individuals may be forced to pay the taxes which were properly owed at the same time as they are found guilty of deliberately not paying their taxes and then made to spend time in jail.

In determining that the failure to pay their fair taxes proved to be intentional, many factors will be contemplated. The most common of these is the financial situation of the payer in an effort to learn if not paying resulted from deliberate fraud or otherwise attempting to hide reportable income from the tax authorities. Failing to pay can be deemed to be fraudulent in those scenarios where the taxpayer endeavored to hide assets by assigning them to a third party or lodging them in overseas bank accounts.

Examples of this are by reporting earned income using a fake name or other personâ€™s social security number. This might also be considered to be identity theft by the appropriate legal authorities. People can be judged as hiding income by not reporting work that did not pay according to traditional means. This might involve receiving cash payments in exchange for services and goods sold. When these sums are not properly reported to the IRS as income in the annual tax filing, then this constitutes willful and deliberate fraud.

There is an important and real distinction between tax evasion and tax avoidance as well. Tax evasion entails illegally making efforts to sidestep paying taxes which are actually owed. Tax avoidance is an entirely legal means of reducing the amounts of taxes owed by a taxpayer. Among these activities could be giving charitably to approved not for profits as well as investing income into tax deferred instruments like IRA individual retirement accounts. With IRAs, no taxes will be owed or paid on invested funds or their returns earned on them unless the funds are withdrawn early before retirement age is fully attained.

# Tax Exemptions

Tax exemptions are special monetary exemptions that decrease the amount of income which is taxable. This can take the form of full tax exempt status that delivers 100 percent relief from a certain form of taxes, partial tax on certain items, or reduced tax rates and bills. Tax exemption can refer to particular groups such as charitable outfits (who receive exemption from income taxes and property taxes), multi-jurisdictional businesses or individuals, and even military veterans.

The phrase tax exemption is commonly utilized to refer to specific scenarios where the law lowers the amount of income that would fall under the taxable label otherwise. With the American Internal Revenue Service, there are two kinds of exemptions which are available to individuals. One example of a tax exemption concerns the decrease in taxes the IRS gives for any dependent children who are under age 18 (who actually live with the head of household income tax filer).

For the year 2015, the Internal Revenue Service permitted individuals who were filing taxes to receive a $4,000 exemption on every one of their permitted tax exemptions. This simply means that any individuals paying taxes who count on three permissible exemptions are able to deduct fully $12,000 off of their taxable income level.

In the cases where they make a higher amount than an IRS pre-determined threshold, the amount in tax exemptions which they are able to utilize becomes phased out slowly and finally eliminated completely. For the tax year 2015, those individuals filing taxes who earned in excess of $258,250, as well as those married filing jointly couples who earned more than $309,900, received a lower amount for their exemptions. This complicated sliding scale with seemingly random numbers in place is all part of the reason why observers claim the American tax system is outdated and overly complex.

There is an important caveat for individuals filing taxes. They can not claim their own personal exemption when someone else claims them as a dependent on their tax return. This is one of the elements that separate exemptions from deductions in the world of tax terminology. Each individual filing is permitted to claim his or her personal deduction.

Looking at a real world example helps to clarify the complicated rules. Young college students who have a job while they go to school will typically be claimed by their parents like a dependent on the parentsâ€™ income tax return. Since the parents are claiming them as a dependent, the students are not permitted to claim their own personal exemption. They can take the standard deduction however. This means that the students who earn $13,000 will be allowed to take the $6,300 standard deduction. This lowers their taxable income to $6,700. If their parents did not claim them, it would mean they were able to also claim the personal exemption, which would reduce their taxable earnings down to $2,700 (derived by subtracting the $4,000 exemption amount from $6,700).

In the majority of cases, individuals who file are also able to obtain a personal deduction for their husbands or wives. This does not apply if the spouse turns out to be claimed by their parents as a dependent on the parentsâ€™ tax return.

There are many scenarios where the dependents of an income tax filer prove to be minor aged children of the primary taxpayer. Regardless of this fact, individuals who pay their taxes may also have other kinds of dependents they can claim for exemption purposes against their income. These dependents are typically relatives of the payer in question, such as a child, parent, sister, brother, uncle, or aunt. They must be truly dependent on the person paying the taxes in order to live for the IRS to accept them as dependents for income tax filing purposes.

It is possible for a person to have no tax liability whatsoever thanks to the combination of personal deductions, personal tax exemptions, and exemptions and deductions for his or her dependents. When this is the case, these individuals are allowed to request an official exemption from withholding tax from their employers. When they do so, their payroll department will only withhold Social Security and Medicare contributions (but not income tax contributions) from their paychecks.

# Tax Rates

Tax Rates refer to the percentage of their income that corporations or individuals will have to pay in taxes to their governing authority or authorities. In the United States, this proves to be the percentage rate that both the federal government and many state governments assess against the taxable income of an individual or the earnings of a corporation. In the U.S., the system utilized is a progressive tax system. This simply means that as the amount of taxable income rises, so will the percentage rate at which taxes are levied on the income or earnings.

Another way of looking at the Tax Rate is that it is the percentage rate that a company or individuals owe form their respective earnings or income. They must pay this to at least the central authority (federal government in the United States), sometimes the state government (or provincial government), and occasionally the municipal governments as well (counties or cities). This makes the tax burden extremely high on these residents and companies. It explains why as much as more than half of earnings or income can be easily taxed in the United States today.

Another feature of these tax rates in progressive systems like the U.S. is that the tax rates are further grouped into tax brackets. There are seven of these brackets. In each of the brackets, the dollar threshold depends on the filer status. These could be single, head of household, married filing jointly, or married filing separately. The two most common statuses for tax filing are single and married filing jointly.

The seven tax brackets include 10 percent, 15 percent, 25 percent, 28 percent, 33 percent, 35 percent, and 39.6 percent. Every tax payer falls into one of these categories in the U.S. As the individualsâ€™ incomes rise, so too does their tax bracket. This means that those who make the most money should in theory pay the most taxes. Yet the way it works is that on the particular income above each threshold, they pay that specific tax rate.

As an example, consider the year 2016. Those individuals who were single filers and earned $450,000 would pay the largest bracket rate of 39.6 percent on only their income in excess of $415,050. On each lower bracket amount, they would be levied the appropriate tax rates on the money earned in that bracket.

For their first $9,275 in income, they would pay 10 percent on this. On the next income up to $37,650, they would be assessed 15 percent. The money from that point up to $91,900 would be levied at 25 percent. The next amount of money up to $190,150 would be assessed taxes at the rate of 28 percent. Money earned up to $413,350 taxes at 33 percent. To $415,050 pays at 35 percent. The remaining money up to the total income of $450,000 would be taxed at 39.6 percent, the top income tax bracket.

If the people were married filing jointly, the bracket threshold amounts would be higher in the example above. For their first $18,650 in income, they would pay 10 percent on this. On the next income up to $75,900, they would be assessed 15 percent. The money from that point up to $151,900 would be levied at 25 percent. The next amount of money up to $231,450 would be assessed taxes at the rate of 28 percent. Money earned up to $413,350 taxes at 33 percent. The remaining money up to the total income of $450,000 would be taxed at 35 percent. If they had earnings above the $466,951 threshold maximum tax bracket income level, this would be assessed at the the top income tax bracket of 39.6 percent.

If this sounds like a complicated and confusing mess, that is because it is. It explains why the United States requires over a million employees at the Internal Revenue Service alone to keep up with the most complicated tax systems in the history of the world.

# Tax Revenue

Tax Revenue refers to money that a government collects. They do this by levying taxes on their own citizens living within their jurisdictions (and living overseas as well in the case of the U.S.). There are many different kinds of taxes collected in the present day and age. Among the most frequently levied taxes are income taxes, property taxes, and sales or VAT taxes.

The revenues from taxes finance government spending. They also go towards maintaining and developing new public works projects. Taxes pay for a variety of other important programs. Some of these are for education, defense, and social welfare expenditures. Practically all governments have laws in effect that provide them with the authority to tax their citizens legally.

Income taxes come from many sources of income which people earn. This might be comprised of commissions, wages, or royalties. There are governments around the world which also tax money earned on speculation, investments, and gambling proceeds (as with the U.S.). The United States and a number of other nations permit their citizens to legally reduce the amount of money they pay in taxes by providing sometimes detailed information on permissible deductions against income. In the majority of cases, tax revenue which comes from income earned becomes payable to both the national and state governments.

Property taxes provide revenue derived from ownership of real property or real estate. These funds are commonly levied and utilized by local governments including provinces, states, counties, and parishes. Such taxes come from possession of land and houses. They typically become due every year. Interestingly, cars and other vehicles also become taxed on an annual basis in most jurisdictions. This tax is levied through the purchase of license plates and vehicle registration which has to be updated annually. These taxes which local governments collect they commonly spend on maintaining state, country, or provincial schools, roads, and other types of public facilities (such as parks). Sometimes these monies are deployed to build up members of the community, as with needy familiesâ€™ support programs.

Sales tax is another way that governments collect a tax revenue every single day of the year. They levy these sales or VAT taxes on practically all purchases. Sometimes exceptions will be made for medicines and some necessary foodstuffs. The rate of taxes which they collect occasionally depends on the kind of item which a person or business purchases. Luxury items often quality for steeper tax rates. There are always higher revenues generated by so-called sin taxes. These are activities which governments attempt to discourage participation in and consumption of for their citizens. On gasoline, this is called carbon tax, while on alcohol and tobacco it is excise taxes.

In many countries of the world (the United States being a notable exception), governments collect a considerable national tax revenue from Value Added Tax. The difference between sales tax and VAT is simple. Sales tax is levied on the final point of sale only. VAT is collected on every stage of production where any value is added to the goods (or service). This is why VAT generates far more income for governments.

For example, in a VAT collecting regime a sweater is a good item to consider. Farmers are VAT taxed on the sales of their wool to factories. Factories which produce a yarn from the wool are also taxed when they go to sell their yarn to producers. Other production facilities that knit the yarn into sweaters also pay VAT when they sell the sweater to the outlet store or shop. Finally, the store which sells the sweater itself will eventually collect a VAT tax from the customer who ultimately purchases the item. VAT taxes are generally included in the sticker price of the item, while sales taxes are not usually included in shelf pricing.

Governments cannot function without tax revenues as the are the most critical types of income for modern age governing. Without such tax revenues, the overwhelming majority of governments would not be able to provide the necessary level of support which businesses and individuals require to live decently and to succeed.

This is why in the majority of nations of the world today, when businesses or individuals do not pay their taxes, they are severely penalized. Such penalties start with fines and can occasionally lead to jail time, in extreme cases of tax avoidance.

# Tax Sheltered Annuities 403(b)

Tax sheltered annuities are retirement savings programs and vehicles that the Internal Revenue Service allows for under the 403(b) section of their tax code. They were created for the benefit of employees who work for churches, educational institutions, and specific not for profit agencies.

They offer the advantage of permitting employees who are eligible to participate to contribute nearly all of their annual income towards retirement savings and investments in the plan. As an example of the generous limits with these particular plans, employers who choose to contribute can put in as much as $53,000 as of 2016 for any single tax year.

This supplemental program for retirement savings gives participating individuals a variety of ways in which they can choose to contribute funds. They may invest on an after tax basis, as with a Roth plan. They may also choose to contribute using funds that are pre-taxed. They can also opt to use a combination of the two methods. These plans and their participating contributions are entirely voluntary. Employees generally make the majority of these contributions as there is not always an employer match involved with them.

A variety of employees of eligible organizations may participate in these tax sheltered annuity plans. Employees of public schools, universities, and state colleges are allowed to participate. Many employees of churches are also allowed to become involved. Those who work for the school systems run by Indian tribes and their governments may participate. Not for profit 501(c)(3) churchesâ€™ and organizationsâ€™ ministers are included in them, as are ministers who are self employed who serve as part of a tax exempt organization. Chaplains are also usually qualified to participate.

There are several good reasons to become involved with these tax sheltered annuity plans. With automatic payroll deductions, it is a simple and relatively painless means of building up extra savings which individuals will require to increase their after retirement income.

They can get involved in a low cost program that is flexible enough to offer a good selection of investment choices. People can make contributions on a Roth after tax basis, a pre tax basis, or a combination of the two. Finally these plans are portable, meaning the owners can take their retirement vehicles with them when they move to a different job or another not for profit organization.

Thanks to these plans and vehicles, account holders are able to invest tax money that would otherwise go to the IRS. They can move money between the various funds in the plans without suffering from capital gains taxes or additional fees. This gives these TSA pre tax accounts a greater return than a taxable account would enjoy if it earned similar returns. For any individuals who use these account vehicles as Roth after tax accounts, all qualified distributions at retirement will be enjoyed completely tax free.

Money from these accounts can not be taken out without penalties until the individual reaches the government mandated minimum retirement age of 59 ½. They must begin taking distributions by the time they turn 70. An exception to the minimum retirement age is for individuals who stop working for their not for profit company before they reach retirement age. In this case, they are allowed to go ahead and begin receiving distributions without having to pay the extra 10% early withdrawal penalty tax. Only any taxes that were due for monies which had been contributed as pre tax dollars would apply in this particular case.

# Term Auction Facility (TAF)

In response to the bank lending freeze that followed the outbreak of the banking and financial crisis in 2007, Ben Bernanke created and launched his Term Auction Facility TAF in December of 2007. The

Fed was able to utilize its long mostly dormant discount window from December 2007 through to March 2010 as a creative new means of helping out struggling banks to access extra funds. They were then able to loan out these additional funds to consumers and businesses at their discretion. A primary new way of lending out such money to the banks lay in this Term Auction Facility.

Using the Term Auction Facility TAF, the Fed set up a system to auction out term funds to interested banking institutions. Any bank or credit union that already was able to borrow money via the primary credit program had eligibility to be a participant in these TAF Fed auctions.

The Fed was willing to accept bad loans as collateral for these funds. At every TAF auction, the Fed loaned out a set amount of money. They utilized the auction process starting with minimum bid rates in order to set the interest rates on these loan facilities. Banks could participate in the bidding process via phone through their local area Reserve Banks. The last of these TAF auctions occurred back on March 8 of 2010.

For the nearly three years that it ran, the Term Auction Facility worked according to a set out regular process. On a two weekly basis, the Federal Reserve would decide on the amount of money which it would then loan out on any given day. They would determine the minimum interest rate at which they would consent to loan out the funds. Banks which were interested in extra funds could then make bids for the dollar amount of money they wished to obtain at the interest rate they would agree to pay. Next the Federal Reserve sorted out the various competing bids by the level of interest rate that each participating bank offered them.

The Fed started with the greatest interest rate and then went on down from there, adding up the totals of money requested until they reached the maximum dollar amount which they were willing to lend out. Interest rates on each loan equaled the lowest interest rate which had been offered by the banks that had bids accepted.

The Fed was willing to do this so that there would not be funding shortfalls at a single institution which might cause the circular flow of credit and money in the whole American banking system to seize up and stop. In reality, most of the banks who borrowed from the Fed through the Term Auction Facility ended up leaving this money in their accounts with the Federal Reserve.

The Term Auction Facility served a useful purpose as the Federal Reserve Bank was willing to offer loans to member banks at rates that were lower than the associated market rates in exchange for putting up collateral in the form of bad loans that no one else would accept. On March 11, 2009, the banks had drawn total credit in the amount of $493.145 billion. The balance sheet of the Fed swelled to nearly a trillion dollars worth of collateral at its maximum extent.

In the end, the program proved to be successful for increasing confidence the banks had in each other, even though they did not loan out these borrowed funds generally. The TAF was originally intended to be more temporary than it turned out to be. Bernanke never envisioned it reaching the trillion dollar mark by June of 2008. All TAF funds have been repaid without taxpayers having to subsidize any of these loans which the Fed issued to the various banks.

# Term Life Insurance

Term life insurance is a form of life insurance. It offers coverage for a preset and limited amount of time that is called the relevant term. The coverage provided is a fixed rate of payment coverage. Once the term expires, the individualâ€™s coverage at the rate of the premiums that were charged before are not assured any more.

The client will be forced to drop their term life insurance coverage or to get a different coverage with varying payments and terms. Should the person who is insured die within the term, the death benefit amounts are paid out to the insured personâ€™s beneficiary. This term life insurance proves to be the most affordable means of buying a major dollar value of death benefit coverage based on the premium cost charged.

Term life insurance turns out to be the first type of life insurance created, and it stands in contrast to permanent forms of life insurance like universal life, whole life, and variable universal life. These coverage types promise an individual pre set premiums that can not go up for the personâ€™s entire life. People do not usually employ term insurance for strategies involving charitable giving or their needs for estate planning. Instead, they are thinking about a need to replace an income if a person passes away on his or her family unexpectedly.

A great number of the permanent life insurance policies also offer the advantage of increasing in value during the personâ€™s contract. This cash value can then be withdrawn when certain conditions are met by the policy holder. Generally, withdrawing these cash amounts closes out the policy. Beneficiaries of permanent life insurance products get the insurance policy face value but not the cash value upon the holderâ€™s death. Because of this, financial advisers will suggest that people purchase term life insurance for their insurance needs and then invest the money saved over permanent products in retirement accounts that provide tax deferred contributions and investment gains, like 401kâ€™s and IRAâ€™s.

Like with the majority of insurance policies, term life insurance pays out claims for the insured, assuming that the contract is current and the premiums are paid as due. Assuming that a claim is not filed, the premium is not given back to the policy holder. This makes term life insurance like home ownersâ€™ insurance policies that pay claims if a home becomes destroyed or damaged as a result of fire, or like car insurance policies that pay drivers if they have a car accident. Premiums are not refunded when the product is no longer required. Because of this, term life insurance like these other products only provides risk protection.

# Title Deed

Title deeds are a form of legal documents. They are utilized to demonstrate that a person owns a certain property. Title deeds are used most often to provide proof of home or vehicle ownership. Title deeds might also be given out on other kinds of property. Title deeds give owners privileges and legal rights. To transfer a property's ownership to another individual, a title deed is required.

Title deeds generally come with detailed descriptions of the property to which they are attached. They are made specific enough so that they can not be mixed up with other properties. They also include the individual's name who owns the piece of property. More than one person can be named as an owner on a title deed. Proof that the title deed is recorded with the appropriate office is provided by the presence of an official seal. Title deeds are commonly signed by the property owner and a person who witnesses the signature, such as a clerk or area government official.

Having a title deed does not mean that a person keeps the car in his or her possession. You can loan a car to a relative to use, even though they are not on the title. If you purchase a car using a loan, then the bank will have the title for its security, even though you would keep the car. You might purchase a house and rent it to a tenant. Although the tenant would not have the title deed, he or she would still possess and occupy the house. The title deed is useful for forcefully retaking possession in any of these scenarios.

When you sell a property, the old title deed is invalidated and a new one is given out that has the new owner's name on it. You might also add another person to a title deed by working with a title company for a property, or the Department of Motor Vehicles for vehicle titles. You have to fill in a request in writing before you receive a new title deed with the other names added to it. Once a person's name has been added to a title deed, they legally control the property along with the original title deed owner.

Title deeds have to be kept safe. As official legal documents, they are not easy to replace when stolen or lost. It is a smart idea to keep title deed copies separate from the original to have proof of ownership while an official replacement title deed is being issued. Physical possession of title deeds allows a person to start a transfer of ownership, so they must be kept where they will not be stolen and then subsequently utilized to transfer your property to another individual.

# Trade Associations

Trade Associations refer to those groups which offer a means for businesses in a certain industry or segment to interact in a way that benefits all parties concerned. Such an organization will be funded by member company contributions. These associations typically work to promote the industry's image to the public.

It might also deliver a single voice in the form of a government legislative lobby. They interact with government officials on issues which will affect the industry itself. Besides such critical functions as these, associations have other roles. These could include a way for the organization to educate the consumers of the general public on the main products and concerns of its particular industry.

Much of the time such industry trade associations will be established as not for profit organizations. This allows companies which associate in the same segment to cooperate together on those issues which affect them all in common. It is also true that these organizations are particularly useful for safeguarding an industry's integrity. This is because they commonly establish behavior standards which all member companies have to honor in order to maintain a good standing record.

Those companies or groups which refuse to live up to the standards the group develops and enforces in common suffer from the consequences. The leaders of the trade association might eventually choose to expel the business from the trade association for continued misbehavior. This would cost the offending company a serious amount of credibility before not only the industry, but also buying customers of the general public.

It is these trade associations which typically maintain all necessary means to ensure the industry's undivided voice will be heard by the law makers in a given nation or jurisdiction. This is why many participating member corporations choose to operate through the trade association in order to encourage industry-friendly legislation which will best help their industry segment to succeed. Similarly, this association could choose to lobby against any legislation that they feel will harm their collective best interests and those of their industry as a whole.

It is true that a number of businesses will elect to back marketing plans and public relations campaigns on their own to increase the exposure of their products and name brand with the relevant consumers. The beauty of a trade association such as this is that it will similarly endeavor to create interest through making members of the public aware and educating them on the industry in general and also the various products it offers. They will not concentrate their efforts on the goods for sale by a given member company. Instead, they will back publicity and marketing or advertising campaigns which lead customers to buy and consume the given industry's goods they produce in general.

This starts with offering the public facts and figures which consumers can easily understand and appreciate. The idea behind such education efforts of the trade association is that it will make it easier for the marketing efforts of the individual companies within the industry to have maximum impact. Besides lobbying, educating, and marketing, these trade associations frequently act as conference sponsors for their member businesses to attend.

Such a conference's purpose and offerings typically center on boosting the industry's overall practical performance. They do this through delivering useful information that every conference participant is able to grasp and remember. Members then take home this information to the other members of their firm and share it with those who could not attend the conference. Practically every business or trade association will sponsor at least one or more of these forms of gatherings or conferences once every year.

# Traditional IRA

The Traditional IRA is the most common type of the various individual retirement accounts available to savers for retirement. Besides this type of IRA, there are also SEP IRAs, Roth IRAs, and Self Directed IRAs. Each of these types of accounts has at least a few features in common with the original and still most popular plain IRA.

These accounts are all particularly designed to help save, grow, and fund individualsâ€™ retirements. They all permit investors to trade a variety of securities, such as stocks, mutual funds, ETFs, and bonds. Different from other kinds of brokerage and investment accounts, IRAs most importantly offer account holders tax benefits. The main difference between traditional IRAs and Roth IRAs centers on the way taxes are paid or deferred by the IRS rules.

With a Roth IRA, owners pay taxes on contributions now. All gains that account holders make in the account then accrue tax free for the entire life of the retirement savings vehicle. The traditional forms of IRAs give holders the advantage of tax deferred contributions. This means that they will not have to pay any taxes on money contributed until they withdraw them later on at retirement time. All gains that they earn in the account over the life of the IRA will be taxable at the time they withdraw them.

With all of these types of IRAs, the annual contribution limits remain the same. For tax year 2016, this amount is $5,500 for individual contributions or $11,000 for married individuals filing jointly. Catch up contributions are also the same in these various kinds of IRAs. When people reach age 50, they can make additional contributions amounting to $1,000 each year for an individual or $2,000 for married people filing jointly.

This means that instead of adding $5,500 individually to the IRA for the year, an individual could contribute $6,500 per year once he or she turns 50. Similarly married individuals would be allowed to add $13,000 per year instead of $11,000 annually once they both reach age 50.

Traditional IRAs do not feature any income limits while Roth IRAs do have these. People can be disqualified from making investments in their Roth IRAs if they earn too much money any given tax year. Single filers are only allowed to make less than $110,000 each year. Above this income, the contribution amount which the IRS allows tapers down until the income reaches $125,000.

Once this income limit is reached, a Roth IRA contribution is disallowed for the tax year. With married filing jointly, the income maximum is higher. With under $173,000 earned for the year, the full $13,000 maximum contribution is permitted. This amount tapers off as the earnings rise to $183,000. Beyond these earnings, two individuals who are married are not allowed to utilize the Roth IRA in that particular tax year.

IRAs are different from 401(k)s, the other popular retirement savings vehicle, in several critical ways. Traditional and the other forms of IRAs can only be set up and maintained by an individual acting on his or her own behalf. 401(k)s are retirement accounts that employers set up on behalf of their employees. Many employers make partially matching contributions to their employees' 401(k) accounts.

IRAs also commonly offer superior choices in different investment possibilities than do the more limited 401(k) plans. Self directed IRAs are allowed to invest in most any type of investment that is not considered to be a collectible item. This means that Self Directed IRAs are allowed to invest in franchises, real estate, precious metals, mortgages, energy, and other alternative investment ideas.

# Trans Pacific Partnership (TPP)

The Trans Pacific Partnership TPP represents a trade agreement that has been put together by twelve countries with borders on the Pacific Rim. Participants signed the final version of the deal in Auckland, New Zealand on February 4, 2016. This signing culminated the end of seven long years of negotiating the treaty. In order to enter into effect, the treaty must be ratified by the member states' legislatures. This includes the U.S. Congress, where opposition to the treaty has been intense and bipartisan from many members of both parties.

There are 30 different chapters to the Trans Pacific Partnership. Their goal is to encourage job creation and retention, economic growth, innovation, higher living standards, competitiveness and productivity, poverty reduction, better government and transparency, and better protection of the environment and labor. This TPP is made up of agreements that reduce tariff and non tariff barriers to trade. It also creates a means of resolving disputes through investor state settlement.

Originally the Trans Pacific Partnership was born from the Trans Pacific Strategic Economic Partnership Agreement that Singapore, New Zealand, Chile, and Brunei signed back in 2005. Starting in 2008, other nations on the Pacific Rim began to discuss a wider arrangement. This included The United States, Vietnam, Peru, Mexico, Malaysia, Japan, Canada, and Australia. This increased the nations who were a part of the trade negotiations to 12 countries.

Previously in force trade agreements of the countries participating will be amended to not conflict with the TPP. Deals that offer better free trade will still be in effect. The Obama administration looks at the TPP as a pair of treaties. Its twin is the still under discussion TTIP Transatlantic Trade and Investment Partnership between the European Union and the United States. The two deals are generally similar.

The original goal of the talks was to conclude negotiations in the year 2012. The final deal stretched on for another three years because of conflicts over difficult issues like intellectual property, agriculture, investments, and services. The 12 nations at last came to an agreement on October 5, 2015. The U.S. Obama administration has made implementing this TPP one of its principle goals for trade. On November 5, 2015, President Obama announced to Congress he would sign the deal and released a public version of the treaty for any interested American individuals and organizations to review.

The U.S. President along with the other 11 leaders all signed the TPP February 4, 2016.

In order for the Trans Pacific Partnership to take effect, all of the signors have to ratify it within two years. In case it is not completely ratified by all parties in advance of the February 4, 2018 deadline, there is an alternative arrangement. It will become effective after minimally 6 signing countries with a combined GDP of greater than 85% of all the signing countries ratify it. This means that the U.S. must ratify if for it to ever take effect.

Other countries may be able to join the trade block in the future. Countries that have shown an interest in joining include South Korea, India, Bangladesh, Cambodia, Indonesia, Laos, Thailand, Colombia, the Philippines, and Taiwan. South Korea did not get involved with the original 2006 agreement. The U.S. invited it to join after South Korea and America concluded their own free trade agreements. South Korea is likely to be the first country to join in a next wave expansion of the group. First it will have to work through TPP treaty issues in agriculture and vehicle manufacturing.

# Trans Union

Trans Union turns out to be one of the three main credit reporting bureaus and information management services that are based in the United States. It delivers these services to around 500 million individual consumers and 45,000 distinct companies found throughout the globe in a significant 33 different countries. This makes it the third biggest credit bureau in the U.S. The firmâ€™s larger and more powerful competitors are Experian and Equifax. This smallest of credit reporting bureaus also sells its credit report and related services directly to the people they are reporting on, the consumers. The firm is headquartered in Chicago, Illinois. It boasted 2014 revenues of $1.3 billion.

The company Trans Union became established back in 1968 as a company with no relationship whatsoever to credit reporting or information gathering. It started out life as a holding company for an organization that leased railroads, the Union Tank Car Company. A year later, it bought out the Credit Bureau of Cook County. This firm owned and kept up files on 3.6 million credit cards.

Chicago-based holding firm the Marmon Group later acquired Trans Union in 1981 in a purchase price valued at $688 million. The company continued operating unobtrusively until 2010 when Goldman Sachs Capital Partners working with Advent International bought it from Madison Dearborn Partners. The firm finally became a publicly traded corporation for the very first time on June 25, 2015 when it started trading on U.S. exchanges via the stock symbol TRU.

As with its two principal rivals, Trans Union has transformed its business lines throughout the decades until it provided services and products pertaining to both consumers and businesses. In business, the company has morphed its fairly long standing credit score product into trending data which assists companies with forecasting the debt and repayment behavior and patterns of consumers. This cutting edged and technologically revolutionary service they call Credit Vision. They rolled it out in October of 2013.

The company similarly has a proprietary service called SmartMoveâ„¢ which assists consumers acting as landlords with background and credit checks. They also bought eScan Data Systems of Austin (Texas) back in September of 2013 in order to deliver to healthcare systems and hospitals after-service eligibility determinations. This impressive technology they integrated into their Clear IQ platform which tracks the insurance and demographically relevant information of patients in order to help with verifying the patientsâ€™ benefits.

Trans Union became the first company back in 2014 to begin accepting monthly rent payment history data from landlords. The company investigated rent payment histories to determine that consumersâ€™ credit scores would benefit from such a move. Resident Credit is their resulting system which makes it simple for property owners to offer up information on their tenantsâ€™ behalf to the credit reporting bureau every month.

Consumers have access to the several Trans Union services which help to protect individuals from both identity and credit theft. These are credit monitoring and identity theft protection services. Credit Lock is their proprietary app which assists individuals in locking and unlocking their credit in order to better safeguard it from activity which turns out to be fraudulent.

The company has been heavily criticized in recent years for hiding charges from consumers. A large number of customers who utilize their services have objected to not being made aware of a $17.95 per month fee for maintaining such a Trans Union account. The company was forced by a March 2015 settlement in conjunction with its two main rivals Equifax and Experian to agree to assisting consumers in finding red flags and mistakes on their credit reports.

# Transatlantic Trade Investment Partnership (TTIP)

The Transatlantic Trade and Investment partnership represents a U.S. and European agreement for mutual trade and investment. In essence it is a free trade deal that the two economic superpowers are working to ratify. The two parties began the initiative in the June of 2013 G8 meeting. U.S. President Obama, European Commission President Barroso, and European Union Council President Van Rompuy introduced the idea and began working on the project.

The goal of the TTIP is to encourage both trade and investment. Governments on both sides believe that this will result in more economic growth and jobs for citizens of both sides of the Atlantic Ocean. Negotiations have been complex and mostly held in secret. The U.S. side is headed by the USTR, or Office of the United States Trade Representative. The Europeans are led by the European Commission. This EC handles negotiations for all 28 EU member countries.

TTIP turns out to be the largest and grandest vision for a trade agreement that has ever been attempted. This is because the United States and European Union economic blocks make up nearly fifty percent of the GDP of the entire world. The impacts on trade are expected to be substantial. Small to medium sized enterprises will gain several benefits in access to the new markets. They will have other countries to which they can export. They will also gain the ability to import input materials from other countries. It is anticipated they will have the ability to gain investments in their businesses at a cheaper, better price as well.

Consumers are supposed to benefit also. Lower prices are expected in both economic blocks because of the reduced tariffs and increased competition. This will improve the purchasing power of residents on both sides of the Atlantic and also help to create more jobs.

Twenty-four different chapters comprise the actual Transatlantic Trade and Investment Partnership. These have been divided into three principal topics. The topics are Market Access, Rules, and Regulatory Cooperation.

Market Access pertains to opening up markets. The goal is to allow for improved competition. Besides this, the architects of the agreement are trying to make it easier for products to flow back and forth across the Atlantic.

The rules section has to do with trade and investment. This areaâ€™s goal is to increase the fairness and ease of importing, exporting, and investing for American businesses in Europe and European businesses in America. Rules cover a number of different important concepts. These include Energy and Raw Materials, Sustainable Development, Small and Medium Sized Enterprises, Customs and Trade Facilitation, Competition, Investment Protection, Geographical Indications, Intellectual Property, and the Government to Government Dispute Settlements.

The area of Regulatory Cooperation pertains to important regulation differences between the United States and the European Union. Both groups often have the same quality and safety levels that they insist on from specific goods. The problem is that each side employs its own procedures in considering the identical product. This imposes high costs on companies who produce the items. It can be prohibitively expensive for smaller to medium sized businesses.

There have been a number of objections raised by protestors to this free trade agreement, particularly in Europe. Many individuals on both sides of the Atlantic oppose the secrecy that surrounds the negotiations. The protesters have concerns that interest groups are creating special rules for larger companies.

The European labor markets are worried that their working conditions and benefits will suffer. Environmental groups are all concerned that environmental standards and safeties that are higher in Europe will be watered down as a result of the free trade initiative.

# Treasury Inflation Protected Securities (TIPS)

Treasury Inflation Protected Securities (TIPS) are a unique and useful form of Treasury issued securities. What makes them special is their expressed and close linkage to inflation levels in their coupon payments. They are set up this way to safeguard investors from the interest destroying impacts of inflation.

TIPS prove to be lower risk investments because they enjoy the expressed and unlimited backing of the U.S. government. Besides this, their par value increases at the same pace as the official rate of inflation as depicted by the CPI Consumer Price Index. The interest rate itself stays fixed with these investments.

The interest earned by these Treasury Inflation Protected Securities pays out twice a year on the same fixed dates. TIPS may be bought directly off of the U.S. government by utilizing the Treasury Direct system. This allows for simple $100 increment purchases of the TIPS in a minimum of only $100 order size. They can be obtained from the site with 30 year, 10 year, and 5 year maturity date options.

Unfortunately for the Treasury Inflation Protected Securities holders, the inflation adjustments of the TIPS bonds fall under the IRS definition of taxable income. This is the case despite the fact that investors do not realize any of those inflation adjusted gains until the point where the bonds mature or they sell out their holdings. Because of this, some investors opt to obtain their TIPS exposure by utilizing a TIPS mutual fund or ETF. Otherwise, they could simply buy and hold them within tax deferred retirement accounts like IRAs. This would save them the tax headaches of having to pay the IRS now on money they will not obtain for possibly years or even decades.

On the other hand, buying TIPS directly means that investors sidestep the costs and fees applied by mutual funds and even ETFs. TIPS bought directly also feature complete exemption from the double or even triple taxation of local income and state income taxes which some investors must pay, depending on where they reside. Residents of Puerto Rico do not have to pay any federal income taxes on these inflation adjusted gains or interest payments because of the Commonwealth's completely unique status which it enjoys within the U.S.

If investors purchased $1,000 worth of TIPS and held them through year end and received one percent coupon rates while there was no CPI measured inflation within the United States, the investors could count on obtaining $10 payments for the entire year in interest payments. Assuming inflation increases by two percent, the principal of the bond would increase by two percent or in this specific instance by $20, to reach a total value of $1,020. The coupon rate would remain locked at one percent, yet it would apply to the entire new principal amount of $1,020 to help the holder receive interest payments of $10.20.

In the extremely unlikely event that deflation reared itself, the bonds would similarly decline in total face value. Should the CPI decline by three percent, the principle would drop by three percent, or $30, resulting in a new par face value of $970 on the formerly $1,000 Treasury bond. This would reduce that next year's interest coupon payments total to $9.70.

When the bonds mature, investors would then get the principal equity which equated either to the $1,000 original par face value, or an applicably higher adjusted principal based on the CPI adjustments higher. Interest payments throughout the life of the bond will be calculated from the principal amount as it rises or falls. This does not apply to the downside if the investors hold their TIPS until they reach maturity. Investors who do not wish to hold their TIPS until this interval can choose to receive a lower amount of principal than the par face value by selling their investment via the secondary bonds market if they so desire.

# Trust

A Trust proves to be a special type of fiduciary arrangement where one participant the trustor grants the other participant the trustee the rights to possess the property title or assets title for the advantages of the beneficiary, often times a third party. When it is utilized in the world of finance, this similarly refers to a kind of closed end investment fund collectively established as a public limited company.

Settlors ultimately establish such trusts. They elect to shift over all or a portion of their possessions (assets) to the trustees of the trust in this action. It is the trustees who ultimately maintain the assets on behalf of the beneficiaries of said trust. The trusts' rules come down to the particular terms that apply to the given trust in question. Some jurisdictions allow for older members of the beneficiaries' class to ascend to the roles of trustee. Some of these jurisdictions actually allow for the grantor to be both a trustee and lifetime beneficiary together at once.

Two different types of trusts exist, the testamentary trust and the living trust. The testamentary trusts are also known as will trusts. These determine the means in which the assets for the individuals will be allocated after they eventually pass away. The document of such a trust comes into play legally following the death of the testator.

On the other hand, living trusts are known as inter vivos or revocable trusts. These written out documents allow for the assets of an individual to be created in the form of a trust. The individual himself or a beneficiary will then enjoy the advantages of and utilization of the resources throughout their remaining lives. Such assets will eventually be transferred to the legal beneficiaries when the individual dies. The trust creator sets a successor trustee who will carry the responsibility of transferring any remaining assets over to the beneficiary in question.

There are a number of different reasons that individuals employ trusts. One of these is to attain a degree of privacy. Wills and their arrangements are often public domain material in many jurisdictions. Trusts can specify the identical conditions which a will may, without the intrusive nature of being public domain documents available for any and all members of the public to read upon demand. This explains why those people who do not wish to have their wills and terms of their estate disposition revealed publically after they are gone will often choose to utilize trusts for their final bequests instead of the will document.

Besides this, trusts are a useful vehicle for planning the payment of taxes. Trusts have different tax arrangements than do standard planning accounts and competing vehicles. The tax consequences for deploying such trusts are typically less negative and expensive than those of other typical means involved in financial planning. This helps to explain why using trusts has become a standard option in the world of efficient tax planning. This is the case not only for individuals but also for corporations.

Finally, trusts find extensive utilization in estate planning procedures. This allows for the assets of deceased people to be passed on to their spouses. The spouses are then able to equally divide up the remaining assets for the benefit of the children who survive the deceased parent. Those children who do not possess the necessary 18 years of age to be considered legal persons (with possession rights) will be required to have trustees to exercise control over all assets in question until they reach the legal age of adulthood.

# Trust Account

A trust account refers to a type of account which a trustee holds on the behalf of the beneficiary. The trustee does not have the ability to utilize the funds in any personal capacity, but merely to safe keep, disburse, and invest them for the advantage of the beneficiary.

An example of this type of arrangement is when an attorney holds funds for the benefit of the client. The attorney will not be able to draw upon the funds until after a certain protocol takes place. As the attorney earns the lawyer fees, the client will have to first review and then actually approve the bill from the attorney before he or she can transfer the client funds from this trust account over to the general account of the attorney for settlement of bills.

There are a number of reasons and situations in which individuals may opt to establish a trust account. In some scenarios, people wish to disperse a pre-determined sum of money to their family or other loved ones over a number of years or throughout the remainder of their natural lives.

As a real world example, consider the following. Parents may wish to establish some trust accounts which will provide money to their dependents and/or children every month if and when they die. In such a scenario, it would normally be banking brokers who would manage such accounts. In fact these broker trustees would draw down the account values by the appropriate amount every month or year as they disbursed the either monthly or yearly funds to the beneficiaries for the individuals who originally formed the trust.

There are other common kinds of trusts as well. One of these is a property tax trust account. Such accounts will be established by entrepreneurs of real estate who own a variety of properties. Rather than have to be concerned about the property tax funds and disbursements to the appropriate taxing authorities themselves, they elect to form a trust account which will pay the taxes. This prevents the entrepreneurs from forfeiting their valuable properties because they forgot to pay the property taxes. There are a number of monetary benefits to having such an account. One of these is that estate taxes will not apply to properties contained in such a trust when the owner dies.

There are two different main types of trust accounts. These are revocable and irrevocable trusts. With revocable trusts, these represent deposit accounts whose owners chose to name one or several beneficiaries. These beneficiaries would then obtain the deposits in the account once the holder of the account died. As the name implies, such revocable trusts may be terminated, revoked, or altered on demand whenever the holder of said account wishes. In this particular case, the owner is the trustor, settlor, or grantor of the revocable trust in question. These types of trusts will be established as either informal or formal. While trustees are powerful and have a broad scope of authority over the assets of the beneficiary, they are not omnipotent, but must be bound by the laws and regulations of the jurisdiction which pertain to trust accounts.

Irrevocable trusts on the other hand are similarly deposit accounts but they are not titled in the name of the owner. Instead these become titled as an irrevocable trust for the name. The owner, trustor, settlor, or grantor also makes deposits of money or other valuable assets to the trust account. The principal difference is that the owners forfeit all ability to alter or cancel the trust once they have established it. These types of trusts also become created once an owner of a revocable type of trust dies. They can be set up through a judicial order as well, or even by a statute as appropriate.

# Uniform Commercial Code (UCC)

The UCC is the acronym for Uniform Commercial Code. This set of standardized rules arose as a means of covering the majority of United Statesâ€™ based commercial transactions. This code does not represent official national law. Yet the potency of it lies in the fact that the majority of American states have chosen to adopt the UCC in some variation. This makes the code legally binding in all but one of the state jurisdictions throughout the U.S. It is safe to say this means most locations in the country.

It also means the Uniform Commercial Code is confusing, as in any given state, interested parties must research it to uncover how that particular jurisdiction has chosen to interpret the code and implement its policy guidelines. In most locales, it lays out the best practices and rules which govern consumer protection regulations, goods' sales, and those commercial transactions which occur between financial institutions (primarily banks and credit card processors) and merchants. The code has a variety of goals, yet one of the most important is to create transparency so that individuals who engage in business at any place in the United States will understand what they can anticipate from other businesses. It also provides them with guidelines on how they should conduct themselves in business in general.

In general though, the intentions of this code center on reducing conflicts and opaqueness between the various laws of states regarding sales and trade. As such, the UCC covers nine separate articles. Among the significant variety of topics it addresses are bank instruments, selling of goods, letters of credit, negotiable instruments, bills of receipts, investment securities, bulk transfers, and secure transactions. Such regulations and guidelines also attempt to reduce the complexity of any and all relevant commercial paper transactions. This would include the ways that checks become processed. The code makes a valid point of distinguishing the differences between consumers who do not understand business well and merchants who must grasp it thoroughly.

Louisiana is now the lone state in the country that has not adopted the overwhelming majority of the Uniform Commercial Code. The reason is because the state of Louisiana still clings to its civil law system which dates back to the early French Napoleonic Code and their lonely tradition as a French colony. This means that they refuse to update their regulations on selling goods. There are some state laws in Louisiana that work hand in glove with the ideas set out in the UCC, yet it is important to realize that this does not mean all of them do.

The Uniform Commercial Code proves to be critically necessary precisely because commerce is hard to consistently regulate in a realm as enormous as the U.S. is. Clearly goods will typically have a point of origin in one side of the nation, be sold in another state and region, then finally become used in a third state or region. When all of the states possess their own rules, regulations, and laws, it becomes confusing and costly for firms to engage in business around the country.

This UCC originally became drafted back in the 1940s decade. The NCCUSL National Conference of Commissioners of Uniform State Laws dating back to 1892 jointly sponsored it with their fellow organization the 1923-originating ALI American Law Institute. While neither groups can claim to make laws, they each possess a vast respect and influence in national and statewide legislations. Professionals and lawyers from all American territories and states receive appointment to the NCCUSL to determine which laws throughout the nation ought to be the same. The ALI is made up of judges and lawyers from the whole of the United States who seek to clarify and explain the common laws in America based upon the changing needs of society.

# Value-Added Tax (VAT)

Value-Added Tax (VAT) turns out to be a kind of tax on consumption which governments place on all products. What makes this different from a sales tax is that whenever any value becomes added along the stages of production as well as at the final register, the VAT tax is applied.

These Value-Added Tax fees are commonly utilized within the European Union which is also the heaviest user of them in the world. The total VAT which end-users pay proves to be the difference between the product's cost minus the materials' cost which were utilized in making the product (which have already been taxed).

A good example to look at is a television set constructed by a manufacturer in Germany. The maker pays VAT on each of the various components it buys in order to produce the TV. After the set arrives in stores, the individuals who buy it must also pay the appropriate amount of Value-Added Tax.

Value-Added Tax is not based on income as with other forms of taxes. Rather it relies on the amount of goods which consumers purchase and consume. Over 160 different nations rely on VAT for at least partial funding of government budgets. The United States is strangely absent from this list of well over 75 percent of the countries on earth.

Advocates for implementing a VAT in the U.S. argue that by replacing the present inefficient income tax system in America with such a national VAT, this would offer numerous advantages. Among these are that it would lower the national deficit and debt, pay for critical social services, and boost government revenues.

Critics of the Value-Added Tax for the U.S. claim that such a tax is inherently regressive. This means that it would require the poor and low income workers to shoulder a greater economic burden and responsibility for funding the government outlays.

Both sides of the debate are in fact correct. In the advantages column, such a Value-Added Tax would bring in massive revenues on every product which traditional American stores, businesses, and Internet-based businesses sell. This would be a boon for government coffers that typically miss out on sales taxes which can not be levied on businesses that avoid sales taxes with customers (in those states where the businesses do not have any physical offices). It would collect presently unpaid billions in taxes from online sales that could be deployed then to pay for law enforcement, schools, and many other social services. Besides this, a VAT would ensure it is far harder to avoid paying taxes. It would further simplify the complicated and bureaucratic federal tax regulations so that the Internal Revenue Service could be massively downsized and made more efficient at the same time.

There are also a number of possible downsides to the VAT, per opponents of the concept. Business owners would suffer from higher costs all along the chain of goods production. A national VAT would also cause potential disputes between the Federal government and those many local and state governments which already charge sales tax rates set on local and statewide levels.

Critics also correctly point out that the consumers bear the ultimate brunt of the tax in the form of higher consumer goods prices, thanks to a VAT. The theory is that the burden of the tax spreads out through each phase of making goods from inputs to the ultimate product. The reality is that higher costs are nearly always passed off on the poor consumers.

As VAT applies equally to all purchases and for all types of salary and wage earners throughout the jurisdiction in which it applies, this would harm lower wage workers than higher ones. Higher wage earners are able to save massive percentages of their income, which would then not be taxed. Lower wage earners live from paycheck to paycheck. As they spend all of their earnings each month, their share of the VAT tax would be proportionally far higher than the wealthy Americansâ€™ share.

# Vested Rights

Vested Rights refers simply to rights that cannot be taken away. In finance, they refer specifically to one of several topics. The most common pertains to employer-provided retirement benefits or stock incentives. They describe the non-forfeitable rights on either employer contributions to the qualified retirement plan or pension plan account or to stock incentives provided as a valuable incentive by the employer. Such vesting will give the employee tangible rights to a portion of the employer-owned assets over time.

This provides a substantial incentive for the employee to deliver his or her best efforts to the company and to stay with it a long time as well. Vesting schedules are always determined by the employing firm. They specify when the employee will then acquire full ownership of the funds, stock, or other asset in question. In general, such non-forfeitable rights will accrue on a time schedule based on the number of years the employee has been with the company.

The amount of time for vested rights to be earned varies from one plan document to the next. It always helps to consider a good example to better understand somewhat complicated topics such as these. An employee could get 100 restricted shares of stock in the firm for which he works as a portion of the yearly bonus. The goal would be to find a way to keep the valuable employee at the firm. The company can do this by spelling out a several year vesting schedule for the stock shares.

For example, it would be common for the stock to vest at the rate of 25 shares (as in 25 percent) per year starting on the completion of the second year. This means that after year three, the employee will be fully vested in 50 shares (50 percent), while after the fourth he or she will have vesting in 75 shares (75 percent), and finally at the end of the fifth year, he or she will entirely own the 100 shares of bonus stock (100 percent vesting). Should the employee part ways with the company at the end of the fourth year, then he or she would have 75 shares of the stock while the remaining 25 would forfeit back to the firm.

There are other benefits where the vested rights are effective immediately. As an example, all employees always gain 100 percent vesting in their own contributions from their salaries to their retirement plans and SIMPLE employer contributions and SEP employer contributions. Generally, any employer contributions to the employee 401(k) plan will also immediately vest. There are other scenarios where this money only vests after a few years on what is called a cliff vesting schedule. This provides the employee ownership of 100 percent of all employer contributions only after completing a pre-determined number of years with the firm. There are also graded vesting schedule options to firms, which mean that the employee gains ownership of a set percentage of all employer contributions made very year. With many traditional pension plans, they will have either a three to seven years long graded vesting schedule, or alternatively a simpler five year cliff vesting schedule built in to their policy.

Becoming one hundred percent vested in an employer retirement plan and employer provided contributions are not a carte blanch to draw out the money on demand though. The rules of the plan will still govern in this regard. They will likely insist that any employees attain legal retirement age before they are allowed to engage in withdrawals without any penalties being assessed.

# Volcker Rule

The Volcker Rule is a controversial much loved or intensely hated part of the Frank-Dodd Wall Street Reform and Consumer Protection Act. This federal regulation made it illegal for banks to pursue specific investment activities using their own money and accounts.

It also restricted their relationship to and ownership of private equity funds and hedge funds. These so called covered funds engaged in a variety of speculative leveraged and high risk investments. Such investments and their ultimate massive failures played a major part in the American and ultimately global financial collapse of the 2008 financial crisis and Great Recession.

The Volcker Rule was originally named for Paul Volcker, the one time legendary Federal Reserve Chairman. This rule eliminates short term bank trading of derivatives, securities, commodity futures, and options on such futures. They may no longer use their own accounts for such trading that does not provide any benefit to the customers of the banks. The end result is that banks may not engage their own proprietary funds in order to participate in investments that may boost their own corporate profits.

This Volcker Rule is spelled out under section 619 of the massive Dodd-Frank Wall Street Reform and Consumer Protection Act. It amended the Bank Holding Company Act of 1956, also known as the BHC Act, by adding in a brand new section 13 that has become universally known as the Volcker Rule. All institutions which accept deposits, as well as any corporate entity that is affiliated with these insured depository groups, are prohibited from pursing this secretive proprietary trading.

They also may no longer have an interest in, acquire, or sponsor any private equity or hedge funds. There are some exemptions, definitions, and restrictions in the legal statute. It provided banking groups with some time until they had to prove they had conformed to the provisions of the rule. Originally this was July of 2014, but it was later extended to July 21, 2015 in order to provide banks with sufficient time to extricate themselves from these trades and practices.

The end form of the regulations had to be approved by five different federal agencies. These included the Federal Deposit Insurance Corporation, the Federal Reserve System Board of Governors, The Commodity Futures Trading Commission, the Office of the Comptroller of the Currency, and the SEC Securities and Exchange Commission. They approved these rules in December of 2013.

The rules became effective on April 1, 2014 and required banks’ complete compliance by July 21, 2015. â€"â€"The Volcker Rule did not completely tie banks’ hands. They are still allowed to keep making markets, hedging, and underwriting government securities. They may also engage in the activities of insurance companies and perform the roles of custodians, brokers, and agents.

They may offer customers private equity funds or hedge funds for their own accounts and benefit. All such services which they provide to their customers they may do in an effort to turn profits. The caveat is that banks may not pursue these activities when it leads to a dangerous conflict of interest, creates instability in the individual bank or the entire United States’ financial system, or opens up the banking institution to dangerous trading strategies or involvement with risky assets.

Banks of certain sizes must report and disclose all of their covered trading activities to the appropriate government regulators. The bigger banks had to create programs that guaranteed they were abiding by the new rules. Besides this, their new compliance programs were subject to further independent analysis and tests. Institutions which were smaller were subjected to fewer reporting and compliance rules and regulations.

# Wash Sale

The Wash Sale refers to an IRS Internal Revenue Service code rule that outlaws any taxpayers from utilizing loss sales on securities in what they cleverly call a â€œwash sale.â€ The rule essentially explains such a sale as any that occurs as the investor trades or sells securities at a loss within 30 days before or after this particular sale, buying a stock or other security that is deemed to be substantially identical, or otherwise obtaining an option to do the same. Such a sale will also occur when investors sell the security and their spouse or a company which they own subsequently purchases the same or substantially the same security back.

Where stocks are concerned at least, one company stock and another is never considered to be substantially the same to the IRS. They also do not count preferred stocks or bonds of one company and another as materially the same. Yet there are cases where the preferred and common stocks of a single company could be considered to be basically the same investment. This is especially true when the preferred stock can be freely converted into the companyâ€™s common stock with no restrictions, or if they both possess voting rights, and if they trade for a price that is near the official conversion ratio of the preferred stock issue.

When such a loss becomes disavowed by the IRS thanks to the wash sale rule, it means that the taxpayer investor will be forced to add his loss back on to the cost of the newer stock. This would then be known as the cost basis on the new stock. Consider an example to help demystify what is at best a confusing topic. An investor might buy 100 shares of JP Morgan common stock at$35 per share, then sell them for $30 per share in a loss, and in less than 30 days later purchase another 100 shares of JPM common stock for $33. The $500 ultimate loss in this scenario would not be permitted for claiming by the IRS thanks to the wash sale rule. Yet it can be added back in to the $3,300 cost of the newer shares. The basis for the new cost then would be $3,800 as the 100 shares times $33 equals $3,300 plus the $500 loss on the prior trade equates to a total new cost basis position of $3,800.

In truth, the only silver lining to a stock or mutual fund trade that goes bad is that the capital loss can help to offset other more profitable investments elsewhere.

The ironic part is that there is no such wash rule for any investor who cashes out on profits on a trade then reenters the trade within 30 days. Tax professionals call this unfair scenario the â€œheads I win, tails you loseâ€ IRS is the master rule. Options are similarly included under the wash rules which mean that you can also have your options loss disavowed if you repurchase the identical ones within 30 days.

Many investors will wonder where the IRS draws the lines on the ever popular newer index mutual funds such as the S&P 500 ones. The IRS throws sand in the eyes of the investor by stating that all circumstances have to be considered when evaluating if securities are in fact substantially identical. No one knows what this really means in point of fact. The general interpretation though is that no two mutual funds are â€œsubstantially the sameâ€ to each other. Yet selling a single S&P 500 index fund for a loss then purchasing another different S&P 500 index fund in 30 days or less would likely be disavowed by the tricky rule.

# Withholding Tax

Withholding Tax refers to the U.S. Federal income tax which they withhold from the wages of any employee. Employers pay these taxes which they collect from their employeesâ€™ payrolls straight to the government. All amounts which they withhold become credited against the employeesâ€™ income taxes. This offsets the amount the employees owe throughout the calendar year. This tax is similarly assessed on other forms of income, including dividends, capital gains, and interest earned by any securities the individual holds. Even non-residents who are American citizens will have to pay these taxes.

The Internal Revenue Service utilizes two different forms of Withholding Taxes in their efforts to be certain that the correct amount of taxes become withheld in various scenarios. By far and away the most commonly utilized and talked about one is the standard means of withholding against personal income. All U.S.-based employers are required to do this on behalf of their employees, whether they are part time or full time. The second and less common method pertains to those nonresidents of the U.S. who earn money in the United States. Their income similarly must be levied to ensure that Uncle Sam receives his full due.

By engaging in Withholding Tax procedures, the United States Department of the Treasury is able to go straight for their share of taxes right at the income source, instead of trying to collect their income taxes after the fact once they are already earned (and potentially spent). They originated this clever, forward thinking system back in 1943 as they instituted a massive tax hike on Americans. Back in the day, the government pondered the issue and believed that they would find it hard to gather up such a huge percentage of income in taxes if they did not get them upfront.

The vast majority of employees fall under the legislation that withholds the taxes when they become hired. The IRS requires all employers to obtain a completely filled in Form W4 at this point before their new employees can receive their first paycheck. This form is utilized to estimate the proper amount of taxes the employee will owe throughout the year and per payroll.

For the majority of people in normal circumstances, they need to have approximately 90 percent of their estimated income taxes be withheld by the Internal Revenue Service this way. Otherwise, they will probably fall behind on the taxes. This oversight comes with stiff penalties. The system is also designed to not overtax individuals as they are paying along the way throughout the year.

Both independent contractors and investors have an exemption from the tedious procedures of Withholding Tax. This does not in any way exempt them from paying the income tax though. When such taxpayers as these get behind on their tax withholding and payment, they can be subjected to backup withholding. This involves a steeper tax rate of withholding that the government sets at a punishing 28 percent.

As if this was not difficult and confusing enough, fully 41 of the individual 50 states utilize a similar withholding scheme for their state income taxes. This way they are sure that they will be able to levy and collect on their own taxes from the state residents. The states rely on both their own worksheets as well as the IRS’™ Form W4 in order to estimate state income tax withholdings for the year and per paycheck. Nine of the states do not collect an income tax.

Such withholding tax is mandatory for the overwhelming majority of Americans or nonresidents who earn income off of a business or a trade within the U.S. Even Americans who live and earn money overseas cannot escape from their income tax obligations. Even nonresident American citizens living and working abroad will be assessed on foreign earned income as well.

# Zoning Laws

Zoning laws are statutes that mandate the ways that you are able to utilize your property holdings. Townships, counties, cities, and alternative local governments affect zoning laws so that they are able to create standards for development that benefit all residents in common.

It does not matter how big or how small a property is; it will be impacted by zoning laws. If you contemplate improving your property or purchasing another piece of property, you should be certain that you are fully aware of zoning restrictions that will affect you in advance of making any kind of commitment.

As an example, properties can be zoned according to residential or commercial restrictions. Commercial buildings will never be permitted to be constructed in a residential area, while residential dwellings can not be put up in commercial zones, unless the zoning laws of the area are changed.

Getting the zoning laws for a property altered proves to be extremely difficult. You would first have to give out public notice before getting an approved variance from the responsible government agencies in charge of zoning plans. Many times, neighbors will stalwartly resist your proposed zoning changes.

Zoning laws allow for a variety of different zoning designations and uses. Among these are commercial zoning, residential zoning, industrial zoning, recreational zoning, and agricultural zoning. These categories are generally further subdivided into other categories. Residential zoning might have sub zoning categories under it including multiple family use, for condominiums or apartments, or single family houses.

Zoning laws include a number of limitations to the property and potential improvements. The total size and height of buildings on the property is commonly restricted. The buildings can only be placed so close to each other. There will be limits to the total area percentage that is allowed to have buildings on it. Perhaps most importantly, the types of buildings that can be built on a given land's zone will be mandated.

You can learn about the zoning laws and ordinances simply by getting in touch with the area planning agency. Alternatively, you might go on the Internet to the local and state search engine to learn about your county and city zoning rules. Local planning organizations will tell you what must be done to get a variance to the area zoning.

## More books by Thomas Herold